A GAME PLAN FOR EFFECTIVE LEADERSHIP

Lessons from 10 Successful Coaches in Moving from Theory to Practice

Robert Palestini

Rowman & Littlefield Education
Lanham, Maryland • Toronto • Plymouth, UK
2008

Published in the United States of America
by Rowman & Littlefield Education
A Division of Rowman & Littlefield Publishers, Inc.
A wholly owned subsidiary of The Rowman & Littlefield Publishing Group, Inc.
4501 Forbes Boulevard, Suite 200, Lanham, Maryland 20706
www.rowmaneducation.com

Estover Road
Plymouth PL6 7PY
United Kingdom

Copyright © 2008 by Robert Palestini

All rights reserved. No part of this publication may be reproduced, stored in a retrieval system, or transmitted in any form or by any means, electronic, mechanical, photocopying, recording, or otherwise, without the prior permission of the publisher.

British Library Cataloguing in Publication Information Available

Library of Congress Cataloging-in-Publication Data

Palestini, Robert H.
  A game plan for effective leadership : lessons from 10 successful coaches in moving from theory to practice / Robert Palestini.
      p. cm.
  Includes bibliographical references and index.
  ISBN-13: 978-1-57886-813-1 (hbk. : alk. paper)
  ISBN-10: 1-57886-813-0 (hbk. : alk. paper)
  ISBN-13: 978-1-57886-814-8 (pbk. : alk. paper)
  ISBN-10: 1-57886-814-9 (pbk. : alk. paper)
  eISBN-13: 978-157886-883-4
  eISBN-10: 1-57886-883-1
  1. Leadership. I. Title.
  HM1261.P34 2008
  303.3'4--dc22

2008004520

∞™ The paper used in this publication meets the minimum requirements of American National Standard for Information Sciences—Permanence of Paper for Printed Library Materials, ANSI/NISO Z39.48-1992.
Manufactured in the United States of America.

CONTENTS

Foreword Phil Martelli v

Preface vii

1 Contemporary Leadership Theory 1

2 Leading with Heart 21

3 Phil Jackson 47

4 Dr. Jack Ramsay 64

5 Pat Riley 92

6 Bobby Knight 107

7 Mike Krzyzewski 120

8 Dean Smith 134

9 Pat Summitt 145

10 John Thompson 172

11 John Wooden 188

12 Bob Hurley 200

13 Leadership Lessons Learned 212

Appendix The Heart Smart Organizational Diagnosis Model	217
Notes	225
References	229
About the Author	231

FOREWORD

It has been my pleasure to watch Bob Palestini work for over 20 years as a graduate dean and professor at Saint Joseph's University as well as a highly successful high school basketball coach in the ultra competitive Philadelphia Catholic League. His expertise and research interest is educational leadership. His eleven books on leadership have been outstanding in their own way but this endeavor relates his theories on leadership to daily coaching. What a great connection.

Having just written my own book, *Don't Call Me Coach*, in which I present the idea that everyone is a coach in his or her own way, I can relate to Dr. Palestini's basic premise that the tenets of situational leadership theory and effective coaching go hand-in-hand whether we are discussing business, educational or social settings.

In this book, Dr. Palestini demonstrates how the use of situational leadership theory by ten successful basketball coaches has contributed to their effectiveness and how these same leadership principles can be appropriately applied to anyone's leadership behavior, whether the individual be a parent, a teacher, an administrator or a CEO. Each of us in our daily lives is asked to assume a degree of responsibility. Bob gives us the road map to follow with excellence being the result. Palestini's book has practical applications that will allow each of us to develop and improve our leadership capabilities.

> Phil Martelli, head basketball coach,
> Saint Joseph's University Hawks

PREFACE

This is a book about leadership. The conventional wisdom is that leaders are born, not made. I disagree! My experience and, more importantly, scholarly research indicate that leadership skills can be learned. Granted, some leaders will be superior to others because of genetics, but the basic leadership skills are learned and can be cultivated and enhanced. The first chapter of this book speaks to the *science* of administration, while the second chapter deals with the *art* of administration and leadership. One needs to lead with both mind (science) and heart (art) to be truly effective.

The effective building blocks of quality leadership are the skills of communication, motivation, organizational development, management, and creativity. Mastering the theory and practice in these areas of study will produce high-quality leadership ability and, in turn, produce successful leaders; doing so with "heart" will result in highly successful and, what some authors have called, heroic leadership.

There is another assumption that many educational practitioners make regarding effective leadership and administration that I would also dispute. Namely, that "nice guys (and gals) finish last." To be a successful administrator, the belief goes, one needs to be firm, direct, even autocratic. Once again, scholarly research, as well as my own experience, indicates that no one singular leadership style is consistently effective in all situations and at all times. Empirical and experiential studies indicate that effective leaders vary their styles depending on the situation. This *situational* approach is a recurring theme in this book. In the concluding chapter, we argue that effective leaders use both their minds and their hearts in the leadership process, and that, in fact, nice guys and gals do oftentimes finish first.

Some 25 years ago, when I was coaching high school basketball, I attended a coaching clinic where the main clinicians were Dean Smith, coach of North Carolina University, and Bobby Knight, then coach of Indiana University. Both coaches were successful then, and three decades later, they remain successful and, in one case at least, revered.

In the morning session Bobby Knight explained how *fear* was the most effective motivator in sports: If you want athletes to listen to you and want to be successful, you need to instill fear in them. In the afternoon session, Dean Smith explained how *love* is the most effective motivator in sports: If you want to win and be successful, you must engender love in the athletes. You can understand my sense of confusion by the end of that clinic. Here were two of the most successful men in sports giving contradictory advice. As a young and impressionable coach, I was puzzled by these apparently mixed messages. Over the intervening years, I have often thought about that clinic and tried to make sense of what I had heard. After these many years, I have drawn two conclusions from this incident, both of which have had a significant impact on my philosophy of leadership and on this book.

The first conclusion has to do with the *situational* nature of leadership. Bobby Knight and Dean Smith impressed upon me the truism that there is no one singular leadership style that is effective at all times and in all situations; and, second, that despite reaping short-term success, the better style for ensuring long-term success is one that inspires love, trust, and respect. Just as athletes become robotic and are fearful of making mistakes when fear is the only motivator, so too are employees who are supervised by an autocratic manager. The leader who instills fear in his or her subordinates stymies all initiative, creativity, and self-sufficiency. Thus, I arrived at my conclusion that effective school administration and leadership, which is my field, and leadership in general begin with love, trust, and respect.

In addition to an emphasis on the nature of leadership, this book focuses on placing *theory* into practice. We cannot underestimate the value and importance of theory. Without theory we have no valid way of analyzing and correcting failed practice. Without a theoretical base, we oftentimes lead by trial and error, or by the proverbial "seat of your pants." On the other hand, however, knowledge of theory without the ability to place it into reflective practice is of no value and not characteristic of effective leadership. Leaders should adopt one of the leadership theories described in this book and place it into reflective practice, modeled after the leadership behavior of some of the coaches that are highlighted here.

This book uses the case study approach in order to facilitate placing theory into effective practice. Each chapter contains an extensive study of one of ten of the most successful basketball coaches of our times. We will analyze each case and see how these coaches were able to place leadership theory into effective practice. I believe that the lessons learned will prove invaluable to leaders and aspiring leaders, whether that is a parent, teacher, school principal, or CEO.

I chose coaches as my subjects because they are basically teachers, and as we shall see, being able to teach one's followers and thus foster a learning organization is a valuable asset if one wishes to be an effective leader. I also chose coaches because their leadership behavior is more observable and more chronicled.

This book also takes an organizational development approach to producing effective leadership. Picture yourself standing in the middle of a dense forest. Suppose you were asked to describe the characteristics of the forest; what types of trees are growing in the forest; how many acres of trees are there; where are the trees thriving; where are they not. Faced with this proposition, most people would not know where to start and "would not be able to see the forest for the trees."

Newly appointed executives and administrators often have this same feeling of confusion when faced with the prospect of having to assume a leadership role in a complex organization like a school or a company. Where does one start? An effective way to start would be to systematically examine the components that make up an organization. Such a system of organizational diagnosis and prescription will lead to a comprehensive and integrated analysis of the organization's strengths and weaknesses and point the way toward possible improvement. Using the leadership implications found in these successful coaches' behaviors as a model, the final chapter of this book suggests such a sequential and systematic approach. Utilizing it effectively can produce dramatic and useful results.

This leads me to what I presumptuously refer to as my "Seven Principles of Effective Leadership." Effective leaders:

- Need to be able to adapt their *leadership style* to the situation.
- Must be keenly aware of the organizational *structure and culture* of the institution.
- Must be able to engender a sense of *trust and respect* in their followers.
- Need to continuously improve their organizations and, therefore, must be *agents for change*.
- Need to be *well organized, creative,* and have a clearly articulated *vision*.
- Must be able to *communicate* effectively.
- Must know how to *motivate* their followers and to be able to *manage the conflicts* that arise.

In my view, which is supported by a prodigious amount of empirical research, if an administrator can master the knowledge and skills encompassed in these seven principles, and do it with heart, he or she will be highly successful.

1

CONTEMPORARY LEADERSHIP THEORY

> The effective functioning of social systems from the local PTA to the United States of America is assumed to be dependent on the quality of their leadership.
>
> —Victor H. Vroom

INTRODUCTION

Leadership is offered as a solution for most of the problems of organizations everywhere. Schools will work, we are told, if principals provide strong instructional leadership. Around the world, administrators and managers say that their organizations would thrive if only senior management provided strategy, vision, and real leadership. Although the call for leadership is universal, there is much less clarity about what the term means.

Historically, researchers in this field have searched for the one best leadership style that would be most effective. Current thought is that there is no one best style. Rather, a combination of styles, depending on the situation the leader finds him- or herself in, has been found to be more appropriate. To understand the evolution of leadership theory thought, we will take an historical approach and trace the progress of leadership theory, beginning with the trait perspective of leadership and moving to the more current contingency theories of leadership.

THE TRAIT THEORY

Trait theory suggests that we can evaluate leadership and propose ways of leading effectively by considering whether an individual possesses certain personality traits, social traits, and physical characteristics. Popular in the 1940s and 1950s, trait theory attempted to predict which individuals would successfully become leaders and then whether they were effective. Leaders differ from nonleaders in their drive, desire to lead, honesty and integrity, self-confidence, cognitive ability, and knowledge of the business they are in. Even the traits judged necessary for top-, middle-, and low-level management differ among leaders of different countries; for example, U.S. and British leaders value resourcefulness; the Japanese, intuition; and the Dutch, imagination, but for lower and middle managers only.[1]

The obvious question is, can you think of any individuals who are effective leaders, but who lack one or more of these characteristics? Chances are that you can. Skills and ability to implement the vision are necessary to transform traits into leadership behavior. Individual capability, which is a function of background predispositions, preferences, cognitive complexity, and technical, human relations, and conceptual skills, also contributes.

The trait approach has more historical than practical interest to managers and administrators, although recent research has once again tied leadership effectiveness to leader traits. One study of senior management jobs suggests that effective leadership requires a broad knowledge of and solid relations within the industry and the company, an excellent reputation, a strong track record, a keen mind, strong interpersonal skills, high integrity, high energy, and a strong drive to lead. In addition, some view the transformational perspective described later in this chapter as a natural evolution of the earlier trait perspective.

THE BEHAVIORAL PERSPECTIVE

The limitations in the ability of traits to predict effective leadership caused researchers during the 1950s to view a person's behavior, rather than that individual's personal traits, as a way of increasing leadership effectiveness. This view also paved the way for later situational theories.

The types of leadership behaviors investigated typically fell into two categories: production oriented and employee oriented. Production-oriented leadership, also called concern for production, initiating structure, or task-focused leadership, involves acting primarily to get the task done. An administrator who tells his or her department chair to do "everything they need to do to get the curriculum developed on time for the start of school" demonstrates production-oriented leadership. So does an administrator who uses an autocratic style or fails to involve workers in any aspect of decision making. Employee-oriented leadership, also called concern for people or consideration, focuses on supporting the individual workers in their activities and involving the workers in decision making. A principal who demonstrates great concern for his or her teachers' satisfaction with their duties and commitment to their work has an employee-oriented leadership style.[2]

Studies in leadership at Ohio State University, which classified individuals' style as initiating structure or consideration, examined the link between style and grievance rate, performance, and turnover. Initiating structure reflects the degree to which the leader structures his or her own role and subordinates' roles toward accomplishing the group's goal through scheduling work, assigning employees to tasks, and maintaining standards of performance. Consideration refers to the degree to which the leader emphasizes individuals' needs through two-way communication, respect for subordinates' ideas, mutual trust between leader and subordinates, and consideration of subordinates' feelings. Although leaders can choose the style to fit the outcomes they desire, in fact, to achieve desirable outcomes on all three dimensions of performance, grievance rate, and turnover, the research suggested that managers should strive to demonstrate both initiating structure and consideration.[3]

A series of leadership studies at the University of Michigan, which looked at managers with an employee orientation and a production orientation, yielded similar results. In these studies, which related differences in high-productivity and low-productivity work groups to differences in supervisors, highly productive supervisors spent more time in planning departmental work and in supervising their employees; they spent less time in working alongside and performing the same tasks as subordinates, accorded their subordinates more freedom in specific task performance, and tended to be employee oriented.

A 30-year research study in Japan examined performance and maintenance leadership behaviors. Performance here refers specifically to forming and reaching group goals through fast work speed; outcomes of high quality, accuracy, and quantity; and observation of rules. Maintenance behaviors preserve the group's social stability by dealing with subordinates' feelings, reducing stress, providing comfort, and showing appreciation. The Japanese, according to this and other studies, prefer leadership high on both dimensions over performance-dominated behavior except when work is done in short-term project groups, where subordinates are prone to anxiety, or when effective performance calls for very low effort.

MANAGERIAL ROLES THEORY

A study of chief executive officers by Henry Mintzberg suggested a different way of looking at leadership. He observed that managerial work encompasses ten roles: three that focus on interpersonal contact: (1) figurehead, (2) leader, (3) liaison; three that involve mainly information processing: (4) monitor, (5) disseminator, (6) spokesman; and four related to decision making: (7) entrepreneur, (8) disturbance handler, (9) resource allocator, and (10) negotiator. Note that almost all roles would include activities that could be construed as leadership—influencing others toward a particular goal. In addition, most of these roles can apply to nonmanagerial positions as well as managerial ones. The role approach resembles the behavioral and trait perspectives because all three call for specific types of behavior independent of the situation; however, the role approach is more compatible with the situation approach and has been shown to be more valid than either the behavioral or trait perspective.[4]

Although not all managers will perform every role, some diversity of role performance must occur. Managers can diagnose their own and others' role performance and then offer strategies for altering it. The choice roles will depend to some extent on the manager's specific job description and the situation in question. For example, managing individual performance and instructing subordinates are less important for middle managers than for first-line supervisors, and less important for executives than for either lower level of manager.

EARLY SITUATIONAL THEORIES

Contingency or situational models differ from the earlier trait and behavioral models in asserting that no single way of leading works in all situations. Rather, appropriate behavior depends on the circumstances at a given time. Effective managers diagnose the situation, identify the leadership style that will be most effective, and then determine whether they can implement the required style. Early situational research suggests that subordinate, supervisor, and task considerations affect the appropriate leadership style in a given situation. The precise aspects of each dimension that influence the most effective leadership style vary.

THEORY X AND THEORY Y

One of the older situational theories, McGregor's Theory X/Theory Y formulation, calls for a leadership style based on individuals' assumptions about other individuals, together with characteristics of the individual, the task, the organization, and environment.[5] Although managers may have many styles, Theories X and Y have received the greatest attention. Theory X managers assume that people are lazy, extrinsically motivated, and incapable of self-discipline or self-control, and that they want security but no responsibility in their jobs. Theory Y managers assume people do not inherently dislike work, are intrinsically motivated, exert self-control, and seek responsibility. A Theory X manager, because of his or her limited view of the world, has only one leadership style available, that is, autocratic. A Theory Y manager has a wide range of styles in his or her repertoire.

How can an administrator use McGregor's theory for ensuring leadership effectiveness? What prescription would McGregor offer for improving the situation? If an administrator had Theory X assumptions, he or she would suggest that the administrator change them and would facilitate this change by sending the administrator to a management development program. If a manager had Theory Y assumptions, McGregor would advise a diagnosis of the situation to ensure that the selected style matched the administrator's assumptions and action tendencies, as well as the internal and external influences on the situation.

FREDERICK FIEDLER'S THEORY

Although McGregor's theory provided a transition from behavioral to situational theories, Frederick Fiedler developed and tested the first leadership theory explicitly called a contingency or situational model. He argued that changing an individual's leadership style is quite difficult, but that organizations should put individuals in situations that fit with their own style. Fiedler's theory suggests that managers can choose between two styles: task oriented and relationship oriented. Then the nature of leader-member relations, task structure, and position power of the leader influences whether a task-oriented or a relationship-oriented leadership style is more likely to be effective. Leader-member relations refer to the extent to which the group trusts and respects the leader and will follow the leader's directions. Task structure describes the degree to which the task is clearly specified and defined or structured, as opposed to ambiguous or unstructured. Position power means the extent to which the leader has official power, that is, the potential or actual ability to influence others in a desired direction, owing to the position he or she holds in the organization.[6]

The style recommended as most effective for each combination of these three situational factors is based on the degree of control or influence the leader can exert in his or her leadership position. In general, high-control situations call for task-oriented leadership because they allow the leader to take charge. Low-control situations also call for task-oriented leadership because they require rather than allow the leader to take charge. Moderate-control situations, in contrast, call for relationship-oriented leadership because the situations challenge leaders to get the cooperation of their subordinates. Despite extensive research to support the theory, critics have questioned the reliability of the measurement of leadership style and the range and appropriateness of the three situational components. This theory, however, is particularly applicable for those who believe that individuals are born with a certain management style, rather than the management style being learned or flexible.[7]

CONTEMPORARY SITUATIONAL LEADERSHIP

Current research suggests that the effect of leader behaviors on performance is altered by such intervening variables as the effort of subordinates, their ability to perform their jobs, the clarity of their job responsibilities, the organization of the work, the cooperation and cohesiveness of the group, the sufficiency of resources and support provided to the group, and the coordination of work group activities with those of other subunits. Thus, leaders must respond to these and broader cultural differences in choosing an appropriate style. A leader-environment-follower interaction theory of leadership notes that effective leaders first analyze deficiencies in the follower's ability, motivation, role perception, and work environment that inhibit performance and then act to eliminate these deficiencies.[8]

PATH-GOAL THEORY

According to path-goal theory, the leader attempts to influence subordinates' perceptions of goals and the path to achieve them. Leaders can then choose among four styles of leadership: directive, supportive, participative, and achievement oriented. In selecting a style, the leader acts to strengthen the expectancy, instrumentality, and valence of a situation, respectively, by providing better technology or training for the employees;

reinforcing desired behaviors with pay, praise, or promotion; and ensuring that the employees value the rewards they receive.[9]

Choosing a style requires a quality diagnosis of the situation to decide which leadership behaviors would be most effective in attaining the desired outcomes. The appropriate leadership style is influenced first by subordinates' characteristics, particularly the subordinates' abilities and the likelihood that the leader's behavior will cause subordinates' satisfaction now or in the future; and, second, by the environment, including the subordinates' tasks, the formal authority system, the primary work group, and organizational culture. According to this theory, the appropriate style for an administrator depends on his or her subordinates' skills, knowledge, and abilities, as well as their attitudes toward the administrator. It also depends on the nature of the activities, the lines of authority in the organization, the integrity of their work group, and the task technology involved. The most desirable leadership style helps the individual achieve satisfaction, meet personal needs, and accomplish goals, while complementing the subordinates' abilities and the characteristics of the situation.

Application of the path-goal theory, then, requires first an assessment of the situation, particularly its participants and environment, and second, a determination of the most congruent leadership style. Although the research about path-goal theory has yielded mixed results, it can provide a leader with help in selecting an effective leadership style.

THE VROOM-YETTON MODEL

The Vroom-Yetton theory involves a procedure for determining the extent to which leaders should involve subordinates in the decision-making process.[10] The manager can choose one of five approaches that range from individual problem solving with available information to joint problem solving to delegation of problem-solving responsibility. Table 1.1 summarizes the possibilities.

Selection of the appropriate decision process involves assessing six factors: (1) the problem's quality requirement, (2) the location of information about the problem, (3) the structure of the problem, (4) the likely acceptance of the decision by those affected, (5) the commonality of

Table 1.1. Decision-Making Processes

For Individual Problems	For Group Problems
AI You solve the problem or make the decision yourself, using information available to you at that time.	**AI** You solve the problem or make the decision yourself, using information available to you at the time.
AII You obtain any necessary information from the subordinate, then decide on the solution to the problem yourself. You may or may not tell the subordinate what the problem is, in getting the information from him. The role played by your subordinate in making the decision is clearly one of providing specific information that you request, rather than generating or evaluating alternative solutions.	**AII** You obtain any necessary information from subordinates, then decide on the solution to the problem yourself. You may or may not tell subordinates what the problem is, in getting the information from them. The role played by your subordinates in making the decision is clearly one of providing specific information that you request, rather than generating or evaluating solutions.
CI You share the problem with the relevant subordinate, getting his ideas and suggestions. Then, you make the decision. This decision may or may not reflect your subordinate's influence.	**CI** You share the problem with the relevant subordinates individually, getting their ideas and suggestions without bringing them together as a group. Then you make the decision. This decision may or may not reflect your subordinates' influence.
GI You share the problem with one of your subordinates, and together you analyze the problem and arrive at a mutually satisfactory solution in an atmosphere of free and open exchange of information and ideas. You both contribute to the resolution of the problem with the relative contribution of each being dependent on knowledge rather than formal authority.	**CII** You share the problem with your subordinates in a group meeting. In this meeting you obtain their ideas and suggestions. Then, you make the decision, which may or may not reflect your subordinates' influence.
DI You delegate the problem to one of your subordinates, providing him or her with any relevant information that you possess, but giving responsibility for solving the problem independently. Any solution that the person reaches will receive your support.	**GII** You share the problem with your subordinates as a group. Together you generate and evaluate alternatives and attempt to reach agreement (consensus) on a solution. Your role is much like that of chairman, coordinating the discussion, keeping it focused on the problem, and making sure that the crucial issues are discussed. You do not try to influence the group to adopt "your" solution and are willing to accept and implement any solution that has the support of the entire group.

A. Is there a quality requirement such that one solution is likely to be more rational than another?
B. Do I have sufficient info to make a high quality decision?
C. Is the problem structured?
D. Is acceptance of decision by subordinates critical to effective implementation?
E. If I were to make the decision by myself, is it reasonably certain that it would be accepted by my subordinates?
F. Do subordinates share the organizational goals to be attained in solving this problem?
G. Is conflict among subordinates likely in preferred solutions? (This question is irrelevant to individual problems.)
H. Do subordinates have sufficient info to make a high quality decision?

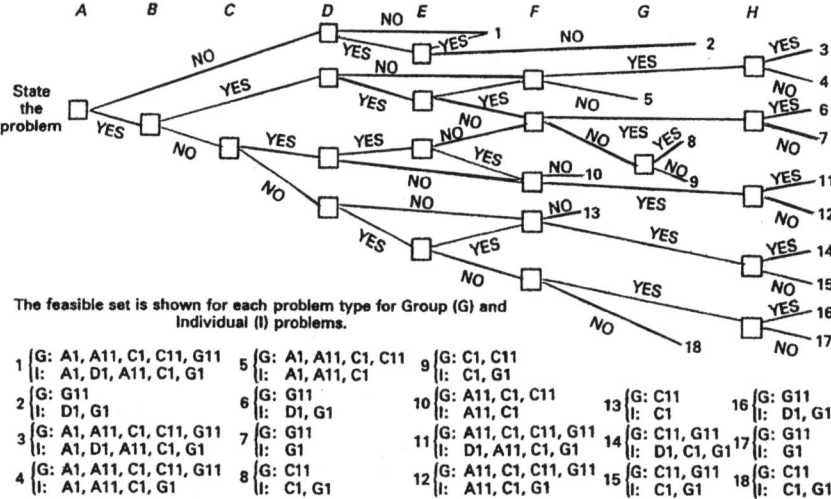

Figure 1.1. Decision process flow chart for both individual and group problems.

organizational goals, and (6) the likely conflict regarding possible problem solutions. Figure 1.1 illustrates the original normative model, expressed as a decision tree. To make a decision, the leader asks each question, A through H, corresponding to each box encountered, from left to right, unless questions may be skipped because the response to the previous question leads to a later one. For example, a no response to question A allows questions B and C to be skipped; a yes response to question B after a yes response to question A allows question C to be skipped. Reaching the end of one branch of the tree results in identification of a problem type (numbered 1 through 18) with an accompanying set of feasible decision processes. When the set of feasible processes for group problems includes more than one process (e.g., a "no response" to each question results in problem type 1, for which every decision style is feasible), final selection of the single approach can use either a minimum number of hours (group processes AI, AII, CI, CII, and GII are preferred in that order) or a secondary criteria. A manager who wishes to make the decision in the shortest time possible, and for whom all processes are appropriate, will choose AI (solving the problem him- or herself using available information) over any other process. A manager who wishes to maximize subordinate involvement in the decision making as a training and development tool, for example, will choose DI or GII (delegating the problem to the subordinate, or together with subordinates reaching a decision) if all processes are feasible and if time is not limited. Similar choices can be made when analyzing individual problems. Research has shown that decisions made using processes from the feasible set result in more effective outcomes than those not included.[11]

Suppose, for example, the teacher evaluation instrument in your institution was in need of revision. Using the decision tree, we would ask the first question: Is there a quality requirement such that one solution is likely to be more rational than another? Our answer would have to be, yes. Do I have sufficient information to make a high-quality decision? The answer is, no. Is the problem structured? Yes. Is acceptance of the decision by subordinates critical to effective implementation? Yes. If I were to make the decision myself, can I be reasonably certain my subordinates would accept it? No. Do subordinates share the organizational goals to be attained in solving this problem? Yes. Is conflict among subordinates likely in preferred solutions? Yes. Do subordinates have sufficient information to make a high-quality decision? Yes.

Following this procedure, the decision tree indicates that GII would be the proper approach to revise the teacher evaluation form. GII indicates that the leader should share the problem with his or her faculty. Together they generate and evaluate alternatives and attempt to reach agreement on a solution. The leader's role is much like that of a chairperson coordinating the discussion, keeping it focused on the problem and making sure that the critical issues are discussed. The leader would not try to influence the group to adopt "his" (or her) solution, and the leader is willing to accept and implement any solution that has the support of the entire faculty.

The recent reformulation of this model uses the same decision processes, AI, AII, CI, CII, GII, GI, DI, as the original model, as well as the criteria of decision quality, decision commitment, time, and subordinate development. It differs by expanding the range of possible responses to include probabilities, rather than yes or no answers, to each diagnostic question, and it uses a computer to process the data. Although both formulations of this model provide a set of diagnostic questions for analyzing a problem, they tend to oversimplify the process. Their narrow focus on the extent of subordinate involvement in decision making also limits their usefulness.

THE HERSEY/BLANCHARD MODEL

In an attempt to integrate previous knowledge about leadership into a prescriptive model of leadership style, the Hersey/Blanchard theory cites the "readiness of followers," defined as their ability and willingness to accomplish a specific task, as the major contingency that influences appropriate leadership style.[12] Follower readiness incorporates the follower's level of achievement motivation, ability, and willingness to assume responsibility for his or her own behavior in accomplishing specific tasks and education and experience relevant to the task. The model combines task and relationship behavior to yield four possible styles, as shown in Figure 1.2. Leaders should use a *telling style*, provide specific instructions, and closely supervise performance when followers are unable, unwilling, or insecure. Leaders should use a *selling style* and explain decisions and provide opportunity for clarification, when followers have moderate to low readiness. Using a *participating style*, where the leader shares ideas and helps facilitate decision making, should occur when followers have moderate to high readiness. Finally, leaders should use a *delegating style* and give responsibility for decisions and implementation to followers, when followers are able, willing, and confident.

Although some researchers have questioned the conceptual clarity, validity, robustness, and utility of the model, as well as the instruments used to measure leadership style, others have supported the utility of the theory. For example, the Leadership Effectiveness and Description Scale (LEAD) and related instruments, developed to measure leadership style by the life cycle researchers, are widely used in industrial training programs. This model can easily be adapted to educational administration and be used analytically to understand leadership deficien-

CONTEMPORARY LEADERSHIP THEORY

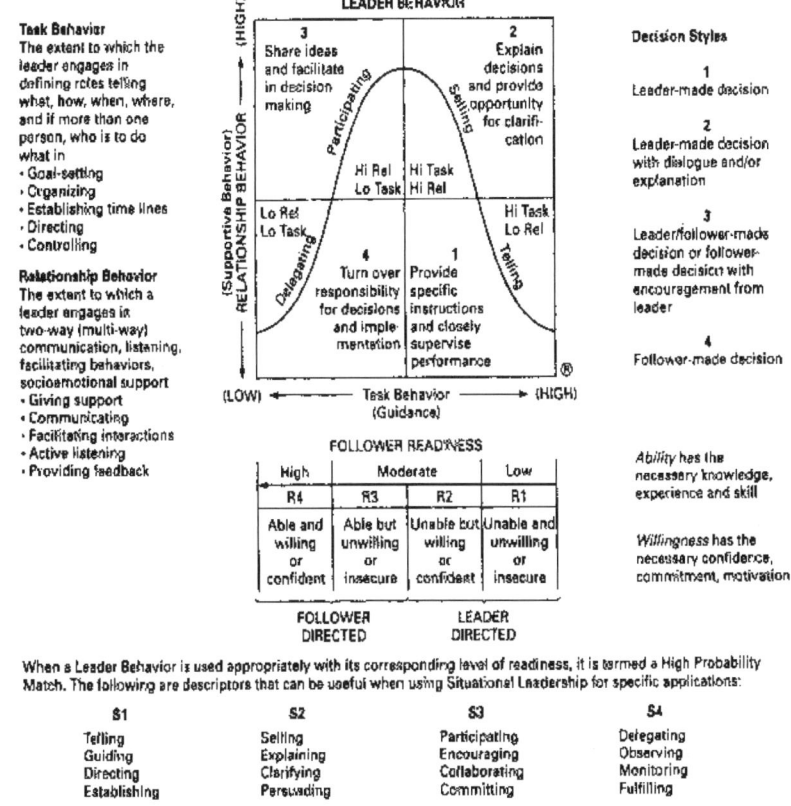

Figure 1.2. Model of Situational Leadership

cies and combine it with the path-goal model to prescribe the appropriate style for a variety of situations.

REFRAMING LEADERSHIP

Lee Bolman and Terrence Deal have developed a unique situational leadership theory that analyzes leadership behavior through four frames of reference: structural, human resource, political, and symbolic. Each of the frames offers a different perspective on what leadership is and how it operates in organizations. Each can result in either effective or ineffective conceptions of leadership.[13]

Structural leaders develop a new model of the relationship of structure, strategy, and environment for their organizations. They focus on implementation. The right answer helps only if it can be implemented. These leaders emphasize rationality, analysis, logic, fact, and data. They are likely to believe strongly in the importance of clear structure and well-developed management systems. A good leader is someone who thinks clearly, makes good decisions, has good analytic skills, and can design structures and systems that get the job done. Structural leaders sometimes fail because they miscalculate the difficulty of putting their designs in place. They often underestimate the resistance that it will generate, and they take few steps to build a base of support for their innovations. In short, they are often undone by human resource, political, and symbolic considerations. Structural leaders do continually experiment, evaluate, and adapt, but because they fail to consider the entire environment in which they are situated, they sometimes are ineffective.

Human resource leaders believe in people and communicate that belief. They are passionate about "productivity through people." They demonstrate this faith in their words and actions and often build it into a philosophy or credo that is central to their vision of their organizations. They believe in the importance of coaching, participation, motivation, teamwork, and good interpersonal relations. A good leader is a facilitator and participative manager who supports and empowers others. Human resource leaders are visible and accessible. Peters and Waterman popularized the notion of "management wandering around," the idea that managers need to get out of their offices and interact with workers and customers. Many educational administrators have adopted this aspect of management.

Effective human resource leaders empower, that is, they increase participation, provide support, share information, and move decision making as far down the organization as possible. Human resource leaders often like to refer to their employees as "partners" or "colleagues." They want to make it clear that employees have a stake in the organization's success and a right to be involved in making decisions. When they are ineffective, however, they are seen as naive or as weaklings and wimps.

Political leaders believe that managers and leaders live in a world of conflict and scarce resources. The central task of management is to mobilize the resources needed to advocate and fight for the unit's or the organization's goals and objectives. They emphasize the importance of building a power base: allies, networks, coalitions. A good leader is an advocate and negotiator, understands politics, and is comfortable with conflict. Political leaders clarify what they want and what they can get. Political leaders are realists above all. They never let what they want cloud their judgment about what is possible. They assess the distribution of power and interests. The political leader needs to think carefully about the players, their interests, and their power; in other words, he or she must map the political terrain. Political leaders ask questions such as: Whose support do I need? How do I go about getting it? Who are my opponents? How much power do they have? What can I do to reduce the opposition? Is the battle winnable? However, if ineffective, these leaders are perceived as being untrustworthy and manipulative.

The symbolic frame provides still a fourth turn of the kaleidoscope of leadership. In this frame, the organization is seen as a stage, a theater in which every actor plays certain roles and attempts to communicate the right impressions to the right audiences. The main premise of this frame is that whenever reason and analysis fail to contain the dark forces of ambiguity, human beings erect symbols, myths, rituals, and ceremonies to bring order, meaning, and predictability out of chaos and confusion. They believe that the essential role of management is to provide inspiration. They rely on personal charisma and a flair for drama to get people excited and committed to the organizational mission. A good leader is a prophet and visionary who uses symbols, tells stories, and frames experience in ways that give people hope and meaning. Transforming leaders are visionary leaders, and visionary leadership is invariably symbolic. Examination of symbolic leaders reveals that they follow a consistent set of practices and rules.

Transforming leaders use symbols to capture attention. When Diana Lam became principal of the Mackey Middle School in Boston in 1985, she knew that she faced a substantial challenge. Mackey found all the usual problems of urban public schools: decaying physical plant, lack of student discipline, racial tension, troubles with the teaching staff, low morale, and limited resources. The only good news was that the situation was so bad that almost any change would be an improvement. In such a situation, symbolic leaders will try to do something visible, even dramatic, to let people know that changes are on the way. During the summer before she assumed her duties, Lam wrote a letter to every teacher to set up an individual meeting. She traveled to meet teachers wherever they wanted, driving 2 hours in one case. She asked teachers how they felt about the school and what changes they wanted.

She also felt that something needed to be done about the school building because nobody likes to work in a dumpy place. She decided that the front door and some of the worst classrooms had to be painted. She had few illusions about getting the bureaucracy of the Boston public school system to provide painters, so she persuaded some of her family members to help her do the painting. When school opened, students and staff members immediately saw that things were going to be different, if only symbolically. Perhaps even more important, staff members received a subtle challenge to make a contribution themselves.

Each of the frames captures significant possibilities for leadership, but each is incomplete. In the early part of the century, leadership as a concept was rarely applied to management, and the implicit models of leadership were narrowly rational. In the 1960s and 1970s, human resource leadership became fashionable. The literature on organizational leadership stressed openness, sensitivity, and participation. In recent years, symbolic leadership had moved to center stage, and the literature now offers advice on how to become a visionary leader with the power to transform organizational cultures. Organizations do need vision, but it is not their only need and not always their most important one. Leaders need to understand their own frame and its limits. Ideally, they will also learn to combine multiple frames into a more comprehensive and powerful style. It is this Bolman/Deal leadership theory on which I will base my conclusions regarding the leadership behavior of the ten basketball coaches profiled in this text.

TRANSFORMATIONAL LEADERSHIP

A charismatic or transformational leader uses charisma to inspire his or her followers and is an example of one who acts primarily in the symbolic frame of leadership outlined above. He or she talks to the followers about how essential their performance is, how confident he or she is in the followers, how exceptional the followers are, and how he or she expects the group's performance to exceed expectations. Lee Iacocca, in industry, and the late Marcus Foster and Notre Dame's Reverend Theodore Hesburgh are examples in education of this type of leader. Such leaders use dominance, self-confidence, a need for influence, and conviction of moral righteousness to increase their charisma and consequently their leadership effectiveness.[14]

A transformational leader changes an organization by recognizing an opportunity and developing a vision, communicating that vision to organizational members, building trust in the vision, and achieving the vision by motivating organizational members. The leader helps subordinates recognize the need for revitalizing the organization by developing a felt need for change, overcoming resistance to change, and avoiding quick-fix solutions to problems. Encouraging subordinates to act as devil's advocates with regard to the leader, building networks outside the organization, visiting other organizations, and changing management processes to reward progress against competition also help them recognize a need for revitalization. Individuals must disengage from and disidentify with the past, as well as view change as a way of dealing with their disenchantments with the past or the status quo. The transformational leader creates a new vision and mobilizes commitment to it by planning or educating others. He or she builds trust through demonstrating personal expertise, self-confidence, and personnel integrity. The charismatic leader can also change the composition of the team, alter management processes, and help organizational members reframe the way they perceive an organizational situation. The charismatic leader must empower others to help achieve the vision. Finally, the transformational leader must institutionalize the change by replacing old technical, political, cultural, and social networks with new ones. For example, the leader can identify key individuals and groups, develop a plan for obtaining their commitment, and institute a monitoring system for following the changes. If an administrator wishes to make an innovative program acceptable to the faculty and the school community, for example, he or she should follow the above plan and identify influential individuals who would agree to champion the new program, develop a plan to gain support of others in the community through personnel contact or other means, and develop a monitoring system to assess the progress of the effort.[15]

A transformational leader motivates subordinates to achieve beyond their original expectations by increasing their awareness about the importance of designated outcomes and ways of attaining them, by getting workers to go beyond their self-interest to that of the team, the school, the school system, and the larger society, and by changing or expanding the individual's needs. Subordinates report that they work harder for such leaders. In addition, their subordinates judge such leaders higher in leadership potential as compared to the more common transactional leader.

One should be cognizant, however, of the negative side of charismatic leadership that may exist if the leader overemphasizes devotion to him- or herself, makes personal needs paramount, or uses highly effective communication skills to mislead or manipulate others. Such leaders may be so driven to achieve a vision that they ignore the costly implications of their goals. The superintendent of schools that overexpands his or her jurisdiction in an effort to form an "empire," only to have the massive system turn into a bureaucratic nightmare, is an example of transformational leadership gone sour. Nevertheless, recent research has verified the overall effectiveness of transformational leadership style.

DEVELOPING A VISION

A requisite for transformational leadership is a vision. Although there seems to be a sense of mystery on the part of some individuals regarding what a vision is and how to create one, the process for developing one is not at all complex. Using education as an example, the first step is to develop a list of broad goals. "All children achieving" is an example of such a goal. These goals should be developed in conjunction with representatives of all segments of the school community, otherwise there will be no sense of "ownership," the absence of which will preclude successful implementation.

The next step in the process is to merge and prioritize the goals and to summarize them in the form of a short and concise vision statement. The following is an example of a typical vision statement:

> Our vision for the Exeter School System is that all of our graduating students, regardless of ability, will say that "I have received an excellent education that has prepared me to be an informed citizen and leader in my community." Our students will have a worldview, and as a result of their experience in the Exeter School System, will be committed to a process of

lifelong learning and the making of a better world by living the ideals of fairness and justice through service to others.

The key concepts in the above vision are: all students achieving, excellence, leadership, multiculturalism, lifelong learning, values, and community service. It is these concepts that the transformational leader stresses in all forms of communication and in all interactions with the school community.

The final step in the process is the institutionalizing of the educational vision. This step ensures that the vision endures when the leadership changes. Operationalizing and placing the important concepts of the vision into the official policies and procedures of the school system is one way of helping to institutionalize the educational vision and incorporating it into the school culture.

IMPLICATIONS FOR LEADERS

The implications of leadership theory for educational and other administrators are rather clear. The successful administrator needs to have a sound grasp of leadership theory and the skills to implement it. The principles of situational and transformational leadership theory are guides to effective administrative behavior. The leadership behavior applied to an inexperienced faculty member may be significantly different from that applied to a more experienced and tested one. Task behavior may be appropriate in dealing with a new teacher, while relationship behavior may be more appropriate when dealing with a seasoned teacher.

The four frames of leadership discussed by Bolman and Deal may be particularly helpful to school leaders and leaders in general. Consideration of the structural, human relations, and political and symbolic implications of leadership behavior can keep an administrator attuned to the various dimensions affecting appropriate leadership behavior. With the need to deal with collective bargaining entities, school boards, and a variety of other power issues, the political frame considerations may be particularly helpful in understanding the complexity of relationships that exist between administrators and these groups. Asking oneself the questions posed earlier under the political frame can be an effective guide to the appropriate leadership behavior in dealing with these groups.

SUMMARY

Recently, a plethora of research studies have been conducted on leadership and leadership styles. The overwhelming evidence indicates that there is no one singular leadership style that is most appropriate in all situations. Rather, an administrator's leadership style should be adapted to the situation so that at various times task behavior or relationship behavior might be appropriate. At other times and in other situations, various degrees of both task and relationship behavior may be most effective.

The emergence of transformational leadership has seen leadership theory come full circle. Transformational leadership theory combines aspects of the early trait theory perspective with the more current situational or contingency models. The personal charisma of the leader, along with his or her ability to formulate an educational vision and to communicate it to others, determines the transformational leader's effectiveness.

Since the effective leader is expected to adapt his or her leadership style to an ever changing environment, administration becomes an even more complex and challenging task. However, a thorough knowledge of leadership theory can make some sense of the apparent chaos that the administrator faces on almost a daily basis.

Among scholars there is an assertion that *theory informs practice and practice informs theory.* This notion posits that to be an effective leader, one must base his or her practice on some form of leadership theory. If the leader consciously based his or her practice on leadership theory, this would be an example of theory informing practice. On the other hand, when a leader utilizes theory-inspired behavior that is continually ineffective, perhaps the theory must be modified to account for this deficiency. In this case, practice would be informing or changing theory. In this book, we will examine the leadership behavior of ten successful basketball coaches to ascertain whether their behavior conforms to the principles of the Bolman/Deal situational leadership theory, and if not, whether their practice or the theory needs to be modified to reflect effective practice. We will also examine how these coaches' leadership practices can be applied to our own leadership behavior to make it more effective.

2

LEADING WITH HEART

> Do unto others what you would have them do unto you.
>
> —The Golden Rule

INTRODUCTION

How the leader utilizes the concepts contained in the preceding chapter depends largely on one's philosophy of life regarding how human beings behave in the workplace. The two extremes of the continuum might be described as those leaders who believe that human beings are basically lazy and will do the very least they need to do to "get by" in the workplace versus those who believe that people are basically industrious and, if given the choice, would opt for doing a quality job. I believe that today's most effective leaders hold the latter view. I agree with Max De Pree, owner and CEO of the highly successful Herman Miller Furniture Company. Writing in his book, *Leadership Is an Art*, he says that a leader's function is to "liberate people to do what is required of them in the most effective and humane way possible."[1] Instead of catching people doing something wrong, our goal as enlightened leaders is to catch them doing something right. I suggest, therefore, that in addition to a rational approach to leadership, a truly enlightened leader leads with heart.

Too often leaders underestimate the skills and qualities of their followers. I remember Bill Faries, the chief custodian at a high school at which I was assistant principal in the mid-1970s. Bill's mother, with whom he had been extraordinarily close, had passed away after a long illness. The school was a religiously affiliated one and the school community went "all out" in its remembrance of Bill's mother. We held a religious service in which almost 3,000 members of the school community participated. Bill, of course, was very grateful. As a token of his gratitude he gave the school a 6-by-8-foot knitted quilt that he had personally sewn. From that point on I did not know if Bill was a custodian who was a quilt weaver, or a quilt weaver who was a custodian. The point is that it took the death of his mother for me and others to realize how truly talented our custodian was. So our effectiveness as leaders begins with an understanding of the diversity of people's gifts, talents, and skills. When we think about the variety of gifts that people bring to organizations and institutions, we can see that leading with heart lies in cultivating, liberating, and enabling those gifts.

LEADERSHIP DEFINED

The first responsibility of a leader is to define reality through a vision; the last is to say thank you. In between, the leader must become the servant of the servants. Being a leader means having the opportunity to make a meaningful difference in the lives of those who allow leaders to lead. This summarizes what I call leading with heart. In a nutshell, leaders do not inflict pain; they bear pain.

Whether one is a successful leader can be determined by looking at the followers. Are they reaching their potential? Are they learning? Are they able to change without bitterness? Are they able to achieve the institution's goals and objectives? Can they manage conflict among themselves? Where the answer to these questions is an emphatic yes is where an effective leader resides.

I prefer to think about leadership in terms of what the gospel writer Luke calls, the "one who serves." The leader owes something to the institution he or she leads. The leader is seen in this context as steward rather than owner or proprietor. Leading with heart requires the leader to think about his or her stewardship in terms of legacy, values, direction, and effectiveness.

Legacy

Too many of today's leaders are interested only in immediate results that bolster their career goals. Long-range goals are left to their successors. This approach fosters autocratic leadership, which oftentimes produces short-term results but militates against creativity and its long-term benefits. In effect this approach is the antithesis of leading with heart.

On the contrary, leaders should build a long-lasting legacy of accomplishment that is institutionalized for posterity. They owe their institutions and their followers a healthy existence and the relationships and reputation that enable continuity of that healthy existence. Leaders are also responsible for future leadership. They need to identify, develop, and nurture future leaders to carry on the legacy.

Values

Along with being responsible for providing future leaders, leaders owe the individuals in their institutions certain other legacies. Leaders need to be concerned with the institutional value system that determines the principles and standards that guide the practices of those in the organization. Leaders need to model their value systems so the individuals in the organization can learn to transmit these values to their colleagues and to future employees. In a civilized institution we see good manners, respect for people, and an appreciation of the way in which we serve one another. A humane, sensitive, and thoughtful leader will transmit his or her value system through his or her daily behavior. This, I believe, is what Peter Senge refers to as a "learning organization."[2]

Direction

Leaders are obliged to provide and maintain direction by developing a vision. I made the point earlier that effective leaders must leave their organizations with a legacy. Part of this legacy should be a sense of progress or momentum. An educational administrator, for instance, should imbue his or her institution with a sense of continuous progress—a sense of constant improvement. Improvement and momentum come from a clear vision of what the institution should be, from a well-planned strategy to achieve that vision, and from carefully developed and articulated directions and plans that allow everyone to participate and be personally accountable for achieving those plans.

Effectiveness

Leaders are also responsible for effectiveness by enabling others to reach their potential both personally and institutionally. The most effective ways of enabling one's colleagues is through participative decision making. It begins with believing in the potential of people—believing in their diversity of gifts. Leaders must realize that to maximize their own power and effectiveness, they need to empower others. Leaders are responsible for setting and attaining the goals in their organizations. Empowering or enabling others to achieve those goals enhances the leader's chances of attaining the goals, ultimately enhancing the leader's effectiveness. Paradoxically, giving up power really amounts to gaining power.

EMPLOYEE OWNERS

We often hear managers suggest that a new program does not have a chance of succeeding unless the employees take "ownership" of the program. Most of us agree to the common sense of such an assertion. But how does a leader promote employee ownership? Let me suggest four steps as a beginning. I am certain that you can think of several more.

1. *Respect people.* As I indicated earlier, respect of people starts with appreciating the diverse gifts that individuals bring to your institution. The key is to dwell on the strengths of your coworkers, rather than on their weaknesses. Try to turn their weaknesses into strengths. This does not mean that disciplinary action or

even dismissal will never become necessary. What it does mean, however, is that the leader should focus on the formative aspect of the employee evaluation process before he or she engages in the summative part.
2. *Let belief guide policy and practice.* Earlier I mentioned developing a culture of civility in your institution. If there is an environment of mutual respect and trust, the organization will flourish. Leaders need to let their belief or value system guide their behavior. Style is merely a consequence of what is believed and what is in our hearts.
3. *Recognize the need for covenants.* Contractual agreements cover such things as salary, fringe benefits, and working conditions. These are part of organizational life, and there is a legitimate need for them. But in today's organizations, especially educational institutions, where the best people working for these institutions are more like volunteers, covenantal relationships are needed. Our best workers may choose their employers. They usually choose the institution where they work based on reasons less tangible than salaries and fringe benefits. They do not need contracts; they need covenants. Covenantal relationships enable educational institutions to be civil, hospitable, and understanding of individuals' differences and unique charisms. They allow administrators to recognize that treating everyone equally does not necessarily mean treating everyone equitably and fairly.
4. *Understand that culture counts more than structure.* An educational institution that I have been associated with recently went through a particularly traumatic time when the credibility of the administration was questioned by the faculty and staff. Various organizational consultants were interviewed to facilitate a "healing" process. Most of the consultants spoke of making the necessary structural changes to create a culture of trust. The institution finally hired a consultant whose attitude was that organizational structure has nothing to do with trust. Interpersonal relations based on mutual respect and an atmosphere of goodwill is what creates a culture of trust. Would you rather work as part of a school with an outstanding reputation or work as part of a group of outstanding individuals? Many times these two characteristics go together, but if

one had to make a choice, I believe that most people would opt to work with outstanding individuals.

IT STARTS WITH TRUST AND SENSITIVITY (HEART)

These are exciting times in education. Revolutionary steps are being taken to restructure schools and rethink the teaching-learning process. The concepts of empowerment, total quality management, the use of technology, and strategic planning are becoming the norm. However, although these activities have the potential to influence education in significantly positive ways, they must be based on a strong foundation to achieve their full potential.

Achieving educational effectiveness is an incremental, sequential improvement process. This improvement process begins by building a sense of security within each individual so that he or she can be flexible in adapting to changes within education. Addressing only skills or techniques, such as communication, motivation, negotiation, or empowerment, is ineffective when individuals in an organization do not trust its systems, themselves, or one another. An institution's resources are wasted when invested only in training programs that assist administrators in mastering quick-fix techniques that at best attempt to manipulate and at worst reinforce mistrust.

The challenge is to transform relationships based on insecurity, adversarialism, and politics to those based on mutual trust. Trust is the beginning of effectiveness and forms the foundation of a principle-centered learning environment that places emphasis on strengths and devises innovative methods to minimize weaknesses. The transformation process requires an internal locus of control that emphasizes individual responsibility and accountability for change and for promoting effectiveness.

TEAMWORK

For many of us, there exists a dichotomy between how we see ourselves as persons and how we see ourselves as workers. Perhaps the following words of a Zen Buddhist will be helpful:

The master in the art of living makes little distinction between his work and his play, his labor and his leisure, his mind and his body, his education and his recreation, his love and his religion. He hardly knows which is which. He simply pursues his vision of excellence in whatever he does, leaving others to decide whether he is working or playing. To him he is always doing both.

Work can be and should be productive, rewarding, enriching, fulfilling, and joyful. Work is one of our greatest privileges, and it is up to leaders to make certain that work is everything that it can and should be. One way to think of work is to envision how a philosopher would lead an organization, as opposed to how a businessman or -woman would lead an organization. Plato's "Republic" speaks of the "philosopher-king," where the king would rule with the philosopher's ideals and values.

Paramount among the ideals that leaders need to recognize in leading an organization is the notion of teamwork and the valuing of each individual's contribution to the final product. The synergy produced by an effective team is greater than the sum of its parts.

The foundation of the team is the recognition that each member needs every other member, and no individual can be successful without the cooperation of others. As a young boy I was a very enthusiastic baseball fan. My favorite player was the Hall of Fame pitcher Robin Roberts of the Philadelphia Phillies. During the early 1950s his fastball dominated the National League. My uncle, who took me to my first ball game, explained that opposing batters were so intimidated by Roberts's fastball that they were automatic "outs" even before they got to the plate. My uncle claimed that Robin Roberts was unstoppable. Even as a young boy I intuitively knew that no one was unstoppable by himself. I told my uncle that I knew how to stop Robin Roberts: "Make me his catcher."

EMPLOYEES AS VOLUNTEERS

Our institutions will not amount to anything without the people who make them what they are. And the individuals most influential in making institutions what they are, are essentially "volunteers." Our very best employees can work anywhere they please. So, in a sense, they volunteer to work where they do. As leaders, we would do far better if we looked upon and treated our employees as volunteers. Earlier I stated that employees should be treat as if they had a covenantal relationship rather than a contractual relationship in the workplace.

Alexander Solzhenitsyn, speaking to the 1978 graduating class of Harvard College, said this about legalistic relationships:

> [A] society based on the letter of the law and never reaching any higher, fails to take advantage of the full range of human possibilities. The letter of the law is too cold and formal to have a beneficial influence on society. Whenever the tissue of life is woven of legalistic relationships, this creates an atmosphere of spiritual mediocrity that paralyzes men's noblest impulses. . . . After a certain level of the problem has been reached, legalistic thinking induces paralysis; it prevents one from seeing the scale and the meaning of events.[3]

Covenantal relationships, on the other hand, induce freedom, not paralysis. As the noted psychiatrist William Glasser explains, "coercion only produces mediocrity; love or a sense of belonging produces excellence."[4] Our goal as leaders is to encourage a covenantal relationship of love, warmth, and personal chemistry among our employee volunteers. Shared ideals, shared goals, shared respect, a sense of integrity, a sense of quality, a sense of advocacy, a sense of caring; these are the basis of an organization's covenant with its employees.

THE VALUE OF HEROES

Leading with heart requires that an organization has its share of heroes, both present and past. We have often heard individuals in various organizations say that so and so is an "institution" around here. Heroes such as these do more to establish the organizational culture of an institution than any manual or policies and procedures handbook ever could. The senior faculty member who is recognized and respected for his or her knowledge as well as his or her humane treatment of students is a valuable asset to an educational institution. He or she is a symbol of what the institution stands for. It is the presence of these heroes that sustains the reputation of the institution and allows the workforce to feel good about itself and about where it works. The deeds and accomplishments of these heroes need to be promulgated and become part of the folklore of the institution.

The deeds of these heroes are usually perpetuated by the "tribal storytellers" in an organization.[5] These are the individuals who know the history of the organization and relate it through stories of its former and present heroes. An effective leader encourages the tribal storytellers, knowing that they are serving an invaluable role in an organization. They work at the process of institutional renewal. They allow the institution to continuously improve. They preserve and revitalize the values of the institution. They mitigate the tendency of institutions, especially educational institutions, to become bureaucratic. These concerns are concerns of everyone in the institution, but they are the special province of the tribal storyteller. Every institution has heroes and storytellers. It is the leader's job to ensure that things like manuals and handbooks do not replace them.

EMPLOYEE OWNERS

If an educational institution is to be successful, everyone in it needs to feel that he or she "owns the place." "This is not the school district's school; it is not the school board's school; it is *my* school." Taking ownership is a sign of one's love for an institution. In his book *Servant Leadership*, Robert Greenleaf says, "Love is an undefinable term, and its manifestations are both subtle and infinite. It has only one absolute condition: unlimited liability!"[6] Although it may run counter to our traditional notion of U.S. capitalism, employees should be encouraged to act as if they own the place. It is a sign of love.

THE SIGNS OF HEARTLESSNESS

Up to now I have dwelled on the characteristics of a healthy organization. In contrast, here are some of the signs that an organization is suffering from a lack of heart:

- When there is a tendency to merely "go through the motions";
- When a dark tension exists among key individuals;

- When a cynical attitude prevails among employees;
- When finding time to celebrate accomplishments becomes impossible;
- When stories and storytellers cease;
- When there is the view that one person's gain needs to be at another's expense;
- When mutual trust and respect erode;
- When leaders accumulate power rather than distribute it;
- When attainment of short-term goals becomes detrimental to the acquisition of long-term goals;
- When individuals abide by the letter of the law, but not its spirit;
- When people treat students or customers as impositions;
- When the accidents become more important than the substance;
- When a loss of grace, style, and civility occurs;
- When leaders use coercion to motivate employees;
- When administrators dwell on individuals' weaknesses rather than strengths;
- When individual turf is protected to the detriment of institutional goals;
- When diversity and individual charisms are not respected;
- When communication is only one way;
- When employees feel exploited and manipulated;
- When arrogance spawns top-down decision making;
- When leaders prefer to be served rather than to serve.

LEADERSHIP AS A MORAL SCIENCE

Here I address how educational administrators and other leaders should be educated and trained for such a position. Traditionally, there has been only one answer: practicing and future administrators should study educational administration in order to learn the scientific basis for decision making and to understand the scientific research that underlies proper administration. Universities train future administrators with texts that stress the scientific research done on administrative behavior, review various studies of teacher and student performance, and provide a few techniques for accomplishing educational goals. Such approaches instill a reverence for the scientific method, but also an unfortunate disregard for any humanistic and critical development of the art of administration.[7]

I suggest a different approach here. Although there is certainly an important place for scientific research in supporting empirically supported administrative behavior, educational administrators must also be *critical humanists.* Humanists appreciate the usual and unusual events of our lives and engage in an effort to develop, challenge, and liberate human souls. They are critical because they too are educators and therefore not satisfied with status quo; rather, they hope to change individuals and institutions for the better and improve social conditions for all. I argue that *administrative* science be reconstructed as a *moral* science. An administrative science can be empirical, but it also must incorporate hermeneutic (the science of interpreting and understanding others) and critical dimensions. Social science has increasingly recognized that it must be informed by moral questions. The paradigm of natural science does not always apply when dealing with human issues. As a moral science, the science of administration is concerned with the resolution of moral dilemmas. Critical and literary models of administration help provide the necessary context and understanding wherein such dilemmas can be wisely resolved, so we can truly actualize our potential as administrators and leaders.

As mentioned in chapter 1 and worth repeating here, one's proclivity to be a critical humanist oftentimes depends on one's philosophy on how human beings behave in the workplace. The two extremes of the continuum might be described as those leaders who believe that human beings are basically lazy and will do the very least that they need to do to "get by" in the workplace, compared to those who believe that people are basically industrious and, if given the choice, would opt for doing the "right thing." Today's most effective leaders should hold the latter view. I agree with Max De Pree, owner and CEO of the highly successful Herman Miller Furniture Company. Writing in his book, *Leadership Is an Art,* De Pree argues that a leader's function is the "liberate people to do what is required of them in the most effective and humane way possible." Instead of catching people doing something *wrong,* our goal as enlightened leaders is to catch them doing something *right.* Such behavior is reflective of a leader who is in the humanist, if not also in the critical tradition.

THE HUMANIST TRADITION

The first responsibility of a leader is to define reality through a vision; the final responsibility is to say thank you. In between, the leader must become the servant of the servants. Being a leader means having the opportunity to make a meaningful difference in the lives of those who allow leaders to lead. This summarizes what it means to be an administrator and leader in the humanist tradition.

Whether one is a successful leader can be determined by looking at one's followers. Are they reaching their potentials? Are they learning? Are they able to change without bitterness? Are they able to achieve the institution's goals and objectives? Can they mange conflict among themselves? Do they have an internal locus of control? Are they concerned with the social implications of educational policy? Where the answer to these questions is an emphatic yes is where an effective and humanist leader resides.

I prefer to think about administration in terms of what the gospel writer Luke calls the "one who serves." The leader owes something to the institution he or she leads. The leader is seen in this context as steward rather than owner or proprietor. Administration as a moral science requires the leader to think about his or her stewardship in terms of legacy, values, direction and effectiveness.

Too many of today's administrators are interested only in immediate results that bolster their career goals. Long-range goals are left to their successors. We believe that this approach fosters autocratic leadership, which often produces short-term results but militates against creativity and its long-term benefits. In effect, this approach is the antithesis of leading humanely. On the contrary, leaders should build a long-lasting legacy of accomplishment that is institutionalized for posterity. They owe their institutions and their followers a healthy existence and the relationships and reputation that enable continuity of that healthy existence. Educational administrators are also responsible for future leadership. They need to identify, develop, and nurture future leaders to carry on the legacy.

Along with being responsible for providing future leaders, administrators owe the individuals in their institutions certain other legacies. Leaders need to be concerned with the institutional value system that determines the principles and standards that guide the practices of those in the organization. Administrators need to model their value systems so that the individuals in the organization can learn to transmit these values to their colleagues and to future employees. In a civilized institution we see good manner, respect for people and an appreciation of the way in which we serve one another. Humane, sensitive and thoughtful leaders will transmit their value systems through their daily behavior.

Administrators are obliged to provide and maintain direction by developing a vision. We made the point earlier that effective leaders must leave their organizations with a legacy. Part of this legacy should be a sense of progress or momentum. An educational administrator, for instance, should imbue his or her institution with a sense of continuous progress—a sense of constant improvement. Improvement and momentum come from a clear vision of what the institution ought to be, from a well-planned strategy to achieve that vision, and from carefully developed and articulated directions and plans that allow everyone to participate and be personally accountable for achieving those plans. Here is where functionalism and critical humanism intertwine. An institution cannot be humane if it is in chaos. It needs to be effectively and efficiently operated.

Leaders are also responsible for effectiveness by being enablers. They need to enable others to reach their potential both personally and institutionally. We believe that the most effective ways of enabling one's colleagues is through participative decision-making. It begins with believing in the potential of people; believing in their diversity of gifts. Leaders must realize that to maximize their own power and effectiveness, they need to empower others. Leaders are responsible for setting and attaining the goals in their organizations. Empowering or enabling others to help achieve those goals enhance the leader's chances of attaining the goals, ultimately enhancing the leader's effectiveness. Paradoxically, giving up power really amounts to gaining power.

THE CRITICAL TRADITION

A postpositivist leader combines the *humanist* tradition with *critical* theory. Dissatisfaction with current administrative approaches for examining social life stems from administrations' inability to deal with questions of value and morality and its inability to fulfill its promise. For example, Griffiths and Ribbins criticize orthodox theories because they "ignore the presence of unions and fail to account for the scarcity of women and minorities in top administrative positions."[8] Erickson asks "Why had educational research had so few real implications for educational policy?" and answers that an empiricist research program modeled on the natural sciences fails to address issues of understanding and interpretation.[9] This failure precludes researchers from reaching a genuine understanding of the human condition. It is time, he argues, to treat educational research as a moral science. The science of administration can also be a moral one, a critically moral one.

The term *moral* is used here in its cultural, professional, spiritual, and ethical sense, not in a religious sense. The moral side of administration has to do with the *dilemmas* that administrators face in education. All educators face three areas of dilemmas: control, curriculum, and societal. Control dilemmas involve the resolution of classroom management and control issues, particularly the issue of who is in charge and to what degree. Control dilemmas center around four questions:

1. Do you treat the child as a student, focusing narrowly on cognitive goals, or as a whole person, focusing more broadly on intellectual, aesthetic, social, and physical dimensions?
2. Who controls classroom time? In some classrooms, children are given latitude in scheduling their activities; in others, class activities follow a strict and mandatory schedule.
3. Who controls operations or what larger context of what it means to be human and how do we resolve the inevitable conflicts that go on in the classroom?
4. Who controls the standards and defines success and failure?

Similar dilemmas occur in the curricular domain and relate to whether the curriculum is considered as received, public knowledge, or whether it is considered private, individualized knowledge, of the type achieved through discoveries and experiments. These curricular difficulties also depend on whether one conceives of the child as customer or as an individual. The customer receives professional services generated from a body of knowledge, whereas the individual receives personal services generated from his or her particular needs and context.

A final set of dilemmas has to do with what children bring to school and how they are to be treated once there. One concern is the distribution of teacher resources. Should one focus more resources on the less talented, in order to bring them up to standards, or on the more talented, in order for them to reach their full potential? The same question arises in regard to the distribution of justice. Should classroom rules be applied uniformly without regard to the differing circumstances of each child, or should family background, economic factors, and other sociological influences be considered? Should a teacher stress a common culture or ethnic differences and subculture consciousness?

Much of teaching involves resolving such dilemmas by making a variety of decisions throughout the school day. Such decisions can be made, however, in a *reflective* or an *unreflective* manner. An unreflective manner means simply teaching as one was taught, without giving consideration to available alternatives. A reflective approach involves an examination of the widest array of alternatives. Thus, reflective teaching suggests that dilemmas need not be simply resolved but can be transformed so that a higher level of teaching expertise is reached.

This same logic can be applied to administration. Administration involves the resolution of various dilemmas, which is the making of moral decisions. One set of dilemmas involves control. How much participation can teachers have in the administration of the school? How much participation can parents and students have? Who evaluates and for what purpose? Is the role of administration collegial or authority centered? The area of the curriculum brings up similar questions. Is the school oriented to basic skills, advanced skills, social skills, or all three? Should the curricula be teacher made or national, state, or system mandated? Should student evaluation be based on teacher assessment or standardized tests? What is authentic assessment? Finally, an additional set of dilemmas pertains to the idea of schooling in society. Should the schools be oriented to ameliorate the apparent deficits that some students bring with them, or should they see different cultures and groups as strengths? Should schools be seen as agents of change, oriented to the creation of a more just society, or as socializers that adapt the young to the current social structure?

Oftentimes these questions are answered unreflectively and simply resolved on an as-needed basis. This approach often resolves the dilemma but does not foster a real *transformation* in one's self, role, or institution. If administration and leadership encompasses transformation, and I argue that it should, then an additional lens to structural functionalism must be found through which these questions can be viewed. I suggest that the additional lens be in the form of critical humanism and the Ignatian vision. In this context, then, administrative leadership can be viewed as a moral science.

THE IGNATIAN VISION

More than 450 years ago Ignatius of Loyola, a young priest who had born to a Spanish aristocratic family, founded the Society of Jesus, the Jesuits, and wrote his seminal book *The Spiritual Exercises*.[10] In this book he suggested a "way of life" and a "way of looking at things" that has been propagated by his religious community and his followers for almost five centuries. His principles have been utilized in a variety of ways. They have been used as an aid in developing one's own spiritual life; they have been used to formulate a way of learning that has become the curriculum and instructional method employed in the 60 high schools and the 28 Jesuit colleges and universities in the United States; and they have been used to develop one's own administrative style. Together, these principles comprise the *Ignatian vision*.[10]

There are five Ignatian principles that I explore here as a foundation for developing an administrative philosophy and leadership style:

1. Ignatius's concept of the *magis*, or the "more."
2. The implications of his notion of *cura personalis*, or "care of the person."
3. The process of *inquiry* or *discernment*.
4. The development of *men and women for others*.
5. Service to the *underserved* and marginalized, or his concept of *social justice*.

At the core of the Ignatian vision is the concept of the *magis*, or the "more." Ignatius spent the greater part of his life seeking perfection in all areas of his personal, spiritual, and professional life. He was never satisfied with status quo. He was constantly seeking to improve his own spiritual life, as well as his secular life as leader of a growing religious community. He was an advocate of "continuous improvement" long before it became a corporate slogan, long before people like Edwards Deming used it to develop his "total quality management" approach to management, and long before Japan used it to revolutionize its economy after World War II.

The idea of constantly seeking "the more" implies change. The *magis* is a movement away from the status quo; and moving away from the status quo defines change. The Ignatian vision requires individuals and institutions to embrace the process of change as a vehicle for personal and institutional improvement. For his followers, frontiers and boundaries are not obstacles or ends, but new challenges to be faced, new opportunities to be welcomed. Thus, change needs to become a way of life. Ignatius further implores his followers to "be the change that you expect in others." In other words, we are called to model desired behavior—to live out our values, to be of ever fuller service to our communities, and to aspire to the more universal good. Ignatius had no patience with mediocrity. He constantly strove for the greater good.

The *magis* principle, then, can be described as the main norm in the selection of information and the interpretation of it. Every real alternative for choice must be conducive to the advancement toward perfection. When some aspect of a particular alternative is *more* conducive to reaching perfection than other alternatives, we have reason to choose that alternative. In the previous chapter, I spoke of the "dilemmas" that educators face during every working day. The *magis* principle is a "way of seeing" that can help us in selecting the better alternative in these dilemmas.

At first hearing, the *magis* principle may sound rigid and frightening. It is absolute, and Ignatius is unyielding, but not rigid, in applying it. On the one hand, he sees it as the expression of our love of humanity, which inexorably seeks to fill all of us with a desire to not be content with what is less good for us. On the other hand, he sees that humanity not only has its particular gifts, but also has its limitations and different stages of growth. If making a choice that in the abstract would be more humane than it would be in the concrete, that choice would not be seen as adhering to the *magis* principle. For example, tracking students according to ability can be seen as humane in the abstract, but in the concrete can be dehumanizing. Ignatius would advise us to focus on the concrete in resolving this dilemma.[11]

In every case, then, accepting and living by the *magis* principle is an expression of our love of humanity. So, whatever the object for choice, the measure of our love of neighbor will be the fundamental satisfaction we will find in choosing and acting by the *magis* principle. Whatever one chooses by this principle, no matter how undesirable in some other respect, will always be how one would most want to be treated as a moral and ethical member of the human race.

Closely related to the principle of the *magis* is the Ignatian principle of *inquiry* and *discernment*. In his writings, he urges us to challenge the status quo through the methods of inquiry and discernment. This is similar to one of the tenants of critical theory. In fact the Ignatian vision and critical theory share a number of norms.

To Ignatius, the need to enter into inquiry and discernment is to determine God's will. However, this process is of value for the purely *secular* purpose of deciding on which "horn of a dilemma" one should come down. To aid us in utilizing inquiry and discernment as useful tools in challenging the status quo and determining the right choice to be made, Ignatius suggests that the ideal disposition for inquiry and discernment is humility. The disposition of humility is especially helpful when, despite one's best efforts, the evidence that one alternative is more conducive to the betterment of society is not compelling. When the discerner cannot find evidence to show that one alternative is more conducive to the common good, Ignatius calls for a judgment in favor of what more assimilates the discerner's life to the life of poverty and humiliation. Thus, when the *greatest* good cannot readily be determined, the *greater* good is more easily discerned in position of humility. These are very demanding standards, but they are consistent with the *magis* principle and the tenets of critical humanism.

In addition to the *magis* principle norm, taking account of what has just been said and of what was said earlier about the norm of humility as a disposition for seeking the greater good, the relationship of the greater good norm to the greatest good norm can be clarified. The latter is absolute, overriding, and always primary. The greater good norm is secondary; it can never, in any choice, have equal weight with the first *magis* principle; it can never justify a choice of actual poverty and humiliation over riches and honors if the latter are seen to be more for the service of humanity in a particular situation for choice, with all its concrete circumstances, including the agent's responsibilities to others and his or her own stage of psychological and spiritual development. In other words, if being financially successful allows one to better serve the poor and underserved, that would be preferred to actual poverty.

Ignatius presents us with several other supplemental norms for facing our "dilemmas." In choices that directly affect the individual person and the underserved or marginalized, especially the poor, Ignatius urges us to give preference to those in need. This brings us to his next guiding principle, *cura personalis* or care of the person.

Another of Ignatius's important and enduring principles is his notion that, despite the primacy of the common good, the need to care for the individual person should never be lost. From the very beginning, the *cura personalis* principle has been included in the mission statement of virtually every high school and college founded by the Jesuits. It also impacts the method of instruction suggested for all Jesuit schools in the *Ratio Studiorum*, or the "course of study" in these institutions. All Jesuit educational institutions are to foster what is now commonly referred to as a "constructivist" classroom, where the student is an active participant in the learning process. This contrasts with the "transmission" method of instruction, where the teacher is paramount and the student is a passive participant in the process. In the Ignatian vision, the care of the person is a requirement not only on a personal needs' basis, but also on a "whole person" basis, which would, of course, include classroom education.

This principle also has implications for how we conduct ourselves as educational administrators. Ignatius calls us to value the gifts and charisms of our colleagues and to address any deficiencies that they might have and turn them into strengths. For example, during the employee evaluation process, Ignatius would urge us to focus of the formative stage of the evaluation far more than on the summative stage. This would be one small way of applying *cura personalis* theory to practice.

The fourth principle to consider is the Ignatian concept of service. Once again, this principle has been propagated from the very outset.

The expressed goal of virtually every Jesuit institution is "to develop men and women for others." Jesuit institutions are called on to create a culture of service as one way of ensuring that the students, faculty, and staff of these institutions reflect the educational, civic, and spiritual values of the Ignatian vision.

Institutions following the Ignatian tradition of service to others have done so through community services programs, and more recently, service learning. Service to the community provides students with a means of helping others, a way to put their value system into action and a tangible way to assist local communities. Although these were valuable benefits, there was no formal integration of the service experience into the curriculum and no formal introspection concerning the impact of service on the individual. During the past 10 years there has been a movement toward creating a more intentional academic relationship. Service has evolved from a modest student activity into an exciting pedagogical opportunity. In the past, service was viewed as a cocurricular activity; today it plays an integral role in the learning process.

Since many institutions are situated in an urban setting, service gives them a chance to share resources with surrounding communities and allows for reciprocal relationships to form between the university and local residents. Immersion into different cultures—economic, racial, educational, social, and religious—is the vehicle by which students make connections. Working side by side with people of varying backgrounds significantly impacts the students, forcing them outside of their comfort zones and into the gritty reality of how others live. Through reflection, these students have the opportunity to integrate these powerful experiences into their lives, opening their eyes and hearts to the larger questions of social justice. Peter-Hans Kolvenbach, the superior general of the Jesuit order, in his address on justice in American Jesuit universities in October 2000, used the words of Pope John Paul II to challenge Jesuit educators to "educate the whole person of solidarity for the real world," not only through concepts learned in the classroom, but also by contact with real people.

Upon assuming the position of superior general in 1973 and echoing the words of Ignatius, Pedro Arrupe declared "our prime educational objective must be to form men and women for others; men and women who will live not for themselves but for others." In the spirit of these words, the service learning movement has legitimized the educational benefit of all experiential activity. The term *service learning* means different things to different people, and debates on service learning have been around for decades, running the gamut from unstructured "programmatic opportunities" to structured "educational philosophies." At Ignatian institutions, service learning is a bridge that connects faculty, staff, and students with community partners and their agency needs. It connects academic and student life views about the educational value of experiential learning. It also connects students' textbooks to human reality, and their minds and hearts with values and action. The programs are built on key components of service learning, including integration into the curriculum, a reciprocal relationship between the community agency and student, and structured time for reflection, which is very much related to the Ignatian principle of *discernment* discussed earlier.[12]

Participation in service by high school and college students, whether as a cocurricular or a course-based experience, correlates to where they are in their developmental process. Service work allows students to explore their skills and limitations, to find what excites and energizes them, to put their values into action, to use their talents to benefit others, and to discover who they are and who they want to become. By encouraging students to reflect on their service, these institutions assist in this self-discovery. The reflection can take many forms: an informal chat, a facilitated group discussion, written dialogue, journal entries, reaction papers, or in-class presentations on articles. By integrating the service experience through critical reflection, students develop self-knowledge of the communities in which they live and knowledge about the world that surrounds them. It is only after the unfolding of this service-based knowledge that the students are able to synthesize what they have learned into their lives. Through this reflection the faculty members also have an opportunity to learn from and about their students. Teachers witness the change and growth of the students firsthand. In short, "service to others" changes lives.

The administrative implications of "service to others" are clear. Not only can educational administrators enhance their effectiveness by including the idea of service to others in their curricula, but also by modeling it in their personal and professional lives. The concept of administrators becoming the "servant of the servants" is essential here. Servant leaders do not inflict pain, they bear pain, and they treat their employees as "volunteers," a concept that we will explore more fully later.

The Ignatian concept of "service" leads into his notion of solidarity with the underserved (poor) and marginalized and his principle of *social justice*. This begins with an attempt to achieve some measure of clarity on the nature and role of social justice in the Ignatian vision. According to some, Ignatius defined justice in both a narrow and wide sense. In the *narrow* sense, it is "justice among men and women" that is involved. In this case it is a matter of "clear obligations" among "members of the human family." The application of this kind of justice would include not only the rendering of material goods, but also immaterial goods such as "reputation, dignity, the possibility of exercising freedom."

Many of his followers also believe Ignatius defined justice in a *wider* sense "where situations are encountered which are humanly intolerable and demand a remedy." Here the situations may be a product of "explicitly unjust acts" caused by "clearly identified people" who cannot be obliged to correct the injustices, yet the dignity of the human person requires that justice be restored; or they may be cause by nonidentifiable people. It is precisely within the structural forces of inequality in society where injustice of this second type is found, where injustice is "institutionalized," that is, built into economic, social, and political structures both national and international, and where people are suffering from poverty and hunger, from the unjust distribution of wealth, resources, and power. The critical theorists, as mentioned earlier, would likely concur with this wider definition of social justice.

It is almost certain that Ignatius was concerned with more than injustices that were purely economic. He often cites injustices about "threats to human life and it quality," "racial and political discrimination," and loss of respect for the "rights of individuals or groups." When one adds to these the "vast range of injustices" enumerated in his writings, one sees that the Ignatian vision understands its mission of justice to include "the widest possible view of justice," involving every area where there is an attack on human rights. Therefore, we can conclude that although Ignatius was to some degree concerned about commutative justice (right relationships between private persons and groups) and distributive justice (the obligations of the state to render to the individual what is his or her due), he is most concerned about what is generally called today social justice, or "justice of the common good." Such justice is comprehensive and includes the above-mentioned strict legal rights and duties, but is more concerned about the natural rights and duties of individuals, families, communities, and the community of nations toward one another as members of the common family of human beings. Every form of justice is included in and presupposed by social justice, but with social justice, it is the social nature of the person that is emphasized, as well as the social significance of all earthly goods, the purpose of which is to aid all members of the human community to attain their dignity as human beings. Many of Ignatius's followers believe that this dignity is being undermined in our world today, and their main efforts are aimed toward restoring that dignity.[14]

In the pursuit of social justice, Ignatius calls on his followers to be "in solidarity with the poor." The next logical question might then be, who are the poor? The poor are usually thought to be those who are economically deprived and politically oppressed. Thus, we can conclude that the promotion of justice means to work to overcome the oppressions or injustices that make the poor truly poor. The fallacy here, however, is that the poor are not necessarily oppressed or suffering injustice, and so Ignatius argues that our obligation toward the poor must be understood to be linking "inhuman levels or poverty and injustice" and not be understood to be concerned with the "lot of those possessing only modest resources," even though those of modest means are often poor and oppressed. So, we can conclude that the poor include those "wrongfully" impoverished or dispossessed.[15]

An extended definition of the poor, one that Ignatius would espouse, would include any of these types of people:

First, those who are economically deprived and socially marginalized and oppressed, especially, but not limited to, those with whom one has immediate contact and is in a position to positively effect.
Second, those who are "poor in spirit," that is, those who lack a value system or an ethical and moral sense.
Third, those who are emotionally poor; those who have psychological and emotional shortcomings and are in need of comfort.

In defining the poor in the broadest way, Ignatius exhorts us to undertake social change in our role as leader; to do what we can do to bring an end to inequality, oppression, and injustice. Once again we can see the close connection between the Ignation principles of social justice and the main tenets of critical theory.[16]

IMPLICATIONS FOR ADMINISTRATION

Each of the principles of the Ignatian vision noted above has a variety of implications for leaders. The *magis* principle has implications for administrators in that it calls for us to continually be seeking perfection in all that we do. In effect, this means that we must seek to continually improve. And, since improvement implies change, we need to be champions of needed change in our institutions. This means that we have to model a tolerance for change and embrace not only our own change initiatives, but also those in other parts of the organization.

The principle of *cura personalis* has additional implications. To practice the Ignatian vision, one must treat people with dignity under all circumstances. *Cura personalis* also requires us to extend ourselves in offering individual attention and attending to the needs of all those in whom we come in contact. Being sensitive to the individual's unique needs is particularly required. Many times in our efforts to treat people equally, we fail to treat them fairly and equitably. Certain individuals have greater needs than others, and many times these needs require exceptions to be made on their behalf. For example, if an adult student does not hand in an assignment on time, but the tardiness is due to the fact that he or she is going through some personal trauma at the moment, the principle of *cura personalis* calls on us to make an exception in this case. It is likely that many would consider such an exception to be unfair to those who made the effort to complete the assignment in a timely manner or, that we cannot possibly be sensitive to the special needs of all of our students and colleagues. However, as long as the exception is made for anyone in the same circumstances, Ignatius would not perceive this exception as being unfair. In fact, the exception would be expected if one is practicing the principle of "care of the person."

The Ignatian process of *discernment* requires educational administrators to be reflective practitioners. It calls on us to be introspective regarding our administrative and leadership behavior. We are asked to reflect on the ramifications of our decisions, especially in light of their cumulative effect on the equitable distribution of power and on the marginalized individuals and groups in our communities. In effect, the principle of discernment galvanizes the other principles embodied in the Ignatian vision. During the discernment process, we are asked to reflect on how our planned behavior will manifest the *magis* principle, *cura personalis*, and service to the community, especially the underserved, marginalized, and oppressed.

The development of men and women for the service of others requires one to have his or her own sense of service toward those with whom the leader interacts as well as developing this spirit of service in others. The concept of "servant leadership" requires us to encourage others toward a life and career of service and to assume the position of being the "servant of the servants." The leader owes something to the institution he or she leads. The leader is seen in this context as steward rather than owner or proprietor.

The implications of Ignatius's notion of social justice are myriad for the administrator. Being concerned about the marginalized among our constituencies is required. We are called to be sensitive to those individuals and groups who do not share equitably in the distribution of power and influence. Participative decision making and collaborative behavior are encouraged among administrators imbued with the Ignatian tradition. Equitable representation of all segments of the school community should be provided whenever feasible. Leadership behavior such as this will ensure that the dominant culture is not perpetuated to the detriment of the minority culture, rendering the minorities powerless. These principles and the ways of applying them will be discussed in later chapters.

SUMMARY

This book began by suggesting that leaders are made, not born. It was posited that if one could master the skills involved in effective leadership, one could become a successful administrator. In this chapter, however, it has been asserted that learning the skills involved in effective leadership is only part of the story. Leadership is as much an art, a belief, a condition of the heart, as it is a set of skills. A truly successful leader, therefore, is one who leads with both the *mind* and the *heart*. In examining the leadership behavior of the ten basketball coaches in the chapters that follow, we should observe not only if their leadership practices conform to the Bolman/Deal situational leadership theory (as presented in Chapter 1), but also if they are leading with *heart*. I believe we will find that those coaches who are most comfortable operating in Bolman and Deal's human resources frame of leadership are most likely to be leading with heart. But the most effective leaders will be those who lead with both mind (structural, political frames) and heart (human resource and symbolic frames).

3

PHIL JACKSON

> One finger cannot lift a pebble.
>
> —Hopi saying

BACKGROUND

Phil Jackson was born on September 17, 1945, in Deer Lodge, Montana, and is the current (as of 2008) coach of the Los Angeles Lakers in the National Basketball Association (NBA). A former player for the New York Knicks, Jackson is widely considered one of the greatest coaches in the history of the NBA. His reputation was established as head coach of the Chicago Bulls from 1989 through 1998. During this tenure in Chicago, Jackson led the team to six NBA titles. His reputation was further enhanced when his next team, the Los Angeles Lakers, won three consecutive NBA titles.

Jackson is known for his use of Tex Winter's triangle offense as well as a holistic approach to coaching that is influenced by Eastern philosophy, earning him the nickname "Zen master." He also applies Native American spiritual practices. The epigraph to this chapter is one of his favorites. He is the author of several candid books about his teams and his basketball strategies. Jackson is also a recipient of the state of North Dakota's Roughrider Award. Jackson was inducted into the Basketball Hall of Fame in 2007.

Interestingly enough, both of Jackson's parents were Assembly of God ministers. In the churches they served, his father generally preached on Sunday mornings and his mother on Sunday evenings. Jackson, his two brothers, and his half-sister grew up in an extremely austere environment in which no movies, dancing, or television were allowed. He did not see his first movie until he was a senior in high school and went to a dance for the first time in college.

In Williston, North Dakota, where Jackson was raised, he played high school basketball and led his team to two state titles. He also played football, was a baseball pitcher, and threw the discus in high school. Jackson attracted the attention of several baseball scouts. Their notes found their way to future NBA coach Bill Fitch, who had previously coached baseball, had been doing some scouting for the Atlanta Braves, and took over as head basketball coach at North Dakota University in the spring of 1962, during Jackson's junior year of high school.

Fitch successfully recruited him to North Dakota, where he was a member of Sigma Alpha Epsilon fraternity. Jackson did well there both academically and athletically, helping the Fighting Sioux to third and fourth place finishes in the NCAA Division II tournament in his sophomore and junior years. Both years, they would be beaten by Southern Illinois. This was the era in which Jackson's future New York Knicks teammate Walt Frazier was the Salukis' biggest star.

Upon graduation, Jackson was drafted in the second round by the Knicks, after they made Frazier their first-round pick. Jackson found that the skills that had served him well at the small-college level were not as effective at the professional level. Although he was a good all-around athlete, with unusually long arms, he was very limited offensively. He compensated for his offensive limitations with sheer hard work and intelligence, especially on defense, and eventually established himself as a fan favorite and one of the NBA's leading sixth men. He was a top reserve on the Knicks team that won the NBA title in 1973. After some of the key starters on that championship team left the Knicks or retired, Jackson found himself in the starting lineup. After going to the New Jersey Nets in 1978 and playing there for two seasons, he retired in 1980.

In the following years, he mainly coached in lower-level professional leagues, notably the Continental Basketball Association (CBA) and the professional leagues of Puerto Rico. While in the CBA, he won his first coaching championship, leading the Albany Patroons to their first CBA title. He regularly sought an NBA job, but was not successful. Finally, however, his persistence paid off, and he was hired as an assistant coach for the Chicago Bulls in 1987. He was promoted to head coach in 1989. It was at this time that he met Tex Winter and became a devotee of Winter's triangle offense. Over nine seasons, Jackson coached the Bulls to six championships in impressive fashion, twice winning three straight championships over separate 3-year periods. The "three-peat" was the first since the Boston Celtics won eight titles in a row from 1959–66, lead by Red Auerbach.

Jackson and the Bulls made the playoffs every year, but won the title only three times. Jackson lost in his first season in 1990. Michael Jordan's first retirement after the 1993 season marked the end of the first "three-peat," and when Jordan returned during the 1996 season, the Bulls won another three championships in a row.

Although he was extraordinarily successful, the tension between Jackson and Bulls general manager Jerry Krause grew. Some believed that Krause felt unappreciated for his work in building the team to a championship level and was jealous of the attention that Jackson and Michael Jordan received. Thus, after the Bulls' final title of the Jordan era in 1998, Jackson left the team. However, after taking a year off, he decided to take a head coaching position with the Los Angeles Lakers.

Jackson took over a talented but underachieving Lakers team and immediately produced results. In his first year in Los Angeles, the Lakers were 67-15 during the regular season and went on to win the NBA championship in 2000. Titles followed in the next 2 years, once again amounting to a "three-peat." Many believed that the Lakers were on their way to a dynasty, but injuries, weak bench play, and public tension between Kobe Bryant and Shaquille O'Neal lead to their eventual downfall.

Prior to the 2003–4 season, the Lakers signed NBA star veterans Karl Malone and Gary Payton, who had been excellent players for their respective former teams. The acquisition of these players lead to speculation that another championship was in order. However, from the first day of training camp, the Lakers were beset by distractions. Bryant's rape trial, continued public sniping between O'Neal and Bryant, and repeated disputes between Jackson and Bryant all negatively affected the team. Despite the distractions, the Lakers made it to the NBA final, but lost to the Detroit Pistons.

On June 18, 2004, three days after Jackson had suffered his first-ever loss in an NBA Finals series, the Lakers announced that Jackson would leave his position as Lakers coach. However, Jackson returned to the Lakers a couple of years later and is currently their head coach. On January 17, 2007, Jackson won his 900th game, currently placing him ninth on the all-time win list for NBA coaches. He is the youngest coach in NBA history to reach that milestone.

SITUATIONAL LEADERSHIP ANALYSIS

Situational models of leadership differ from earlier trait and behavioral models in asserting that no single way of leading works in all situations. Rather, appropriate behavior depends on the circumstances at a given time. Effective managers diagnose the situation, identify the leadership style or behavior that will be most effective, and then determine whether they can implement the required style.

Phil Jackson is very adept at adapting his leadership behavior to the situation in which he finds himself. There is ample evidence that he utilizes all four of Bolman/Deal's frames of leadership in different situations. He assumes the role of the structural leader in his thorough preparation for the season and for particular games. In dealing with his players, he uses the human resource frame of leadership behavior at appropriate moments. His use of the symbolic frame of leadership is almost legendary, giving him the nickname of the "Zen master." And, although the use of the political frame is not prominent, there are documented instances when he engaged in political behavior when appropriate.

Adjusting to the situation by utilizing the different frames of leadership behavior is one of Phil Jackson's strengths as a leader. He realized the situational nature of leadership very early in his coaching career when be observed: "Pro basketball may be a man's world, but working with the Patroons I discovered that I was far more effective as a coach when I balanced the masculine and feminine sides of my nature. In my case, healing the split between feminine and masculine, heart and mind—as symbolized by my compassionate father and analytic mother—has been an essential aspect of my growth both as a coach and a human being" (Jackson & Delehanty, 1995, p. 67; all cites in this chapter, unless otherwise noted, are from this source).

In another instance, he observed that these are occasions when a firm hand is needed. He learned early that one of the most important qualities of a leader is listening without judgment, or with what Buddhists call bare attention. He found that when he could be truly present with impartial, open awareness, he got a much better feel for the players' concerns than when he tried to impose his own agenda. And, paradoxically, when he backed off and just listened, he got much better results on the court.

Jackson quotes John Heider from his book *The Tao of Leadership*: "The wise leader is of service: receptive, yielding, following. The group member's vibration dominates and leads, while the leader follows. But soon it is the member's consciousness that is transformed. It is the job of the leaders to be aware of the group member's process; it is the need of the group member to be received and paid attention to. Both get what they need, if the leader has the wisdom to serve and follow." (p. 68).

Jackson learned that there is only so much a coach can do to influence the outcome of the game. If you push too hard to control what happens, resistance builds and reality smacks you in your face. In Zen it is said that the gap between accepting things the way they are and wishing them to be otherwise is the tenth of an inch of difference between heaven and hell. If we can accept whatever hand we've been dealt—no matter how unwelcome—the way to proceed eventually becomes clear.

Jackson further recognizes the need to adjust one's leadership behavior to the situation when he cites James O'Toole's book, *Leading Change*. Jackson points out that in his book, "management consultant O'Toole talks about a different style of leadership, known as 'value based' management that closely resembles his approach. Value based leaders enlist the hearts and minds of their followers through inclusion and participation. They listen carefully to their followers out of deep respect for them as individuals and develop a vision that they will embrace because it is based on their highest aspirations. 'To be effective,' writes O'Toole, 'leaders must begin by setting aside that culturally conditioned natural instinct to lead by push, particularly when times are tough.

Leaders must instead adapt to the unnatural behavior of always leading by the pull of inspiring values'" (p. 154).

This view is very similar to what is advocated in Chapter 2 of this book regarding the necessity of the effective leader to lead both with mind *and* heart.

What O'Toole is suggesting is compassionate or servant leadership. Jackson agrees and points out that "In the Buddhist tradition, compassion flows from an understanding that everything derives its essential nature, or Buddha nature, from its dependence on everything else." In applying this approach to one of his players, Jackson says, "What I needed to do was open my heart and try to understand the situation from his point of view. I need to practice the same selflessness and compassion with Horace Grant [one of his players] that I expected from him on the court" (p. 154).

Jackson acknowledges that in order for him to be continuously improving as a leader and to continue to be an effective one, he needed to adapt his style or behavior to the ever-changing situations. He indicates that the challenge was not to try to repeat themselves but to use what they had learned to re-create themselves—to conjure up a new vision for the team. In placing this flexibility into practice, he cites a situation with one of his best players, Scottie Pippen. "My guess was that frustration had blurred Scottie's thinking. And I knew that if I came down too hard on him, it would only make matters worse. Scottie is a brooder. When things go wrong for him, he often falls into a deep funk that lasts for days. I knew the incident would weigh on his mind like a Sisyphean boulder" (p. 191). In such situations, Jackson instinctively knew that the leadership behavior he needed to apply to Scootie Pippen would be radically different from what he may have used on another player with a different temperament [situation].

THE STRUCTURAL FRAME

Structural leaders develop a new model of the relationship of structure, strategy, and environment for their organizations. Phil Jackson knows the importance of leadership behavior that comes out of the structural frame. However, he is also acutely aware of the need to temper structural leadership behavior with human resource behavior. "Obviously, there's an intellectual component to playing and coaching basketball. Strategy is important. But once you've done the mental work, there comes a point when you have to throw yourself into the action and put your heart on the line. That means not only being brave, but also being compassionate, toward yourself, your teammates, and your opponents. This idea was an important building block of my philosophy as a coach. More than anything else, what allowed the Bulls to sustain a high level of excellence was the players' compassion for each other" (p. 52).

Jackson intuitively knew that although the structural approach was critical for success, using it exclusively would lead to disaster. Pro basketball is a macho sport. Many coaches worry about showing any sign of weakness, tend to shut down emotionally and ostracize players. This can have a disturbing ripple effect on the players that ultimately undermines team unity. Late in Jackson's playing career the Knicks acquired Spencer Haywood, one of the game's premier forwards, to strengthen the front line. When he arrived, he announced to the press that he was going to be the next Dave DeBusschere and was so cocky everybody on the team, not to mention the fans, started secretly waiting for him to fail. No leader will be hired for any position if his or her boss does not think that the leader is capable of acting out of the structural frame. In speaking of the general manager who first gave him a chance at coaching, Jackson asserts that he didn't care about Jackson's overblown reputation as a sixties flower child. All he wanted to know was whether he could help turn his team into a winner. Jackson's first act after being named head coach of the Bulls was to formulate a vision (structural leadership behavior) for the team. He reminded himself that it could not be unrealistic. He had to take into account not only what he wanted to achieve, but how he was going to get there.

Overemphasizing the human resource frame to the detriment of the structural frame can actually lead to a decline in performance. Jackson says: "Throughout the game they'd look over at the bench, nervously trying to read my mind. I immediately cut them off. 'Why are you looking at me?' I'd ask. 'You already know you made a mistake.' If the players were going to learn the offense, they would have to have the confidence to make decisions on their own. That would never happen if they were constantly searching for direction from me. I wanted them to disconnect themselves from me, so they could connect with their teammates—and the game" (p. 105).

What his father sometimes called righteous anger was the most skillful means to shake up a team. But it has to be dispensed judiciously. And it's got to be genuine. "If you're not really angry, the players will detect it immediately," Jackson says. "Most importantly, eruptions shouldn't be directed at one or two members of a group; they should encompass the whole pack" (p. 142). Jackson acknowledges the need for structural behavior when he determines that every leader has weaknesses and makes mistakes; an effective leader learns to admit it." Finally, though most players find Jackson compassionate, he's not a touchy-feely kind of guy who'll slap a player on the back and console him when he doesn't perform. Times like these call for structural frame behavior, not human resource frame behavior.

THE HUMAN RESOURCE FRAME

Human resource leaders believe in people and communicate that belief. They are passionate about *productivity through people*. There are abundant instances when Phil Jackson acknowledges the effectiveness of human resource frame leadership behavior. Even though it was important to have good players in place and the "triangle offense" that he so effectively used (structural), he says: "The real reason the Bulls won three straight NBA championships from 1991 to 1993 was that we plugged in to the power of oneness instead of the power of one man, and transcended the divisive forces of the ego that have crippled far more gifted teams. Center Bill Cartwright said it best: 'Most teams have guys who want to win, but aren't willing to do what it takes. What it takes is to give yourself over to the team and play your part. That may not always make you happy, but you've got to do it, because when you do, that's when you win'" (p. 6). And, motivating a team to play as one is oftentimes the result of applying human resource frame behavior like compassion. What appealed to Jackson about the sixties—and what he carried away with him when it was over—was the emphasis on compassion and brotherhood, getting together and loving one another right now, to paraphrase one of his favorite recording groups, *The Youngbloods*. Many people were on the same path, trying to escape from their parents' archaic views and reinvent the world. Jackson no longer felt so isolated from his peers. For the first time in his life, he was no longer an outsider.

According to Jackson, compassion is where Zen and Christianity intersect. Though he still had reservations about the more rigid aspects of Christianity, he remained deeply moved by the fundamental insight that love is a conquering force. In [I] Corinthians 13:1–2, St. Paul writes: If I speak in the tongues of men and angels but do not have love, I am a noisy gong or clanging cymbal. And if I have prophetic power, and understand all mysteries and knowledge, and I have all faith, so as to remove mountains, but do not have love, I am nothing. What does all this have to do with professional basketball? Compassion is not exactly the first quality one looks for in a basketball player. But as his practice matured, Jackson began to appreciate the importance of playing with an open heart. He believed that love is a force that ignites the spirit and binds teams together.

In his work as a coach, Jackson discovered that approaching problems of this kind from a compassionate perspective, trying to empathize with the player and look at the situation from the player's point of view, can have a transformative effect on the team. Not only does it reduce the player's anxiety and make him feel as if someone understands what he's going through, it also inspires the other players to respond in kind and be more conscious of each other's needs. The most dramatic example of this phenomenon occurred in 1990 when Scottie Pippen's father died while they were in the middle of a tough playoff series against the Philadelphia 76ers. Pippen skipped Game 4 to attend the funeral and was still in a solemn mood before the start of the next game. Jackson thought it was important for the team to acknowledge what was going on in Scottie's life and give him support. He asked the players to form a circle around him in the locker room and recite the Lord's Prayer. Jackson knew the value of using human resource frame leadership behavior in the form of empowering individuals. His ultimate goal was to find a structure that would empower everybody on the team, not just the stars, and allow the players to grow as individuals as they surrendered themselves to the group. For example, giving everybody playing time helped defuse a lot of the petty jealousy that usually fragments teams. It worked so well, in fact, that it became one of Jackson's trademarks as a coach.

According to Jackson, his players were skeptical, at first, but toward the end of his first season, they realized what could happen if they really supported each other: they beat the CBA All-Stars in an exhibition game. After that, they started paying closer attention when Jackson talked about what selfless team play could accomplish. In effect, by sharing power, the whole becomes greater than the sum of the parts.

Other instances when Jackson used human resource leadership behavior in the appropriate situations included when he contradicted his own owner. The Bulls' owner, Jerry Reinsdorf, once told Jackson he thought most people were motivated by one of two forces: fear or greed. However, Jackson thought that people were also motivated by love. Even in installing his famous triangle offense, which required unselfish teamwork to succeed, Jackson considered the effect that it would have on the human beings involved, his players. In essence, the triangle offense was a process for integrating mind and body, sport and spirit in a practical and elementary form that anyone could learn. It was awareness in action. What appealed to Jackson about the system was that it empowered everybody on the team by making them more involved in the offense, and demanded that they put their individual needs aside for the good of the group.

The triangle offense made relatively unskilled players feel like they had an integral role in the team's ultimate success. The players knew that it was a team concept rather than an individual concept, so they understand that the coach is not attacking them personally when he or she corrects a mistake, but only trying to improve their knowledge of the system so that the team will have greater success.

According to Jackson, that's what the system teaches players. There's a lot of freedom built into the process, but it's the freedom that one of Jackson's players, John Paxson, talks about as the freedom to shape one's role for oneself and use all of one's creative resources to work in unison with others. During Jackson's playing days, the Knicks had that kind of feeling. Everyone loved playing with each other so much, they had an unspoken rule among ourselves about not skipping games, no matter what the excuse. If the leader is not sensitive to the followers' needs, the team won't buy the coach's plan and everyone—most of all the coach—will end up frustrated and disappointed. But when your vision is based on a clear-sighted, realistic assessment of your resources (structural behavior) and a concern for the individual (human resource behavior), alchemy often mysteriously occurs and a team transforms into a force greater than the sum of its parts. Visions are never the sole property of one person. Before a vision can become a reality, it must be owned by every single member of the group.

Jackson believes that some coaches feel threatened when their players start asserting their independence, but he thinks it's much more effective to open up the decision-making process to everybody. His approach is to follow a middle path. Rather than the two extremes of coddling players or making their lives miserable, he tries to create a supportive environment that has a definite structure but also gives them the freedom to realize their potential. He also tries to cultivate everybody's leadership abilities, to make the players and coaches feel that they've all got a stake in the team. No leader can create a successful team alone, no matter how gifted that leader is.

Jackson believes that the way to tap into that energy is not by being autocratic, but by working with the players and giving them increasing responsibility to shape their own roles. No one is doing it for money. It may seem that way, but that's just an external reward. You're doing it for the internal rewards. You're doing it for each other and the love of the game, asserts Jackson.

Jackson is acutely aware of the need to adapt his leadership behavior to the situation, especially the use of human resource frame behavior. He says: "In Buddhist teachings the term *skillful means* is used to describe an approach to making decisions and dealing with problems in a way that is appropriate to the situation and causes no harm (p. 162)." Skillful means always arise out of compassion, and when a problem emerges, the idea is to address the offense without denying the humanity of the offender. Athletes are not known to be the most verbal breed. That's why bare attention and listening without judgment are so important to Jackson. When you're a leader, you have to be able to read accurately the subtle messages players send. To do that means being fully present with a beginner's mind. Over the years Jackson learned to listen closely to his players—not just to what they say—but also to their body language and the silence between their words relate.

Coach Jackson's appropriate use of human resources leadership behavior has been recognized by one of his most famous players. Michael

Jordan told Jackson that his approach to the game reminded Jordan of his mentor, former University of of North Carolina coach Dean Smith, which may have something to do with why they worked so well together. In Jackson's mind, Jordan was the epitome of the peaceful warrior. Day in and day out, he had endured more punishment than any other player in the league, but he rarely showed any sign of anger.

We can see clearly from these instances that Phil Jackson makes human resource frame leadership behavior an integral part of his overall leadership style.

THE SYMBOLIC FRAME

In the symbolic frame, the organization is seen as a stage, a theater in which every actor plays certain roles and the symbolic leader attempts to communicate the right impressions to the right audiences. One could argue that Phil Jackson's frequent use of symbolic leadership behavior differentiates him from many of his coaching colleagues.

"I sensed that there was a link between spirit and sport. Besides, winning at any cost didn't interest me. From my years as a member of the championship New York Knicks, I'd already learned that winning is ephemeral. Yes, victory is sweet, but it doesn't necessarily make life any easier the next season or even the next day (p. 4)." The day he took over the Bulls, he vowed to create an environment based on the principles of selflessness and compassion that he had learned as a Christian in his parents' home, sitting on a cushion practicing Zen, and studying the teaching of the Lakota Sioux. He knew that the only way to win consistently was to give everyone—from the stars to the number 12 player on the bench—a vital role on the team, and inspire them to be acutely aware of what was happening, even when the spotlight was on somebody else. More than anything, he wanted to build a team that would blend individual talent with a heightened group consciousness. As head coach of the Bulls he had learned that the most effective way to forge a winning team is to call on his players' need to connect with something larger than themselves. He felt that even for those who didn't consider themselves spiritual in a conventional sense, creating a successful team—whether it's an NBA champion, a gold medal school, or a record-setting sales force—is essentially a spiritual act. It requires the individuals involved to surrender their self-interest for the common good so that the whole adds up to more than the sum of the parts.

According to Jackson, one of his team leaders, Bill Cartwright, was particularly adept at using symbolic leadership behavior. Cartwright applied *basketball jargon* to anything he did: if someone paid him a compliment, he'd say, 'nice assist'; if a taxicab nearly mowed him down, he'd shout, 'great pick.' It was amusing. But, for Jackson basketball is an expression of life, a single, sometimes glittering thread that reflects the whole. Like life, basketball is messy and unpredictable. It has its way with you, no matter how hard you try to control it. According to Jackson, the trick is to experience each moment with a clear mind and open heart. When you do that, he believes that the game of life will take care of itself.

Jackson had the locker room decorated in such a way as to be a symbol of his expectations of the team. He had the locker room decorated this way to reinforce in the players' minds that their journey together each year, from the start of the training camp to the last whistle in the playoffs, is a sacred quest. The locker room was their holy sanctuary, the place where the players and the coaches come together and prepared their mind, body, and soul for the battle, hidden from the probing eyes of the media and the harsh realities of the outside world. This is the room where the spirit of the team took form. "For example, there's a passage from Rudyard Kipling's *Second Jungle* book that was on the wall of our locker room, and I often read it during the playoffs to remind the team of this basic principle" (p. 12):

> Now this is the Law of the Jungle—
> as old as true as the sky:
> And the Wolf that shall keep it may prosper,
> but the Wolf that shall break it must die.
> As the creeper that girdles the tree truck,
> the Law runneth forward and back—
> For the strength of the Pack is the Wolf,
> and the strength of the Wolf is the Pack.

Coach Jackson's thinking on the value of symbolic leadership behavior evolved over time, however. Initially, Jackson would have scoffed at anyone who suggested that selflessness and compassion were the secrets to success. Those were qualities that counted in church, not battling under the boards with Wilt Chamberlain and Kareem Abdul-Jabbar. But after searching long and hard for meaning everywhere else, Jackson discovered that the game itself operated according to laws far more profound than anything that might be found in a coach's playbook. According to Jackson, inside the lines of the court, the mystery of life gets played out night after night.

Jackson came by his reliance on symbolic behavior from his parents during his formative years. His mother, Elisabeth, was as passionate about spirituality as anyone he'd ever known. She got her calling to become an evangelist when she was a teenager living on a small farm in eastern Montana. His father, Charles, was a warm, compassionate man with a view of life based on a literal translation of the King James version of the Bible. Their lives were determined by the rhythms of church life. In fact, in his first four years, they actually lived in the basement of the church until the parish could afford a parsonage.

Over time, his ideology was influenced by the tenets of Zen Buddhism. When first introduced to Zen, Jackson found it puzzling. The monk's description of Zen baffled him. How could you have a religion that didn't involve belief in God, Jackson wondered. What did Zen practitioners do? The monk indicated that they simply tried to clear their minds and be in the present. To someone raised in a Pentecostal household—where attention was focused more on the hereafter rather than the here and now—this was a mind-boggling concept. It struck Jackson in listening to the monk that he had inherited his mother's mind and his father's heart, and those two sides of his character were still in conflict, according to Jackson.

"There's a passage in Carlos Castaneda's *The Teaching of Don Juan*, in which Don Juan advises Castaneda: 'Look at every path closely and deliberately. Try it as many times as you think necessary, then ask yourself, and yourself alone the question. Does this path have a heart? If it does, the path is good. If it doesn't, it is of no use'" (p. 45). According to Jackson, what pollutes the mind in the Buddhist view is the desire to get life to conform to our peculiar notion of how things should be, as opposed to how they really are. There is an old Zen story that illustrates this point. Two monks were traveling together in a heavy downpour when they came upon a beautiful woman in a silk kimono who was having trouble crossing a muddy intersection. "Come on," said the first monk to the woman, and carried her in his arms to a dry spot. The second monk didn't say anything until later. Then he couldn't contain himself anymore. "We monks don't go near females," he said. "Why did you do that?" "I left the woman back there," the first monk replied. "Are you still carrying her?" The point of Zen practice is to make you aware of the thoughts that run your life and diminish their power over you. The goal of Zen is not just to clear the mind, but to open the heart as well. The two, of course, are interrelated.

When the legendary Vince Lombardi was basketball coach at Fordham in the early 1940s he used to have his players make a pledge before each practice. He'd stand them behind the end line and say "God has ordained me to teach you young men about basketball today. I want all those who want that training to step across that line." This wasn't just an empty symbolic gesture. Lombardi understood the power of making a conscious act of commitment. That's why he wanted his players to cross that line every day. Jackson believed in Lombardi's philosophy.

Jackson would utilize symbolic leadership behavior to instill his philosophy of selflessness in his players by posting inspirational poems such as the following on the locker room wall (p. 99):

Fish Don't Fly

When a fish swims in the ocean, there is no limit to the
water, no matter how far it swims.
When a bird flies in the sky, there is no limit to the air,
no matter how far it flies.
However, no fish or bird has ever left its element since the beginning.

"This ancient Zen teaching," Jackson says, "holds great wisdom for anyone envisioning how to get the most out of a group. Just as fish don't fly and elephants don't play rock and roll, you can't expect a team to perform in a way that's out of tune with its basic abilities" (p. 100).

Jackson has created video intertwining game shots with movie scenes to get his points across to his team in a symbolic way. He used scenes from *The Wizard of Oz* video tape. One sequence showed B.J. Armstrong dribbling to the basket and being flattened by the Detroit front line, followed by a shot of Dorothy arriving in the Land of Oz, looking around and saying to her faithful dog, "This isn't Kansas anymore, Toto," B.J. got the message. Another sequence showed Horace Grant, who needed to develop court savvy, being faked out by Isiah Thomas on a screen-and-roll play, followed by the Scarecrow talking about how great it would be to have a brain. Horace also got the symbolic message.

If there was ever a doubt about whether the Jackson's symbolic messages had been internalized by his players, those doubts vanished when John Paxson came across a Chinese fable in the *Harvard Business Review* that he said reminded him of Jackson's leadership style. The story was about Emperor Liu Bang, who, in the third century B.C., became the first ruler to consolidate China into a unified empire. Seated at the central table with Liu Bang was his illustrious high command. First there was Xiao He, an eminent general whose knowledge of military logistics was second to none. Next to him was Han Xin, a legendary tactician who'd won every battle he'd ever fought. Last was Chang Yang, a shrewd diplomat who was gifted at convincing heads of state to form alliances and surrender without fighting.

Chang Yang asked the Emperor's disciples what determined the strength of a wheel? "Is it not the sturdiness of the spokes?" one responded. "Then why is it that two wheels made of identical spokes differ in strength?" asked Chang Yang. After a moment, he continued, "See beyond what is seen. Never forget that a wheel is made not only of spokes but also of the space between the spokes. Sturdy spokes poorly placed make a weak wheel. Whether their full potential is realized depends on the harmony between. The essence of wheel making lies in the craftsman's ability to conceive and create the space that holds and balances the spokes within the wheel. Think now, who is the craftsman here?"

The disciples were silent until one of them said, "But master, how does a craftsman secure the harmony between the spokes?" Chang Yang asked them to think of sunlight. "The sun nurtures and vitalizes the trees and flowers," he said. "It does so by giving away its light. But in the end, in which direction do they grow? So it is with a master craftsman like Liu Bang. After planning individuals in positions that fully realize their potential, he secures harmony among them by giving them all credit for their distinctive achievements. And in the end, as the trees and flowers grow towards the giver, the sun, individuals grow toward Liu Bang with devotion."

Phil Jackson's use of the symbolic leadership frame was not only extensive, but also effective.

THE POLITICAL FRAME

Leaders operating out of the political frame clarify what they want and what they can get. Political leaders are realists above all. They never let what they want cloud their judgment about what is possible. They assess the distribution of power and interests.

Phil Jackson is very astute at utilizing the political frame of leadership behavior when appropriate. One need only observe that he is one of the highest paid men in his profession. In negotiating his salary and benefits, he utilized political frame leadership behavior. However, he also recognizes the limits of power. When comparing the power that an NBA coach has over his players as compared to a college coach, Jackson observes that while it is true that NBA coaches don't have the autocratic power of someone like Bobby Knight, they have far more power than it appears. The source of the power is the fact that coaches have played a central role in the players' lives since they were youngsters.

On the contrary, Jackson understands the misuse of political frame behavior. He refers to such an instance in recalling a time when he compromised his principles to placate his boss, and the players picked up on his ambivalence immediately. The solidarity that had taken so long to build suddenly evaporated. Not only did they lose the playoff series, they were lost as a team.

CONCLUSION

Phil Jackson's success is no accident. He is the epitome of a situational leader in the Bolman/Deal mold. He effectively utilizes all four frames of leadership behavior suggested by the Bolman/Deal situational leadership theory. Additionally, he utilizes the four frames in the appropriate circumstances. He is especially adept at behaving out of the human relations and symbolic leadership frames. Leaders and aspiring leaders can learn much from studying Phil Jackson's leadership style and applying it to their own particular situations.

④

DR. JACK RAMSAY

Trust yourself when men doubt you, but make allowance for their doubting too.

—Rudyard Kipling

BACKGROUND

Jack Ramsay was born on February 21, 1925, in Philadelphia and now is a former college and professional basketball coach. He is a 1942 graduate of Upper Darby High School outside of Philadelphia. He was inducted into the school's Wall of Fame in 1979. He received his bachelor's degree from Saint Joseph's College in 1949, and his master's and doctorate degrees from the University of Pennsylvania in 1952 and 1963, respectively. He has the most formal education of any of the coaches studied in this book.

In the fall of 1942, after a celebrated high school athletic career, Ramsay attended Saint Joseph's College for one year, joined the navy and then was sent to Villanova University in the navy's V-12 program to complete academic requirements for officer training school. He was commissioned an ensign in December 1944. He spent most of his active duty as a platoon leader in the Underwater Demolition Team (later known as the Navy SEALS) and then as a captain of a cargo ship. The physical regimen that he endured to qualify for the Navy SEALS has continued into his adult life.

After graduating from Saint Joseph's College, he began his basketball coaching career at Saint James High School in Chester, Pennsylvania, where he coached and taught for 3 years. He then took a position at Mount Pleasant High School in Wilmington, Delaware. During the 6 years that he spent coaching at the high school level, he played professional basketball in the Eastern League for Harrisburg and then, Sunbury. He did so to supplement his teaching/coaching salary, which was $2,400 per year.

After 6 successful years as a high school coach, Ramsay became head coach at his alma mater, Saint Joseph's College, in 1955. In his first season, Ramsay would lead the Hawks to their first Big 5 crown (Villanova, LaSalle, Penn, Temple, and Saint Joseph's) and their first-ever postseason berth (in the National Invitation Tournament). Ramsay would remain at Saint Joseph's through the 1966 season, leading the Hawks to six more Big 5 crowns and ten postseason appearances.

Immediately after leaving Saint Joseph's, he was hired as general manager of the Philadelphia 76ers, who won a National Basketball Association (NBA) title in his first season in the front office. In 1968, he left the front office to take over as head coach of the 76ers. In his four seasons as coach, he led the team to three playoff appearances. After the 1971–72 season, he took the head coaching job with the Buffalo Braves. His tenure was almost a mirror image of his time with the 76ers—four seasons, three playoff berths.

Ramsay's next coaching stop was his most famous, with the Portland Trail Blazers. When he arrived in 1976, the Blazers had not made the playoffs or compiled a winning record in their 6-year history. However, he arrived just as a young team, led by Bill Walton, started to gel, and also benefited from the ABA dispersal draft in the 1976 off-season, in which the Blazers picked up hard-nosed forward Maurice Lucas. In his first season in Portland (1977), Ramsay led the Blazers to their only NBA title to date. In his second season, the Blazers were 50-10 after 60 games and favored to repeat as champions before Walton, in the midst of a season in which he would be named the league's most valuable player (MVP), broke his foot, the first of the numerous major injuries that radically shortened his career. Ramsay continued to coach the Blazers until 1986 with general success, although he was never able to approach the level of his first seasons there. He was also a coach in the 1978 All-Star Game. Ramsay coached the Indiana Pacers for the 1986–88 seasons before retiring early in 1988-89. At that time, he was second on the all-time wins list for NBA coaches, trailing only the legendary Red Auerbach.

Dr. Jack later spent 9 years as a television color commentator for the Philadelphia 76ers and the Miami Heat, and continues to do commentary for ESPN on television and radio. He was the color commentator for the Miami Heat from 1992 until 2002. Ramsay worked alongside announcer Eric Reid, who was still working Miami Heat games in 2008. During Ramsay's tenure as the Heat's commentator, he developed some memorable nicknames and phrases for the Heat players. Whenever All-Star point guard Tim Hardaway would make a three-point shot, Dr. Jack would shout, "This away, that away, Hardaway!" Or if any Heat player made a nice shot, you would hear Dr. Jack shout "Bottom of the net!"

Ramsay prided himself on his physical fitness and mental toughness and tried to be a model for his players. Well into his 80s, Ramsay participated in triathlons (running, swimming, and cycling great distances) in his age class at the national level. He was enshrined in the Basketball Hall of Fame in 1992 and was named one of the ten greatest coaches of all time in 1996. He has authored several highly rated books, including *The Coach's Art* and *Dr. Jack's Leadership Lessons Learned From a Lifetime in Basketball*.

SITUATIONAL LEADERSHIP BEHAVIOR

Situational leadership models differ from the earlier trait and behavioral models in asserting that no single way of leading works in all situations. Rather, appropriate behavior depends on the circumstances at a given time. Effective managers diagnose the situation, identify the leadership style or behavior that will be most effective, and then determine whether they can implement the required style.

Jack Ramsay realized the importance of adapting his leadership behavior to the situation very early on in his professional life. In recalling his days as a high school coach, he remembered that he adopted a "system" to which his athletes would have to adjust. However, he saw the futility of that approach when he lost some games because "I played a fast-break game, but my players lacked the skills to play it well, and I made no adjustments" (Ramsay, 2004, p. 41; all cites in this chapter, unless otherwise noted, are from this source).

From these unfortunate experiences and from observing the behavior of successful leaders, he was soon convinced of the situational nature of leadership. In observing the behavior of Tim Duncan, the San Antonio Spurs' great center, Ramsay says, "He remains somewhat quiet, but is a vocal, forceful leader when the occasion demands." And in observing the leadership behavior of Duncan's coach, Gregg Popovich, Ramsey observes, "Like all successful leaders, Pop is true to himself and is unique. He is extremely well organized in handling the myriad coaching duties; he knows the NBA game thoroughly, works hard at developing an effective team game, and is very demanding of his players [structural behavior]. Popovich says, 'I tell our players from the beginning that I won't play any mind or motivational games with them, that I'm going to be honest and open with them [human resource behavior].'" Ramsay continues, "And he doesn't play favorites—he'll even jump all over Duncan. All the players accept his approach and respond positively because they respect him and know what they need to do on the floor to satisfy him."

"Popovich says of one his star players, Tony Parker, 'If I've been a little tough on Tony, I'll take him to a restaurant for dinner [when we're] on the road and order a bottle of French wine, then explain why I went after him hard and give him a chance to tell his side of the story'" (p. 54).

In observing the former New York Knicks' coach Red Holzman's approach toward his players, Ramsay notes, "He was harder on some than others, but he knew how to push the right buttons—and no one got away with anything. He was clearly the man in charge. I learned a lot just being around him" (p. 58).

On the other hand, Ramsay observed what could happen when a leader does not act in a situational manner. "Bill Russell was another great player who tried to transfer his winning ways to coaching, only to meet with frustration and unfamiliar defeat. I had tremendous respect for him as a player and liked him personally; I wanted to understand why he could not make the transition from player to coach. He was gentler, softer, then the media pictured him to be, and some players might have taken advantage of that. And like a lot of great players, Bill expected players to play like he did, even though they weren't at his ability level, and he couldn't get them there with motivational talks. It was very frustrating for him. Unfortunately, he did not have Bill Russell playing for him" (p. 86).

In contrast to the superstar Russell, in speaking of Alex Hannum, his predecessor at Philadelphia, Ramsay says, "He had great rapport with his players, and was a stand-up guy. Though he'd had only modest success as an NBA player, he had a great sense of the game as a coach. Known as 'Sarge' for his no-nonsense approach with players, he was widely admired by players throughout the league" (p. 86).

In speaking of Billy Cunningham, one of his successors with the Philadelphia 76ers, Ramsay observes that "Cunningham found that he got the best performance from them by dealing with each as an individual. 'Some I could criticize in front of the team; others I did in private.'" Ramsay continues, referring to his own leadership practices, "Adjustments are almost always necessary in any leader's communication, to account for changes especially in personnel. Two episodes from my coaching career stand out in my mind" (p. 91).

At a team meeting where each player was asked to offer an opinion regarding the team's play, "Maurice Lucas was the last to respond [to Ramsay's screaming from the bench]. He said that I should calm down, that the players were getting negative vibes from my conduct on the sidelines, and it was hurting their confidence. Instead of jumping all over players at timeouts, Luke suggested, 'Just tell us we [messed] up, and let it go at that.' With that, everyone in the room, including me, broke up laughing. I agreed to more patience, but said that I still wanted each player to lift his game. There was a united nodding of heads, the meeting ended on an upbeat note, and our play picked up after that" (p. 92).

The second incident came after a big win in the league playoffs when Dr. Jack was coaching the 76ers. One of his stars (Archie Clark) had spent a lot of time on the bench during this particular game. After the game, he berated Ramsay in front of the team about his lack of playing time. "Caught up in the euphoria of our biggest win of the season, I was at first stunned, then angered by his outburst. We got into a shouting match that almost came to blows. I tried to clear the air the next day at the team meeting, but the team's high spirits were deflated, and the Bucks blew us away in Game 3, then won the next two to end our season" (p. 93).

"In retrospect, the Clark incident was an example of poor communication and personnel management on my part," Ramsay said. "I had ignored the warning signs. I should have tried harder to find a solution to the problem, to find more personal one-on-one time with Clark to reach a common ground. It was a lesson I learned the hard way in my first years of NBA coaching. Perhaps nothing would have worked, because Clark had such a strong, self-centered personality. But I hadn't done my job well, and that bothers me to this day" (p. 93).

Jack Ramsay was obviously influenced in his own leadership behavior by some of the other basketball coaches he knew and respected. As indicated earlier, one of them was Red Auerbach. When Ramsay asked Auerbach how he handled so many star players so well, he gave Dr. Jack a very situational theory-like answer. "First of all," he said, "you don't *handle* people. You handle animals; you treat people like human beings. That was always the most important thing with me." "And that's what Auerbach did," says Ramsay, "He treated each player with respect and got the same in return" (p. 94).

Ramsay continues, "Just as leaders in other fields bring their personalities to bear on their particular style of leadership, there have been all kind of personalities among notable coaches. They range from domineering types, like Vince Lombardi and Bob Knight, to quiet, orderly directors like John Wooden. The vital factor was that all three of them were who they were; they didn't try to be someone else. In his study on the principles of leadership, Bruce Oglivie found that those in authority who achieved high levels of success shared three characteristics: intense intellectual curiosity about their jobs, a burning desire for success, and 'transparent personalities'—what you see is what you get" (p. 139).

"That position lets coaches create their own philosophy and style of playing, allows for developing individualized methods of teaching, affords great motivational circumstances, and gives them freedom to determine how they conduct their game. After a lot of trial and error, the survivors become the kind of coach they really want to be. I use the term 'survivors' deliberately, because each level of coaching demands adjustments that not everyone can make. I recounted how unprepared I was for my first job. But I learned from it and then was better prepared for college coaching" (p. 139).

Ramsay also recognizes the situational nature of leadership when conversing with his acquaintances involved in other sports. For example, in a conversation with Gary Bettman, the commissioner of the National Hockey League (NHL), in comparing the NBA with the NHL, Bettman said: "The culture of the NHL is not the same as that of the NBA. Hockey is a different sport from basketball, so some of the things we do are different. But those internal qualities I just mentioned are effective everywhere. That's why David Stern [commissioner of the NBA] could step into an executive position with any Fortune 500 company and have the same success that he's had in the NBA." He would merely have to adjust his leadership behavior to the new situation.

Another Ramsay friend, Joe Dumars, general manager of the Detroit Pistons, is cited by Ramsay as being astute at adjusting his leadership behavior to the situation. "Although he appeared to be somewhat reserved and reticent as a player, Dumars says that he has 'always been vocal enough when needed to convey my vision and had never had a problem saying what needed to be said.' But, he adds, 'I don't pontificate beyond that. I'm not a soapbox kind of guy'" (p. 183).

Ramsay also pointed out how the former Detroit Piston star Dave Bing was able to apply the leadership skills that he developed as a player to another venue by adapting his behavior to the new situation (business). "Dave [Bing] has received much recognition for his success in the business world. In 1984, he was named the Nation's Outstanding Minority Small-Business Entrepreneur and was honored at the White House by President Ronald Reagan. In 1990, he received the first Schick Achievement Award for prominence following an NBA career. He is also a highly visible and productive member of the Detroit community. In 1987, he made a six-figure contribution to the United Negro College Fund. And in July 1989, when the Detroit public school system was set to eliminate sports from the curriculum due to budget cuts, Bing was asked to head up a committee to raise the necessary $600,000 to continue programs in sports, music, and the arts. In August, he handed over a check for the full amount. He then initiated a concerted appeal to the voters to pass a levy that would provide funds for those activities in the future. The levy passed in September of the same year" (p. 236). When asked to elaborate on his success, Bing said, "Your plans have to be flexible enough to accommodate changing conditions in the economy. And never, never allow complacency" (p. 237).

The notion of situational leadership was also noted in a conversation between Bill Bradley and Ramsay. "Recently, Bill Bradley told me more about his approach to leadership. He said that, in new situations, he waits for an appropriate time to become an active leader. 'I was a vocal leader in high school and college; it was needed and I had no problem doing that. When I first came to the Knicks, I was new on the scene and didn't play a lot, so I deferred to the more established veterans. It was the same way when I went to the Senate. As a junior senator, I waited my turn and did the best work that I could. Gradually, I took advantage of opportunities to lead'" (p. 246).

THE STRUCTURAL FRAME

Structural leaders develop a new model of the relationship of structure, strategy, and environment for their organizations. Although there is ample evidence that Jack Ramsay utilized all of the frames of leadership behavior, one could argue that he is basically a structural leader. We started this chapter with one of Dr. Jack's favorite quotes by Rudyard Kipling. Kipling is urging that we never be so overconfident that we do not learn from our mistakes. Jack Ramsay can be characterized as one who lives by this credo. He learned to be a leader by observing others and by learning from his own mistakes.

In observing his counterpart Big 5 coaches, Ramsay says: "The influence these men had on their teams fascinated me. Each team had its unique style that those outstanding coaches put in place. The high level of team play that I saw as I played against them maximized the skills of the best players. Those teams were among the nation's best every year, and it was obvious that their coaches played a leading role in that success. I wanted to have that experience with a team of my own. It was then that I decided on coaching as a profession" (p. 11).

Ramsay realizes the need to behave in the structural frame in order to achieve success. He says, "Preparation is very important. Everybody has the will to win, but only those who prepare are going to get there" (p. 25). Furthermore, "Confident people analyze the situation, make logical plans to improve it, then go to work to achieve their goals" (p. 26).

Being willing to learn from one's mistakes is evident in Ramsay's depiction of his own behavior as a beginning coach. "I showed my young players how I played without teaching them how they should play. I failed to break down the game into its basic elements and taught whole concepts instead of part to whole" (p. 41). In keeping with Ramsay's propensity to learn from others and from his own mistakes, he recalls his observations of a respected coaching colleague, Pete Newell. "Because of his highly developed sense of the game and how to teach it, Newell was connected with one NBA team or another for all of the 22 years that I was involved with the league. I hadn't paid enough attention to detail, and admitted as much. Pete had obviously noticed that my players weren't consistent in the way they received the ball at the side-court position, and asked me if I had ever thought about it? This was his way of offering a suggestion" (p. 44).

On another occasion, Ramsay reports: "I learned about the zone press—a defense I was often given credit for originating—from Woody Ludwig, a coach at Pennsylvania Military College (now Widener College). Like St. James High School, PMC was located in Chester, Pennsylvania. In my senior year at St. Joseph's, we scrimmaged PMC. They played a small college schedule and weren't considered a very strong team. The scrimmage went easily for St. Joe's—until Ludwig applied full-court, zone pressure late in the workout. We had never seen anything like it before and proceeded to turn over the ball frequently. That tactic took us completely out of our game. I tucked away that experience in my memory bank, and when I was at St. James, I learned all the adjustments Ludwig used in that defense. By the time I was coaching at St. Joseph's, the zone press was part of my defensive game plan—thanks to Woody Ludwig" (p. 44). Ramsay's adoption of the zone press as a strategy is an instance of utilizing structural frame leadership behavior.

DR. JACK RAMSAY

In speaking of his coaching counterpart, Pat Riley's structural leadership behavior, Ramsay recalls: "As a launching point, he [Pat Riley] recalled principles implemented by his former coaches: in high school, Walt Przbylo, and in college, the legendary Adolph Rupp. Both were strong disciplinarians." Ramsay says that Riley also made use of structural leadership behavior in the form of what he called "Backs to the Bleachers." Whenever Riley was not happy with the performance of his players, he would bring them together for a team meeting and had them sit with their backs to the bleachers. "He called it 'Backs to the Bleachers' because that's where his squad sat while he talked to them about the status of their game and what they would work on that day on the court" (p. 45).

"He [Riley] has a rigid, well-thought-out game plan; he works his players very hard on the practice floor; he talks to them back-to-the-bleachers style before each practice [structural behavior]; and he makes time to speak to individuals to bolster confidence and inspire their continued efforts [human resource behavior]." Ramsay speaks of the importance of appropriately applying structural behavior in his observation of Tim Duncan, the great San Antonio Spurs center. "Like his coach [Gregg Popovich], Duncan doesn't hesitate to take responsibility for how the team plays, frequently announcing to his teammates in the locker room after a tough defeat that the loss was on his shoulders. And despite his dominance as a player, he is completely unselfish, following Pop's game plan fully and productively and never losing sight of the role his teammates play in his own success." Speaking further about Duncan's coach, Gregg Popovich, Ramsay notes, "Shrug it off though he might, Gregg Popovich has become an outstanding coach. He has a workable game plan, uses his personnel extremely well, and makes in-game adjustments effectively" (p. 51). These qualities are characteristic of structural frame leadership behavior and are also part of Jack Ramsay's leadership behavior.

Ramsay endorses the need for structural leadership behavior by citing the behavior of two of this protégés, Jim Lynam, former coach of the Philadelphia 76ers, Washington Bullets, and Saint Joseph's University, and Bill Walton, the great Portland Trailblazer and UCLA star. "The best teachers learn from their students. I've learned a lot about the game from many players. Jim Lynam was one of them. When Jim was senior at St. Joseph's, I wanted to install an offense similar to St. Bonaventure's because I felt our personnel was well suited to it. We had spent weeks working on pass and cut moves, when Lynam suggested including a high post screener in the attack. I was skeptical at first because I thought it would clog the middle. Instead, I found that the screener freed up cutters with back-picks and gave us opportunities to score a lot of layups. It became part of the offense I used in college and in the pros" (p. 59). In a similar situation, Bill Walton suggested to Ramsay when he first became coach of the Portland Trailblazers, "Don't assume we know anything, coach." Ramsay said that "Bill, who had played for the legendary John Wooden at UCLA for four years, had seen how valuable Wooden's emphasis on fundamentals had been to those teams. He wanted that same kind of focus for this young Portland team, which at the time had never had a winning season, and so was suggesting that I take nothing for granted" (p. 59). Ramsay was evidently happy to oblige.

Ramsay acknowledges the need for structural behavior to be an effective leader especially if one does not have the knowledge needed to be such a leader himself. In speaking about his friend Billy Cunningham, the former coach of the NBA champion Philadelphia 76ers, he recalls that "Billy Cunningham got into it [coaching] by accident. He was doing television commentary for Sixers' games the year after the team lost to my Portland team in the 1977 NBA Finals. Sixers' management was unhappy with that loss, and when the team struggled early in the following season, Gene Shue was fired, and Billy went from the television booth to the coaching bench" (p. 66). Since he did not have the basketball knowledge of a head coach, "Billy hired Chuck Daley, and excellent X-and-O guy, away from the University of Pennsylvania. 'That's when I think my real leadership qualities developed,' Billy added, 'I literally looked myself in the mirror and asked, "What can I do to make this team the best team it can be?"' I started thinking about how I could utilize each player to the best of his abilities, how to get them to overachieve and how to motivate them to play within the team game. When the games began, I'd chart their called plays, paying particular attention to the coach's tendencies—which plays he called when the shot clock wound down, how plays were set up for the star players, and any characteristics of the defense that I thought my team could exploit" (p. 66). And the learning process all began by hiring someone who could act as a structural leader until Cunningham had a chance to learn to do so for himself.

As a structural leader, Jack Ramsay is a stickler for details. He maintains: "A combination of numerous little things make the final result effective, but six guidelines can capture the main characteristics of a good coach: (1) know the game thoroughly and develop a successful game plan; (2) teach the skills fitting the game plan; (3) set high standards and motivate your players to play that game; (4) be ready to make effective adjustments during the game when necessary; (5) know the competition; and (6) never stop trying to reach stated goals" (p. 71). Of course, all of these characteristics are manifestations of the structural frame of leadership.

The ability to teach effectively, another structural frame trait, is thought by Ramsay to be a key to success as a leader. "The ability to teach is the basis of good coaching or leading in any field. Teaching is demonstrating, telling, motivating, demanding, encouraging, correcting and criticizing, and showing approval. Learning is the product of teaching. If there has been no learning, there has been no teaching. When teaching is successful, the result is palpable: a light comes on in the eyes of the student that actually radiates over that person's countenance. There is an instant communication of change. The student feels it, and the teacher sees it" (p. 72).

"Classroom teachers are in wonderful positions of leadership. It is my perception that every person who has gone through an educational system has had teachers who have had a profound effect on their lives. Too often, this kind of leadership goes unappreciated. I remember with gratitude all the teachers who were part of my educational life, though certain ones occupy a special niche in my memory bank: Miss Platt, the grade school teacher in Milford—who demonstrated her love of children and teaching every day; Miss Kerr, our class advisor at Upper Darby High School (whom everybody adored); my professor of philosophy at St. Joseph's, Father Edward Gannon, SJ; and the esteemed Dr. McMullin, my professor at the University of Pennsylvania. Each helped me to achieve whatever success I've had in life" (p. 138).

Oftentimes structural frame behavior is necessary in encountering a new situation. Ramsay recalls an incident when he was first named coach of the Portland Trailblazers. Basketball practice started at 7:00.

"They [Bill Walton, Maurice Lucas, and Herman Gilliam] strolled in together at 7:05. I knew my authority was being challenged. I pointedly checked my watch, then announced that the three players—and I named them—who were five minutes late would be fined $5 a minute, an accepted rate for tardiness in those days. Years later, Larry Steele, a reserve swingman on that team, observed that fining those three players was my most significant act in getting the team off to a good start. He said that it established team unity and made it clear that everyone would be treated the same." "Everybody likes the person in charge to *be* in charge," says Ramsay. "There is nothing worse than an administrator who won't exercise authority. That applies to all walks of life. It is certainly true in sports" (p. 88).

Mental preparation, a structural frame behavior, is a Ramsay trademark. "To that end, I do crossword puzzles, cryptograms, and word puzzles while I am eating my breakfast" (p. 111). "I tape the games . . . and replay them when I get home. It [taping] became a great tool for evaluation, which I continue to use in both television and radio work" (p. 126). Ramsay says "Great leaders know where they want to go and how they plan to get there. They are well-organized, are comfortable delegating authority, know how to communicate pertinent information appropriately and effectively and are able to prepare their personnel thoroughly." To illustrate these points, Ramsay recalls a story about Sir Ernest Shackleton, the 1914 explorer who survived after being stranded in the Arctic for almost 2 years. "Sir Ernest accomplished that feat by never losing his poise; maintaining his confidence that they would all survive; organizing the group's activities in a meaningful manner; establishing excellent rapport with every member of the group, which brought them closer together as individuals; and adjusting his game plan to meet changing conditions" (p. 136).

According to Ramsay, no one in sports exemplifies the qualities of leadership better than the NBA's David Stern, who is widely regarded as the most successful sports commissioner of all time. "When I asked him [Stern] about his qualities as a leader, he hedged a bit: 'I'm not one for introspection,' he said, 'but I always had the ability to set a tone. I've always been compulsively interested in acquiring facts, forming an opinion, then pursuing that opinion with conviction. I did that in grade school, in camp, in high school—and I still like to debate issues.'" Stern told Ramsay, "We established the motto, 'The relentless pursuit of perfection' before Lexus [the car manufacturer] did, knowing that true perfection is never reached. Our first concern, after we've done what we consider to be a great job is 'how can we do it better?'" (p. 143).

In support of the need for structural frame behavior for effective leadership, Ramsay cites a book by Micheal Useem and Warren Bennis, *The Leadership Moment*, in which they "write that leadership is the act of making a difference. [It] entails changing a failed strategy or revamping a languishing organization. It requires us to make an active choice among plausible alternatives, and it depends on bringing others along, on mobilizing them to get the job done. "It struck me that all those characteristics apply to a coach who takes on the challenge of a struggling franchise. Three of the four teams that I coached fit that description perfectly. Consequently, I was afforded great opportunities of leadership" (p. 148).

The need for rules and regulations as a manifestation of structural behavior is important to Ramsay. "The rules I felt called on most often to enforce with my teams mainly had to do with time, place, physical condition, and equipment. I required players (and coaches) to be punctual and at the designated site for all team activities, to be physically prepared to do their jobs and to have the necessary equipment to carry them out. Players recognize the need for discipline, because they all know it's the only way for a team to succeed. But they want the same rules to apply to everyone—they don't want double standards. The rules must apply equally to the stars of the team as to the role players and the benchwarmers" (pp. 153–154).

Ramsay recalls an incident where he did not apply the rules in an equitable way. The incident involved one of his star players, Chuck Person, with whom Ramsay got into a heated argument about Person taking bad shots. Ramsay told Person to leave the gym. Person left the floor, but not the gym. Instead of fining him, Ramsay just let the incident go. Ramsay noted: "The rest of the squad regarded my action as backing down in the face-to-face confrontation. Team morale wasn't the same after that, and I had no one to blame but myself. I should have taken a strong stand. When Person didn't leave the gym, I should have told him he would be suspended if he didn't. If he had left the gym, I would probably have retained my position of authority. If he had still refused to leave, I would have had to make certain that he was suspended" (p. 167).

"I agree with David Stern: Those in leadership positions don't often analyze themselves while in that role. Looking back at myself now, I think my players would say that I led by example and by doing. I was a hands-on coach. I tried to stay in top physical condition, ate a proper diet, abstained from drugs, and consumed only modest amounts of alcohol, to show that what I was demanding of them, I was also demanding of myself. While I didn't have NBA-level basketball skills, I was able to demonstrate adequately what I wanted done on the floor. I worked hard at developing an effective team game, spent long hours analyzing opponents, and never gave up on an opportunity—no matter how slight—to win a game" (p. 169).

Translating these ideas to nonbasketball situations, Ramsay says, "Being successful in life takes careful planning. You have to make decisions on a continuous basis and as often as possible, you want them to be the right ones. Ideally, you should have time to study a situation or condition and reach a sound, rational conclusion; but often, you must make the decision 'on the fly'" (p. 189). "In business, long-range planning is often referred to as the 'mission statement'; in sports it's called the 'game plan.' This is a unified plan for the group; it helps all members understand how their individual roles influence the end result and defines for those involved in a specific activity the purpose and direction of their actions. For the game plan to succeed, everyone in the group must understand it, believe that they can accomplish it, and that the result will meet the goals of the group" (p. 190). This thinking on the part of Ramsay reflects his clear understanding of the need for appropriately applied structural frame leadership behavior.

THE HUMAN RESOURCE FRAME

Human resource leaders believe in people and communicate that belief. They are passionate about *productivity through people*. There are a number of instances when Jack Ramsay acknowledges the necessity of applying human resource leadership behavior to certain situations in order to be effective. For example, early in his basketball training as a member of the Saint Joseph's College team, he learned the value of human resource leadership behavior. His coach was the legendary Billy

Ferguson, who was famous for coaching an overachieving group of players nicknamed the Mighty Mites because of their propensity for defeating nationally ranked teams with no player over 6 feet 2 inches tall. The Mighty Mites prospered during the 1930s, but Ramsay played for Ferguson toward the end of his career. In his senior year, after having been a starter for half the season, Ramsay was suddenly benched with no explanation. In recalling that time in his life, Ramsay says, "I held no malice toward Ferg for the incident, but I tucked it in the back of my mind as an inappropriate way for a coach to deal with a player" (p. 6).

Ramsay learned from that incident that human resource leadership behavior is necessary at times for a leader to maximize his or her effectiveness. Dr. Jack was so effective in applying human resource behavior that four of his former players at Saint Joseph's followed his example and became head coaches in the NBA (Jack McKinney, Matty Goukas, Jim Lynam, and Paul Westhead). This is still an NBA record.

Over time Ramsay garnered the reputation of being able to relate to his players. As a result, his teams were very successful. He recalls: "I had the honor of being associated with two truly great teams: the Sixers of 1967 and the Portland Trail Blazers of 1977. Those Blazers, molded around Bill Walton's pinpoint passing and the intimidating presence of Maurice Lucas, represent my closest brush with basketball Nirvana. That group remains one of the joys of my life" (p. 16).

In another instance of the effectiveness of the timely use of human resource behavior, Ramsay recalls an incident when Mark Cuban, the controversial owner of the Dallas Mavericks, held a team meeting before practice to introduce himself to the players and to outline his goals as the owner of the franchise. To get the players undivided attention, he challenged Dirk Nowitzki, one of his star players, to a game of one-on-one. As Ramsay recalls, "Needless to say, he came away a loser, but it served his greater purpose: to open the doors of communication" (p. 23).

Reflecting on his own human resource practices, Ramsay cites Mark Cuban's attitude toward winning. Although winning is important, "Having fun is important too," Cuban emphasizes. "We have a nice environment for our players and a beautiful new arena. Our locker room is first-rate. Our players like playing here. I want our fans to enjoy the total experience of Mavericks basketball. We work hard to make that happen. When they have fun, we have fun" (p. 25).

Cuban is a master of finding creative ways of effectively applying human resource leadership behavior to a given situation. "If you want to get the most from the people working with you, it's important to acknowledge their efforts, make them feel appreciated." For example, "Having the players' cars washed when they get back from a road trip is one of those. These are little things, but they show people that we care about them." In a more subtle application of human resource behavior, Ramsay tries to always be positive rather than negative in his instructions. For example, "Block out" and "Head up" are cryptic and positive. They carry a "do this" message, rather than a "don't do that" message. Along these lines, Ramsay "made it a point to say something constructive to my team immediately after every game—win or lose" (p. 36).

Ramsay cites Michael Jordan as a leader in the human resource mold. Jordan was not shy about taking over a game; "However, he also appreciated and showed great trust in his less-talented (by NBA standards) teammates who played big in the clutch—players like Bobby Hansen, John Paxson, and Steve Kerr, all of whom made game-winning plays orchestrated by MJ" (p. 32).

Another human resource–type leader was the former coach of the Los Angeles Lakers, Bill Sharman. Ramsay credits his knowledge of good player communications to Sharman. Sharman was an innovative coach for his time. He was the first coach to make day-of-game shootarounds a mandatory practice. Wilt Chamberlain, a notorious free-spirit, preferred going to the beach to play volleyball on mornings of a home game. "Eventually," says Ramsay, "Sharman cajoled Wilt into trying out the shootaround routine, which he came to enjoy. Coincidentally, the Lakers began a winning streak that reached a yet-unbroken record of 33 straight games. Ramsey says that Sharman also "made it a practice to talk with each of the reserve players at least once a week" (p. 46).

In referring to another of his coaching friends, Gregg Popovich, Ramsay quotes him as saying, "I want the players to know that we [he and his staff] care about them beyond basketball. We feel a responsibility for doing that." "Pop recognizes the value of off-court communication as well, and out to that end, he organizes team dinners and other social events for players, coaches, and their significant others to engender a family atmosphere." He says, "I want the players to see the stability that we [coaches] have in our families, and encourage the same quality in theirs. We also try to demonstrate humility that comes from knowing how fleeting success is, and that we're privileged to have the opportunity that we have. We're not going to gloat over wins nor make excuses for losses." Acknowledging Popovich's popularity with his players, Ramsay notes, "To be that well liked is a rare achievement for a leader" (p. 55).

Taking a page out of Sharman's and Popovich's books, Ramsay says, "It was my practice when I took a new coaching job to meet with each player individually in his home, to get to know him personally and to give him an idea of the game we'd play and his role" (p. 59). Telling people where they stand—on a team, in a relationship, in a family, at work—requires the ability to communicate effectively. "To that end," says Ramsay, "I make it a practice to speak to every player on my team each day that we meet, which was almost every day during the season. I try to make eye contact with them as well, and if that proved impossible, it was clear sign that I had to try harder to communicate" (p. 80).

"As a coach, in addition to talking directly with each player on my team every day, I took an interest in their families as well as their general well-being. And I gave players who weren't getting any playing time extra, personalized practice with me" (p. 83). A proponent of this approach is Phil Jackson, who became closely associated with the Native American culture and used many of their unity concepts—like the human circle that stays in constant physical and spiritual touch—to bring his team together. The premise for this approach was to tell the players: "We care about you; we want you to take care of yourselves." "These were Phil Jackson's ways of showing a genuine personal interest in each player and enabled the Bulls to become a family as much as they were an NBA championship team" (p. 83), says Ramsay. This human resource approach worked well when, much to Kobe Bryant's chagrin, "Jackson explained to Shaq [Shaquille O'Neal] the offense would run through him at the post, where he'd have the opportunity to display his scoring and passing skills. In the end, Kobe agreed, with some reluctance, to a slower-paced game plan. Although it wasn't a perfect fit for him—and there were times during the season when he was openly at odds with both Jackson and O'Neal—Bryant stayed in the team concept and the Lakers thrived," says Ramsay (p. 85).

In recalling his great NBA championship Portland Blazer team, Ramsay says, "There was an open, almost lighthearted atmosphere, with time for laughs as well as a serious down-to-business attitude." Ramsay was always open to player suggestions. "My feeling was that if the idea was sound technically, it had a stronger likelihood of success because the players had a personal investment in making it happen." There was such a camaraderie on that team that, "To this day, Bill Walton continues to lift my spirits. For the past 10 years, there hasn't been a holiday—Christmas, Easter, Fourth of July, or Thanksgiving—that Bill Walton didn't call me to say, 'I just want to say hello, thank you for all you did for me, and to tell you that we love you and Jean [his wife] very much'" (p. 60).

A great deal of Ramsay's philosophy regarding the need for human resource leadership behavior was the result of a very unfortunate incident that occurred in 1961 when three of his players were convicted of point-shaving. "I had a hard time coming to grips with my failure to prevent these young men from getting involved in an activity so contrary to the aims of the sport. I thought seriously about giving up coaching, but Father Geib [the athletic director at Saint Joseph's] and others encouraged me to stay in it. I had allowed myself to get too caught up with coaching success and had lost sight of my main responsibility as a leader: to serve as guide in the development of the athletes in my charge" (p. 218).

Lastly, Ramsay alludes to Jerry West's approach in applying the human resource frame to his leadership behavior. "West believes that an individual's personality dictates the kind of leader that person can be. 'I think I have a way of relating to people and getting along with them. I don't talk down to people. I don't try to boss or manage people; I work with them. I'm candid and honest.'" Both West and Ramsay agree that "Mutual trust is very important in leadership." And it is effective. Kobe Bryant says, "'It's great to listen to Jerry West—he's been there: I could always trust Jerry'" (p. 233). West recognized that "Being successful in both basketball and business is all about teamwork. I was a pretty good scorer, but I couldn't score unless someone set picks for me to get open and someone else passed me the ball" (p. 236).

Judging from these instances, we can see clearly the importance that Jack Ramsay places on the human resource aspect of his leadership behavior.

THE SYMBOLIC FRAME

In the symbolic frame, the organization is seen as a stage, a theater in which every actor plays certain roles and the symbolic leader attempts to communicate the right impressions to the right audiences. Jack Ramsay often made use of symbolic leadership behavior. As a college coach, he was one of the first coaches to leave his seat on the bench and "prowl the sidelines" as a symbol to his players and the fans that, like the players, he was an active participant in the game. He was also prone to remove his sports jacket at a critical time and toss it into the crowd as a sign to his team that it was time to "get down to business." In a humorous anecdote to this jacket-tossing tradition, Jack McKinney, Ramsay's assistant at the time, alluded to a time when it did not work out exactly as planned. In those early days of coaching, the head coach oftentimes would be given the team's meal and transportation money for away games. Ramsay had a habit of putting the money in an envelope and keeping it in his sports jacket pocket. You guessed it! In one game, he threw his jacket into the crowd and it was returned intact, except for one thing—the meal money was gone. There is a happy ending to this story, however. A Wake Forest student found the envelope and returned it to Ramsay. From then on, Dr. Jack made sure to keep the meal money in his pants pocket (McKinney & Gordon, 2005, p. 69).

Ramsay projects the image of a hard-working, no-nonsense person of great moral integrity. Considering what author David Halberstam has to say about Dr. Jack, that image remains very much intact. "I have come to admire him [Jack Ramsay]. Jack has no con to him, no artifice. He's an old-fashioned man, direct, sometimes a bit blunt, with a highly developed ethical sense, one in which there is still a clear and well-drawn line between right and wrong. In a sports world however one finds, with increasing frequency, altogether too many big-name coaches with a dual value system—a benign one created specifically for export to the larger public and projected through calculated media appearances, then a real value system, albeit a covert one, where the line between right and wrong is crossed all the time—Jack remains a throwback. There is not two of him—there is only the one. What you see is what you get" (as cited in Ramsay, 2004, p. x).

Halberstam continues on about Ramsay's symbolic behavior during "hard times." "Jack might be the most passionate of coaches, and defeat might still be unbearably painful—you did not want to go out to dinner with him after a losing game that season—but he never changed as a man, and he never blamed others for what was going on. He was as passionate, ethical, and honorable when everything was collapsing on him as he had been when everything was going right just a few years earlier and he was obviously on his way to becoming coach of the year" (as cited in Ramsay, 2004, p. xi).

Ramsay recognizes the value of symbolic leadership behavior in recalling one of the idiosyncrasies of the great John Wooden. "Master coach, John Wooden, thought lacing one's shoes was so important that he always taught a session on the manner in which players should lace their sneakers. Coach Wooden felt that unless a player's feet were sound and secure, he couldn't be expected to perform the game's basic functions. When I coached the Trail Blazers, I noticed that Bill Walton, one of Wooden's prize pupils, always pulled his laces tighter just before practice began. He still adhered to Wooden's message; Lace 'em up tight!" (p. 20).

In an effort to build confidence in his team after losing the first two playoff games to the 76ers in the Blazers' championship year, Ramsay was careful not to indicate that the losses were due to lack of ability. If he did, "It would say, in effect, that we weren't good enough to beat the Sixers. I didn't want to send a negative signal, so I decided not to change anything *except* the way we played" (p. 31).

Ramsay also used symbolic leadership behavior in defining "winning." "An important aspect of a winning attitude is the recognition that there are different definitions of winning, depending on the situation. The will to win is no less meaningful when it gathers only a very personal sense of achievement, as opposed to public acclaim." Ramsay remembers a former player asking him about a swimming competition that he had entered, "'Are you going to win it?' he asked. When I told him that I didn't expect to, that there would be about 300 contestants—some at the world-class level—and that I'd be satisfied to finish the race within the two-hour time limit, he looked shocked. 'I can't believe I'd ever hear you say that you didn't think you could win!' But for me and many others in that event, the definition of winning was finishing the swim in less than two hours. I tried to explain that to the player, but he had watched me go all-out as a coach to win too many basketball games and couldn't imagine that I'd be any different in other competitions" (p. 37).

Dr. Jack recognizes the strength of symbolic behavior in recalling Phil Jackson's approach. "He gave his rookies a booklet put out by the Church of Scientology on ways to achieve happiness in life. It was all about living the good life . . . some Golden Rule principles, some on the ways to get along well with others. The premise of this approach was to tell the players: 'We care about you; we want you to take care of yourselves.' These were Phil's ways of showing a genuine personal interest in each player and enabled the Bulls to become a family as much as an NBA team" (p. 83).

Ramsay prided himself on being in top physical condition and was very public about his regimen. It was a symbolic way of demonstrating to his players that he was not asking any more of them than he demanded of himself. "It was March when I entered a triathlon competition in August. That seemed like enough time to get in shape, so I agreed to enter the race and set out a training program for myself. I finished the race in the middle of the pack, third in my 50–54 age group, but feeling good physically; and I was determined to do better the next time. I was impressed by the competence of so many men and women as well as by their spirited and upbeat attitudes. It was an exhilarating experience" (p. 107).

"I upgraded my bicycle and did at least one triathlon competition a year for the next 20 years. I also competed in many road runs of half-marathon, 10K and 5K distances, and ocean swims of up to 3 miles. I had learned the importance of top-level conditioning and liked how it made me feel, both physically and mentally. By successfully bringing myself beyond what I thought were my physical limits, I was able to call on my team to play through fatigue and push themselves to maintain a high level of performance. I had done it myself and knew they could do it, too" (p. 108).

Ramsay is a great believer in the importance of the image that one projects. When he first took over the helm of the Buffalo Braves, he remembers, "They dressed in sweat suits and sneakers to travel, wore floppy caps, and carried their boom boxes with them in airports and on flight—with the volume at near-peak levels. You could hear the Braves coming before you saw them" (p. 155).

"That wasn't the attitude or the image that I wanted for a team I was coaching. I believe that, deep down, everyone wants to be proud of the organization with which they're associated. Members may gripe about their superiors or working conditions but innately they want success for their group; and when it comes, they are quick to identify themselves as members, and do so with great pride. Therefore, I instituted some rules for travel including mandatory travel attire. Suit jackets, dress slacks (no jeans), collared shirts and dress shoes became mandatory for my Braves. Hats, if worn, had to be removed on planes and in dining areas. I established a curfew hour, based on arrival time at a game site and the time the game ended, and placed a prohibition against visitors in a team member's hotel room. I also required players to wear a headset when listening to their personal music" (p. 155).

Ramsay took pride in establishing a sense of trust and respect in all his relationships and tried to model the desired behavior. "Many passages from Shakespeare's plays seemed to speak directly to me, but one in particular, from Hamlet, stood out: 'To thine own self be true; and it must follow, as the night and the day, Thou canst not then be false to any man'" (p. 156).

"I wanted the team to know that when I said I would do something, they could count on it getting done. I also expected the same treatment in return. In almost every instance, in my personal life and throughout my years of schooling, military service, and professional life in sports and in the field of communications, I felt satisfied that my associates and I had established mutual trust in whatever project was at hand" (p. 157).

Establishing a bond of trust produces valuable by-products, says Ramsay. "Internal leadership is vital to establishing a strong core of discipline and rapport among team members. It is created when one or more members of a group set positive standards, in addition to those that the leader espouses. This internal example has the potential to forge goals or modes of conduct and behavior that the group leader cannot achieve alone" (p. 171).

Ramsay recognizes the symbolic behavior of others and uses it to inform his own practice. "[Billy] Cunningham learned another leadership lesson: 'If you want to motivate people, show them first how highly motivated you are. I always want people to work with me, not for me,' Cunningham says. That formula worked well for Billy Cunningham—the player, the coach, and the business executive. He's been at the top of the heap in everything he's done" (p. 240).

Bill Bradley is another example of someone Ramsay admires for his demonstration of symbolic behavior. After his basketball career, Bradley was a stockholder and executive at Sports Potential, Inc. When the CEO of the company, Steve Spinner, was asked by Ramsay what most impressed him about Bradley, he responded, "his integrity." "'He's the most ethical individual I've ever met. And now the company reflects that same quality.'" Bradley simply says, "'Never doubt who you're dealing with. If there are any questions about a person's character, you don't want him'" (p. 246).

Although his public image does not always reflect it, Charles Barkley is also an individual that Ramsay admires. When a new trainer, Tony Harris, was hired by the 76ers and had to leave his family in Cleveland for financial reasons, "Charles told him to get a place for his family and bring them to Philadelphia, promising to take care of the additional costs until they sold their house. Charles kept his word, and kept his peace—he never said anything to anyone about it. I leaned about the incident from Harris," said Ramsay (p. 257).

"Loyalty is another admirable Barkley trait. After I left the Sixers and became affiliated with the Miami Heat and ESPN, whenever either group requested an interview with Charles and he knew that I was available, he would say he'd only do the interview if I conducted it—and he never turned me down. When Phoenix was in the NBA Finals with Chicago in 1993, I was among a horde of media waiting outside the arena after a shootaround on a game day. ESPN had sent a camera, a producer, and me, in hopes of getting something of interest to air on the early SportsCenter show. The Suns finished their work, came out of the building, and headed for the team bus. Charles was among them, but when he saw me, he stopped, came over, and answered a couple of my questions before joining his teammates" (p. 257).

Modeling desired behavior is a form of symbolic frame leadership. Dr. Jack places great emphasis on being an example of the behavior he hopes to find in others. The use of such symbolic behavior is a significant part of his overall leadership style. Projecting the image of a "family man" is important to Ramsay. "I believe my greatest achievement is that I am a parent of a strong family. Winning games and championships, with the acclaim that accompanies them, seems highly important at the time, but the love and caring shared within a good family yield the richest of all rewards or honors. For me, the family is really what life is all about" (p. 263).

THE POLITICAL FRAME

Leaders operating out of the political frame clarify what they want and what they can get. Political leaders are realists above all. They never let what they want cloud their judgment about what is possible. They assess the distribution of power and interests. Every coach has to behave in the political frame at some point in his or her career in order to be a truly effective leader. Much of the political frame behavior for coaches revolves around their own contract negotiations, as well as their relationships with their owners, general managers, and star players. Accurately assessing the power distribution in these relationships will often determine whether the coach attains his or her goals.

Ramsay, of course, is no exception to this fact of life. He recalls an incident that occurred at the end of his days with the Portland Trail Blazers. Immediately after the Blazers had lost to Denver in the 1986 playoffs, the team's owner, Larry Weinberg, came to the locker room after all the players had dressed and left, and quietly expressed his disappointment. He then said that he might want to make a coaching change. Ramsay told him that was certainly his prerogative and, in fact, he wasn't sure he wanted to continue to coach the team. They were both aware that Ramsay had a year left on his contract with Portland for which the Blazers were responsible if they terminated his coaching position. He said he would let Ramsay know and not to say anything publically about it. Ramsay agreed.

Ramsay heard nothing from Weinberg for several weeks, then received a call from him saying that the Blazers were going to replace him with Mike Schuler. Later, he called again to say that as he remembered their meeting after the Denver game, Ramsay had initiated the conversation about not returning as coach. If he had, that could be construed as resigning, and the Blazers would not be responsible for paying him for the last year of his contract. When Ramsay reminded him exactly how the conversation had gone, he quickly dropped the issue. That was not the first time the Blazers had tried to avoid paying Ramsay for an agreed-upon amount. When he signed his first contract with Portland for the 1976–77 season, Weinberg offered him a series of bonuses: $5,000 for making the playoffs, another $5,000 for advancing to the Conference Finals, and $25,000 if they won it all.

In those days, the NBA gave the head coach a playoff sum equal to what the players received. As Ramsay recalls, the league's share that season was about $20,000. About a week after the Finals ended, Harry Glickman, the team's president, called him into his office and said that as he remembered the contract negotiations, the bonus amount due Ramsay from the Blazers was to be decreased by the amount he received from the NBA. There had been no mention of that condition in Ramsay's negotiations with Weinberg—and Glickman had not been a part of any of those discussions. Ramsay told Glickman as much and stormed out of his office. The subject was never mentioned again, and the Blazers paid him what was due.

With this as a backdrop, Ramsay later agreed to coach the Indiana Pacers, but engaged in a little subterfuge of his own. He specified to Indiana that he would take only $100,000 of the $400,000 due him in the first year and defer the balance until after he had finished coaching in the NBA. With the offset stipulation of his Portland contract, the Blazers were still responsible for $250,000 of the final year of his contract. Weinberg was irate and accused Ramsay of "double-dipping." He refused to pay anything, and they were at a stalemate for several months.

Finally, Ramsay called Weinberg and suggested that they split the difference. He continued to object, saying that taking a salary of only $100,000 was unrealistic. "You're Jack Ramsay," Weinberg exclaimed. Ramsay reminded him that he had been Jack Ramsay when Weinberg offered him $75,000 to take the job in Portland, even though he had made $100,000 the year before in Buffalo. Weinberg paused, agreed to the settlement, then added, "'I guess we were both wrong'" (p. 163).

Recalling this incident, Ramsay said, "I had won a small victory, but I didn't feel good about any of it. I had always fulfilled my obligations in every job I'd ever had in a straightforward manner and I didn't like the revenge motives that had prompted my actions in this matter. That wasn't how I had lived my life. In my disgruntlement, I had forgotten that line from Shakespeare: 'to thine own self be true . . .' I vowed I'd never do that kind of thing again. And I never have" (p. 164).

In another instance of the use of raw power, Ramsay recalls a violent disagreement with the Buffalo Braves management when he was coaching there. The Buffalo Braves at the time had won 10 home games in a row, but after a crushing defeat at the hands of the Chicago Bulls, Paul Snyder, the team owner, and Bob MacKinnon, the general manager, were waiting outside the locker room. As soon as Ramsay walked into the room, Snyder said angrily, "It's your fault we lost." Ramsay wasn't feeling good about the way his team had played and was in no mood to listen to Snyder—who was a typical owner and knew nothing about the intricacies of the game—tell him what he was doing wrong that caused the defeat. So, Ramsay said, "Paul, I don't want to hear it, "and started to leave the room. Snyder grabbed his arm and said, 'You're going to listen to me!' Ramsay wrenched his hand from his arm and said, 'Like hell I am,' and stormed out. As Ramsay was leaving, Snyder shouted, 'I want to see you in my office.' Ramsay responded, 'I'm not coming. I won't have you telling me how to coach this team'" (p. 220).

Soon MacKinnon came in and pleaded with Ramsay to go to Snyder's office. Ramsay still refused to go. "Bob, I'm not going to listen to that guy tell me how to run this team." He said, "He'll fire you, Jack." Ramsay said, "that's okay; let him do it."

"When I calmed down, I realized I had to answer one question: Did I want to continue my stubborn reaction to Snyder's tirade or could I find a way to maintain my authority yet show a modicum of appeasement? I had calmed down enough to agree to go with him to Snyder's office. When we walked into his office, Snyder had calmed down, too, and he spoke about his right as owner to know what was going on with the team and that I should be willing to talk with him about it. I agreed to that, but added that after a loss wasn't the best time to have such a meeting" (pp. 220–221).

The Braves went on to win the next four games on the road, and when the team returned home, Snyder claimed that the outburst had been the reason why the team had come together. Ramsay agreed that since the team had seen him stand up to management, they coalesced in support of him. These incidents reflect Jack Ramsay's use of the political frame of leadership behavior when the situation calls for it.

CONCLUSION

It is readily apparent that Jack Ramsay utilizes all four of the Bolman/Deal frames of leadership, where appropriate. Although one could make the assertion that Ramsay is basically a structural leader because of his intense preparation, his organizational skills, and his attention to detail, there is no doubt that he aptly uses the other three frames of leadership behavior as well. The loyalty that his players have to him, even years after they have retired, attests to his extensive use of the human resource frame of leadership.

Ramsay's use of the symbolic frame of leadership is particularly interesting. He leads by example. He wants his players to be in top mental and physical condition, industrious, trustworthy, and good family men. In his own life, he models these behaviors in hopes that his players will assume the same characteristics. He is very proud of the physical and mental regimen that he religiously follows, even into his eighties. He is equally proud of his reputation for personal and moral integrity. Finally, he is enormously proud of the accomplishments of his family and the fact that he has been married to his wife, Jean, for more than 50 years. No wonder he is such a revered leader in his native Philadelphia and beyond.

5

PAT RILEY

It's a little like wrestling a gorilla. You don't quit when you're tired—
you quit when the gorilla is tired.

—Robert Strauss

BACKGROUND

Pat Riley was born in Rome, New York, and raised in Schenectady. He played for Linton High School in Schenectady under New York State legendary coach Walt Przybylo, where most notably he was a member of the team that defeated New York City's vaunted Power Memorial Academy whose star player, Kareem Abdul-Jabbar (formerly Lew Alcindor), would become one of Riley's players when he coached the Los Angeles Lakers. Riley was a versatile athlete in college, participating in both basketball and football. He led the 1966 Kentucky basketball team, coached by the legendary Adolph Rupp, to the National Collegiate Athletic Association's championship game, where they lost to Texas Western, a game that was immortalized in the movie *Glory Road*. He was selected by the San Diego Rockets in the first round of the 1967 National Basketball Association (NBA) draft and was also drafted as a flanker by the Dallas Cowboys in the National Football League. He joined the Rockets and later signed with the Los Angeles Lakers, helping them win the 1972 NBA Championship. After a relatively undistinguished playing career, he retired in 1976 as a member of the Phoenix Suns.

Riley then worked as a broadcaster for the Lakers. During the 1979–80 season, when the team's head coach, Jack McKinney, was incapacitated following a bicycle accident, assistant coach Paul Westhead took over the team's head coaching duties. Riley then moved from the broadcast booth to the bench as one of Westhead's assistant coaches. Six games into the 1981–82 season, Magic Johnson began to publicly express his unhappiness with the head coach. Lakers' owner Jerry Buss fired Westhead, and eventually named Riley to the head coaching position.

Riley led the Lakers to four consecutive NBA finals appearances, winning twice, in 1982 and 1985. His teams featured a fast-break style that coined the term "Showtime." Riley won the NBA title once again in 1987, with a Lakers team that was considered one of the greatest teams of all time. With future Hall of Famers Magic Johnson, James Worthy, and Kareem Abdul-Jabbar, and important role players such as Michael Cooper, Byron Scott, A. C. Green, Mychal Thompson, and Kurt Rambis, the Lakers finished 65-17 in the regular season, third best in league history. They met with similar success in the playoffs, beating the Celtics to win Riley his third NBA Championship.

One of Riley's most famous moments came when he guaranteed the crowd a repeat championship during the Lakers' championship parade. Although the 1988 Lakers did not produce as many wins in the regular season as the 1987 Lakers, they still managed to win an NBA title, becoming the first team in 20 years to repeat as champions. The Lakers beat the Detroit Pistons in seven games in the 1988 NBA finals, making good on Riley's promise. Riley stepped down as coach of the Lakers after they lost to the Phoenix Suns in the 1990 NBA playoffs, despite being named NBA Coach of the Year for the first time.

After stepping down as coach, Riley accepted a job as a television commentator for NBC. However, this job only lasted 1 year, as he became head coach of the New York Knicks in 1991. In 1993, he led the Knicks to the best regular season record in team history and received his second coach of the year award. He was especially admired for his ability to work with the physical, deliberate Knicks, considering that he was associated with the fast-break style of the Lakers in the 1980s. Riley returned to the NBA finals in 1994, but his Knicks lost in seven games to the Houston Rockets.

In 1995, Riley resigned from the Knicks and became head coach of the Miami Heat. In 1997, the Heat defeated his old team, the Knicks, in a physical seven-game series to advance to the Eastern conference finals for the first time in franchise history. However, they proved no match for Phil Jackson's Chicago Bull's, featuring the great Michael Jordan. Riley was selected as coach of the year for the third time, after leading Miami to a 61-21 regular season record. In 2006, the Miami Heat reached the NBA finals for the first time. Riley's Heat beat the Dallas Mavericks to win their first NBA title. It was Riley's fifth championship as a head coach. He joined Alex Hannum and Phil Jackson as the only coaches to coach two different teams to NBA titles.

SITUATIONAL LEADERSHIP ANALYSIS

Situational leadership models differ from the earlier trait and behavioral models in asserting that no single way of leading works in all situations. Rather, appropriate behavior depends on the circumstances at a given time. Effective managers diagnose the situation, identify the leadership style or behavior that will be most effective, and then determine whether they can implement the required style.

Perhaps Pat Riley's most dramatic demonstration of his situational leadership skills came with his ability to adapt his leadership behavior in leading two very different teams, the fast-paced Los Angeles Lakers and the deliberate New York Knicks. In this instance he recognized that he did not have the personnel with the athleticism needed to run the floor as he did with the Lakers. As a result, he adapted his leadership behavior to the situation and utilized the strengths that his Knicks team had. Although they were not fast, his players were strong and intelligent. So he used a deliberate style of offense, which featured hard screens, a tight defense, and strong rebounding, capitalizing on the physicality of his players.

Another instance of Riley's use of situational leadership behavior is in his "temporary insanity" philosophy. He maintains that displaying temporary insanity on occasion can have a motivating effect on one's followers. But, "a leader's aggrieved outburst is not an explosion, nor is it a regular or predictable event. It is the art of being angry at the right time, to the right degree, with the right people. Temporary Insanity requires plenty of advanced thought—a real and focused mental plan, not emotion-driven monologue." However, "a dose of Temporary Insanity demands a rapid follow-up of compassion." In addition, "The Temporary Insanity leader should always send out someone to complete the damage report and get a quick, accurate reading of the emotional wounding done by the rampage" (Riley, 1993, p. 175; all cites in this chapter, unless otherwise noted, are from this source).

Riley also recognizes the need to alter ones leadership behavior in order to continuously improve. To improve, an organization needs to change. Change implies doing something *different.* Doing something different often requires different leadership behavior. Endorsing this rationale, Riley indicates that eventually every team has to learn that excellence isn't a destination. It's a process that must be continually improved, just as the Japanese view quality to be. The challenge of competition always involves finding *new* ways to win. If your company makes a great product, you can be sure that other companies will do everything they can to adopt its best features.

Riley's theme of constantly changing to adapt to a new situation and to remain competitive is further elaborated upon in his "Winning Mission Recipe." Riley says that a business mission is likely to succeed if it adheres to the five points of his "Winning Mission Recipe." Two of the five points relate to adapting one's leadership behavior to the situation. Riley says that any organization is likely to be effective if the mission is constantly adjusted for changes in competition and if the mission is updated to keep pace with the company's success

THE STRUCTURAL FRAME

Structural leaders develop a new model of the relationship of structure, strategy, and environment for their organizations. Pat Riley recognizes that a leader has to behave in the structural frame in order to be effective. Structural leaders are well organized, well prepared, and plan ahead. Riley refers to the "covenant" or agreement that he had with all of his teams. Although the covenant required some human resource–related behavior on the part of the leader, "another role of leadership is to the *enforcer* of the covenant." Riley told his players, "We as a group will monitor each other. And I as your coach will enforce them. The team understood and accepted the rightness of our covenant, and some of them knew that if they stayed out [of the covenant] it might mean the bench. The essence of the covenant is totally positive peer pressure. It replaces blaming and finger pointing— two vicious enemies of teamwork—with mutual monitoring and mutual reinforcement" (p. 71).

Riley also shows his respect for behaving in the structural frame in "Riles' Guide to Bolt Proofing." This is Riley's guide to prevent "thunderbolts" or surprises from negatively affecting the organization:

Riles' Guide to Bolt Proofing

- Stick to your strengths and core values. They will be your emergency generator when a bolt strikes.
- Ground the bolt's shock value by involving your core team.
- Exploit the "equivalent benefit" in any adversity and milk it for as much personal development as you can get. Coming back from a thunderbolt has little to do with a grand strategy and great deal to do with strength of heart and the conviction to follow a basic plan.
- And, for God's sake, get the weather report before you go out the door! Meaning: stay attuned to any regulatory hearings, competitive innovations, new twists in behavior or attitude of a key teammate, or slippage in standards or procedures that give the inkling a thunderbolt may be unleashed. (p. 92)

Riley's "Rule of Total Preparation" is also an indication of the importance of structural frame leadership behavior. He points out that being ready in not enough. One has to be prepared for a promotion or any other significant change. Preparation demands mental and physical conditioning and conscious planning. A player who is just ready and not totally prepared simply increases the risk and is a liability to the team. In speaking about one of his star players, James Worthy, Riley indicates that he loves the hunger and the willingness in that kind of player's attitude, but that he needs to coach them one step more, so that they understand the amount of work they must still invest.

Another instance of Riley's acknowledgment of the necessity of appropriate structural frame behavior is in his attitude toward complacency. Riley says that complacency is the success disease. It takes root when you're feeling good about who you are and what you've achieved. Considering one of his coaching counterparts, he points out that his non-complacent attitude is always far ahead of potential problems. He is constantly fixing it before it's broken.

Riley suggests that we take a look at the competition between the U.S. and Japan. At the end of World War II, American industries began some incredible years of prosperity. But as Peter Drucker, the famous business expert, once pointed out, there are an enormous number of managers who have retired while still on the job. Riley agrees that the recovering industrialized nations saw their openings at that time. The Japanese embraced the thinking of the American Dr. W. Edwards Deming. Deming had strong beliefs about the best way for business to be organized—with deep respect for quality, total attention to the needs of the consumer, commitment to continual improvement, and a supportive attitude toward the people who get the job done. Deming was responsible for the Total Quality Management movement. W. Edwards Deming was a prophet without honor in his own land, while in Japan his message was taken to heart. We see the result of this complacency on the part of the U.S. corporations. So, what have we learned? Riley says that we've learned that you can't go up against principles such as total quality or continuous improvement and win.

To Riley the structural frame behaviors of planning and practice are crucial to success. He refers to an incident in his coaching career: "Trying to exhort the team to raise its effort level, I leaned on them during a mid-December practice. One veteran on the team responded: 'I only got so much use left in my legs, and I'm not going to use it up in practice. I'm a game player.'" Riley's response to this: "A classic game player is a fraud. Sloughing off in practice and workouts kills conditioning, invites the 'thunderbolt' of injury, and ensures game-losing fatigue. A 'game player' is committing a flagrant foul against the team's work ethic and its 'covenant'" (p. 140).

Appropriately applied structural frame leadership behavior is necessary for continued success, for overcoming complacency, and for responding to adversity. Pat Riley recalls a time when Ralph Sampson made an impossible game-winning shot to deny the Lakers the NBA Championship. He says that new and greater efforts were put into practice among a group of proud athletes who, collectively, had been evolving their winning ways for a long time. "What was the force that led us to mastery? Did it all begin with what Ralph Sampson called his 'funky' shot?" Whatever it was, it motivated the championship Lakers. They all achieved through an unceasing drive to be the best. They would also all tell you that hard, intelligent, relentless work is the way to winning. Excellence is the way. Mastery is the way. And, challenge is the way.

Developing a sense of mission is a structural leadership behavior. Riley agees that having a sense of mission that reaches beyond the present defines the final steps to individual and team effectiveness. That means going beyond simply being the best, going so far that you leave footprints. Riley believes that in your life, in your career, there may be only two or three times when you're truly on a mission of greatness. When you are, you have to know how to behave. A coach never stops coaching. And he knew it was right time for the Lakers to embark on a that mission.

Companies and other organizations embark on missions just as individuals and teams do. Riley points out three striking examples from the business world when tremendous success has been the direct outgrowth of a clear mission: the New York Knicks franchise, HBO, and Rodale Press. In all these cases, Riley quotes Francis Bacon in asserting: "A wise man will make more opportunities than he finds (p. 192)." In the case of Rodale Press, Riley speaks of a J. I. Rodale, who in the early 1940s, bought a farm in rural Pennsylvania and put his organic gardening ideas to the test. The farm had hardpan, run-down soil, but gradually turned into some of the most productive land in the region. In May 1942, Rodale printed the first issue of a magazine called *Organic Farming and Gardening*. By 1950 he was ready to add *Prevention*, a magazine dedicated to personal health. Riley indicates that their dedication to a clear mission, with the topic of health, has make Rodal Press the dynasty in its segment of the publishing industry.

According to Riley, the resurrection of the New York Knicks franchise in the 1990s is another example of an organization dedicated to a clearly formed mission. He remembers talking with his team and trying to get them to internalize the mission. "To drive home the point, I said: 'Well, we're the New York Knicks. Our culture is very aggressive. We seek to dominate. That's how we play.'" Then he gave them an abbreviated version of the mission (p. 245):

- Our culture is hardworking.
- Our philosophy is defense-focused.
- Our defense in aggressive.
- Our aggressiveness is domination-driven.

THE HUMAN RESOURCE FRAME

Human resource leaders believe in people and communicate that belief. They are passionate about *productivity through people*. Pat Riley knows the importance of human resource frame leadership behavior in building teamwork. However, he points out that building teamwork isn't simple. In fact, it can be a frustrating, elusive commodity. That's why there are so many bad teams out there, stuck in neutral or going downhill. "Teamwork doesn't appear magically, just because someone mouths the words. It doesn't thrive just because of the presence of talent or ambition. It doesn't flourish simply because a team has tasted success" (p. 16).

According to Riley, teamwork is the essence of life. All of us are team players, whether we know it or not. Our significance arrives through our vital connections with other people, through all the teams in our lives. Family life, for example, is a central experience. You can be the one who elevates it, and the one who sets the stage for its greatest accomplishments. That is what can make you great, posits Riley.

Riley believes that the answer to developing teamwork is to be found in what he calls "innocence" (p. 19). He defines innocence as a selfless attitude and a humility that individuals have whereby they think that they can accomplish very little by themselves. What being innocent means is understanding territoriality and knowing that each player has his space and then putting it aside for the common good. Innocence is about trust in a team. It's an attitude: doing your best for the team will always bring something good for you. It means believing that everything you deserve will eventually come your way. And, it's more than just innocence. It's innocence with experience. Only experienced innocence can combat the cynicism and pessimism that comes through inexperience. Riley believes that some of his Knicks teams reflected this "innocence." Those players were ready to join their strengths for the Knicks. They were ready to declare their innocence and place it into practice. Riley's rule for detecting innocence is to be conscious of the exact moment when a gifted team dedicates itself to unselfish trust and combines instinct with boldness and effort. It is only then that it is ready to rise to innocence, says Riley. For example, Magic Johnson had both style and efficiency and knew when to let one dominate the other. According to Riley, he quickly established himself as a dominant player, but he did it in a unique way. He was an avid student of basketball. Instead of crushing his teammates under his own greatness, he studied their styles and figured out how he, as the man controlling the movement of the ball, could help them get the most out of their abilities.

Another way of binding people together, according to Riley, is to develop a covenantal relationship with them. "A covenant is an agreement that binds people together," says Riley (p. 57). The Constructive Covenant:

Binding people together,
creates an equal footing,
helps people shoulder their own responsibilities,
prescribes terms for the help and support of others,
and creates a foundation for teamwork.

According to Riley, every team must decide, very consciously, to uphold the covenant terms, that represent the best values—voluntary cooperation, love, hard work, and total concentration on the good of the team. The greatness flowing through the heart of the team must be distributed to all extremities. Luckily for Riley, the opportunity to step to the forefront came at exactly the moment in time when the players themselves were ready to surrender their negativity to the core covenant.

He remembers how he and his team talked for hours about the stresses within the team and what might be going through the players' heads. We knew that restoring trust was the way to turning around their mental state. According to Riley, athletes, especially professionals, are hypersensitive to issues of trust. They've worked hard to reach a place where justice is uncomplicated: you give effort, go by the rules, produce results, and you will be rewarded.

Riley believes that "Positive covenants are born

> in the depths of crisis,
> when hidden agendas are brought to light,
> after the supply of scapegoats is exhausted,
> if the first seeds of real trust are sown,
> as teammates start acting positively for each other,
> when the barriers to enthusiasm are overturned."

Riley once told Magic Johnson and his Lakers' running mates that they could play ten years together and go down as the greatest trio of guards in the history of the league. You should want to be godfathers to each others' children. That's how close you ought to be.

Human resource leadership behavior can bring about mutual trust and respect, according to Riley. Trust is known to be the key that makes it possible for organizations to succeed. When trust is present, leadership knows immediately who is with them and who is against them. Borderline performance and clique-joining become untenable. And, it is all enabled by trust, according to Riley. Mutual trust and the power of the covenant are principles known and experienced by every great business, every significant team, and every extraordinary organization in the world. Kareem Abdul-Jabbar was a player that Pat Riley believes is among the most team-oriented individuals that he has coached. Kareem knew that if a player of his status could accept criticism without complaint, the others on the team would follow suit. Riley said that Kareem strengthened the team's backbone in the way that he took criticism. He knew that the more Riley could target him, our star, the stronger his teammates would become. On the other hand, Riley points out that Kareem needed to be rewarded for his positive behavior, so even though Riley had a policy of not having friends and relatives traveling with the team, when Jabbar asked if his father could travel with the team, he made an exception. He knew that he was breaking his own rules, but he also knew that Kareem mightily deserved it.

Riley uses human resource frame behavior in a rather unique way when he evaluates his players' performance. Rather than do what most coaches do, which is arbitrarily rake people over the coals, Riley's system focuses on the positive use of information. First, instead of ranking our players against each other, he compared them to people on opposing teams with similar positions and similar roles.

Riley learned to be human resource oriented by reading about and observing human behavior in nonbasketball settings. He observed that time-and-motion studies were considered to be degrading and inhuman. He points to Paul Adler, a business school professor at the University of Southern California who indicates that procedures that are designed by the workers themselves in a continuous successful effort to improve productivity, quality, skills, and understanding can humanize even the most disciplined forms of bureaucracy like a basketball team.

In conclusion, Riley fully recognizes the need for the appropriate use of human resource leadership behavior in order to be effective when he points out that compassion is a vital component of any effective organization. Without it, anger degenerates into brutality and tears the fabric of the team or organization.

THE SYMBOLIC FRAME

In the symbolic frame, the organization is seen as a stage, a theater in which every actor plays certain roles and the symbolic leader attempts to communicate the right impressions to the right audiences. Starting with the trend-setting way he dresses and ending with his liberal use of slogans and inspirational devises, Pat Riley makes very astute use of symbolic frame leadership behavior. He refers to his players as "Showtime Warriors." He uses the term "Constructive Covenant" to describe the mutual understanding that he and his team have with one another to be unselfish and sensitive to one another. He refers to "Riles Rules of the Heart" to describe his family-oriented relationship with his team, and refers to unforeseen circumstances as "Thunderbolts." Selfish players are referred to as "The Disease of Me," and planned outbursts on his part are called "Temporary Insanity."

Riley also makes liberal use of inspirational poems and quotes. Some of his favorites are:

PAT RILEY

> *The world is full of willing people, some willing to work, the others willing to let them.*—Robert Frost
>
> *Complacency is the last hurdle standing between a team and its potential greatness.*—Pat Riley
>
> *The will to win is important, but the will to prepare is vital.*—Joe Paterno
>
> *It's a little like wrestling a gorilla. You don't quit when you're tired—you quit when the gorilla is tired.*—Robert Strauss
>
> *What the inner voice says will not disappoint the hoping soul.*—Friedrich Schiller

Riley's rule on beating the "Sympathy Syndrome" is another instance of his use of symbolic leadership behavior. Riley says that if you give permission to lose, you will guarantee a loss. If you don't protect yourself from other people's sympathy, you cheat yourself and your team. Shoulda, coulda, and woulda, won't get it done. In overcoming adversity, only a positive attitude, alertness and returing to the basics can make you a winner. Psychologists call it the self-fulfilling prophecy. Unconsciously, we try to shape our reality to fit our own preconceptions, even when those preconceptions are self-destructive, Riley asserts.

Spirituality, another symbolic behavior, is important to Riley. He credits his wife's mother, Dorothy Rodstrom, for unlocking the power of the Bible for him as a source of wisdom in the fight against Thunderbolts, Chokes, and other such adversities. Whenever he has been tested in his life—in basketball or in anything else—Dorothy Rodstrom had trained him to use the Bible as a problem-solving tool.

"Riles' Rule of the Leading Voice" is another demonstration of Riley's reliance on symbolic behavior. According to Riley, when a breakthrough arrives, there will generally be some message, some voice that captures the essence of the work to be done. It could be a movie, a novel, a song, a speech, or a sentence rich in images . . . . Or, perhaps, Three Wise Men following a star in the sky. Whatever it may be, it is more than just a Sign. There are marching orders that come with it. To energize a team or an organization to break through to its goal, some message must act as a catylist to ignite that energy,

In referring to one of his former players who had undergone some life-threatening experiences, he indicates that the player was sustained through those times by a wonderful mother and devoted uncles, whose voices he heard from his most profound inner reaches. According to Riley, all of us have at least one great voice deep inside of us.

In evaluating his teams' performances, Riley likes to use symbolic leadership behavior when appropriate. He points out that statistics are one part of the performance analysis that leads to mastery. Images are another. We live in a high-tech world. Athletics are a natural for the use of technology. Riley is an avid user of video data, and he likes to pull together scenes and concept themed lines to instruct and motivate his players.

Riley is fully aware of the symbolic nature of athletics. Athletic teams inspire people so often because they are small enough to be real teams. Big companies try to be teams, and so do large government departments, but most can be teams only in very general terms. According to Riley, in order to be a real team, the organization must work together almost daily; it must constantly be aware of its own performance; and, it must be in tune with its own morale. Riley posits that if the organization can't do these things, the group is not a real team.

In a specific example of how Pat Riley used symbolic leadership behavior to motivate his team, he recalls his team waiting to play the winner of the Dallas Mavericks–Seattle Supersonics playoff series. After a 26-point Seattle win, the headline in a Dallas newspaper read DALLAS CHOKES. Riley showed a copy of the paper to his team and said, "My question to you is, do you want to read the same kind of headlines in the *Los Angeles Times*?" (p. 178).

In another instance, Riley recalls that before his Knicks went up against the Chicago Bulls in game six of their last playoff series, trailing the series three to two, he told the players a story about a scorpion and a frog now familiar to all those who had seen the movie *The Crying Game*. It seems that the frog was about to jump in the frog pond and paddle himself to the other side. Before he plunged in, a scorpion came rustling up next to him and asked a favor. He said "take me across on your back." "Oh no," the frog said. "You might sting me" "Why would I do that?" the scorpion said, "If I kill you, I'll die too." So the frog invited the scorpion to climb on his back, and started swimming over the water. Before he got halfway to the other side, he felt a burning jolt at the base of his neck. "Why did you sting me?" the frog said, "Now we're both going to die!" "I stung you because that's what I do," the scorpion answered. "I sting frogs. That's my nature." In driving home the point, Riley added that the New York Knicks are known to be aggressive and dominating. That's who they were.

THE POLITICAL FRAME

Leaders operating out of the political frame clarify what they want and what they can get. Political leaders are realists above all. They never let what they want cloud their judgment about what is possible. They assess the distribution of power and interest.

Having reached the point where he is recognized as one of the top two or three professional basketball coaches in the world and commands a salary that is commensurate with that status, one can assume that Pat Riley has acted out of the political frame of leadership behavior on many occasions, when appropriate. This does not even include his many business interests outside of basketball. For example, Riley is known for his friendship with Giorgio Armani, preferring to wear Armani suits during basketball games, and even modeling once at an Armani show. There are two incidents, however, where Riley clearly exercised political frame behavior.

During the 1979–80 NBA season, when the Lakers' head coach Jack McKinney was incapacitated with serious head injuries after a bicycle accident, assistant coach Paul Westhead took over the team's head coaching duties. At the time, Pat Riley moved from the broadcast booth to the bench as one of Westhead's assistants. Although the Lakers were very successful during the next year or so, six games into the 1981–82 season, Magic Johnson began to publicly express his unhappiness with Westhead's style of coaching. Lakers owner Jerry Buss immediately called a press conference and fired Westhead, and then immediately named general manager Jerry West head coach. West, at the conference, refused the job on the spot. Buss then turned to Riley and asked, "Do you want the job?" Riley reluctantly agreed, but only if West would sit on the bench for a few games until he felt comfortable. West agreed, Riley took the job, and the rest is history.

Another occasion when Riley utilized political frame leadership behavior was when he stepped down as Miami Heat coach at the beginning of the 2003–4 season to fully dedicate his attention to his duties as general manager. Longtime assistant Stan Van Gundy took over and guided the Heat to the playoffs. Van Gundy lead the Heat to the Eastern conference finals during the 2005 playoffs, although they lost to the Detroit Pistons after being up 3-2 in the series.

Riley resumed coaching the Heat on December 12, 2005, replacing Stan Van Gundy after the Heat started the season with a disappointing 11-10 record. Van Gundy had resigned in order to "spend more time with [his] family." Although Van Gundy maintained that his decision to resign was his own, there has been speculation that he was pushed out by Riley. Whatever the true story is, this is definitely an example of the use of political leadership behavior.

CONCLUSION

Pat Riley is successful in utilizing all four situational leadership frames as described by Bolman/Deal. Although he makes liberal use of all four frames, one could argue that he is a symbolic leader at heart. The stylish way in which he dresses and his meticulous grooming practices portray him as a "modern-day coach." His branding of his teams' fast-paced style of play as "Showtime" adds to this image. Slogans, such as "Riles' Rule of Rebirth," "Riles' Rule for Detecting Innocence," "Riles' Rules of Reverse 20/80," "The Constructive Covenant," "Riles' Rule of the Heart," "Riles' Rule on Beating the Sympathy Syndrome," "Riles' Guide to Bolt Proofing," "Riles' Rule to Total Preparation," "Riles' Rule of the Leading Voice," "Riles' Rule on Game Players," "Riles' Rule of the Brilliant Loss," "Riles' Rule of Micro-Teams," "Riles' Rule of the Missing Part," "The Temporary Insanity Textbook," "Riles' Rule for Footprints," "The Winning Mission Recipe," "Riles' Rule of Enlightened Self-Interest," and "Riles' Rule of the Warrior" are further indications of the importance that he attaches to symbolic leadership behavior.

As we have observed with other coaches profiled in this book, we see in Pat Riley a successful and effective leader who is intentional about how he applies leadership theory to his behavior and introspective in analyzing its appropriateness and effectiveness. There is much to be learned about effective leadership behavior from "Coach Riles."

6

BOBBY KNIGHT

Enthusiasm, that certain something that pulls us out of the mediocre and commonplace, and fills us with power. If we have it, we should thank God for it. If we don't have it, we should get down on our knees and pray for it.

—Ralph Waldo Emerson

BACKGROUND

Bobby Knight was born on October 25, 1940, in Massillon, Ohio. Known as "The General," in 2008 he was the head men's basketball coach at Texas Tech. He was previously head coach at Indiana University and at Army. Knight has won more National Collegiate Athletic Association (NCAA) Division I men's basketball games than any other head coach.

Knight has won three NCAA championships, one National Invitation Tournament championship, and led the U.S. Olympic basketball team to a gold medal in 1984. This is considered collegiate basketball's Triple Crown. Knight also led Indiana University to eleven Big 10 Conference championships, and is a four-time National Coach of the Year.

Knight is one of NCAA Division I college basketball's most controversial coaches because of his behavior. He has thrown a chair across the court during a game, been arrested for physical assault, and has repeatedly displayed a combative nature during his encounters with members of the press. However, he is simultaneously commended for running clean programs and for his high percentage of graduating players.

He began his career as a player at Orrville High School where he played football and basketball. He continued under Hall of Fame coach Fred Taylor at Ohio State University in 1958. He was a reserve on the Buckeyes' 1960 NCAA Division I national championship team, which featured future Hall of Fame players John Havlicek and Jerry Lucas. In addition to lettering in basketball at Ohio State, Knight also lettered in football and baseball.

After graduation in 1962, Bobby Knight coached junior varsity basketball at Cuyahoga Falls High School in Ohio. After that, he accepted an assistant coaching position at Army in 1963, where, 2 years later he was named the head coach at the relatively young age of 24. In six seasons at West Point, Knight won 102 games. One of his players was Hall of Fame coach Mike Krzyzewski.

Knight was recognized as a rising star, and when Indiana University was seeking a new coach in 1971, they turned to Knight. Knight immediately endeared himself to the basketball-mad state of Indiana with his disciplined approach to the game. Educated in military history, Knight was given the nickname "The General" by former University of Detroit and Detroit Pistons coach-turned-broadcaster Dick Vitale.

Indiana reached the Final Four in 1973, losing to UCLA. In 1976, the Hoosiers were undefeated at 32-0 and won the NCAA Championship, beating conference rivals Michigan University. Knight's Hoosiers also won championships in 1981, with future NBA and Hall of Fame point guard Isiah Thomas, beating North Carolina; and in 1987 with guard Steve Alford, beating Syracuse University. Indiana won the 1979 National Invitation Tournament (NIT) Championship, and Knight led the U.S. national team to a gold medal in the Olympic games as coach of the Michael Jordan–led 1984 team. He also won eleven Big 10 Conference titles. Knight is one of only four coaches to win NCAA, NIT, and Olympic championships, joining Dean Smith of North Carolina, Adolph Rupp of Kentucky, and Pete Newell of California. Knight is the only coach to win the NCAA, the NIT, the Olympic gold, and the Pan-Am gold. In 1991, Bob Knight was elected to the basketball Hall of Fame.

In 2000, after a history of negative incidents, Myles Brand, the Indiana University president, announced that he had adopted a "zero tolerance" policy with regard to Bobby Knight's behavior.

In September 2000, an Indiana University freshman, Kent Harvey, reportedly said, "Hey, Knight, what's up?" to him. According to Harvey, Knight grabbed him by the arm and berated him for not showing him proper respect. Brand stated that this incident was only one of numerous complaints that occurred after the zero-tolerance policy had been placed on Knight. He asked Knight to resign. When Knight refused, however, he then relieved Knight of his duties immediately.

After taking the next season off, Knight accepted the head coaching job at Texas Tech. Knight quickly improved the program, which had not been to an NCAA tournament since 1996. He led the Red Raiders to postseason appearances in each of his first 4 years at the school. During Knight's first 6 years at Texas Tech, the Red Raiders has won 126 games, an average of 21 wins per season. On January 1, 2007, at Texas Tech, Knight achieved his 880th career win, passing retired North Carolina coach Dean Smith for the most career NCAA Division I men's college basketball victories. The Red Raiders' participation in the 2007 NCAA men's Division I basketball tournament marked another record. With their inclusion as the number ten seed in the East Regional, Knight became the coach to lead his team to more NCAA tournaments than any other.

In 1987, Knight was the first person to be honored with the Naismith Men's College Coach of the Year Award. Five years later he received the Clair Bee Coach of the Year Award. And, in 2007, he was the recipient of the Naismith award for "Men's Outstanding Contribution to Basketball." Knight announced his retirement from college basketball in February 2008.

SITUATIONAL LEADERSHIP ANALYSIS

Situational leadership models differ from the earlier trait and behavioral models in asserting that no single way of leading works in all situations.

Rather, appropriate behavior depends on the circumstances at a given time. Effective managers diagnose the situation, identify the leadership style or behavior that will be most effective, and then determine whether they can implement the required style.

On the surface, Bobby Knight has a reputation for being the quintessential autocrat. In reality, however, when we examine the total spectrum of his leadership behavior, there is ample evidence that it is at least somewhat situational. For example, the common perception is that Bobby Knight would have a rigid set of rules for his team. The reality is that he has but one rule: "If you do anything in any way, when ever or where ever, that I think is detrimental to the good of this basketball team, to the school, or to yourself, I'll handle it as I see fit" (Knight & Hammel, 2002, p. 15; all cites in this chapter, unless otherwise noted, are from this source). This rule was recommended to Knight by one of his mentors, the former professional coach and coach of Saint John's University, Joe Lapchick.

The reason that Knight has but one very flexible rule is so he can be situational in his enforcement of it and so he does not back himself into the proverbial "corner." In considering his rule, Knight says that he thinks it as did Joe Lapchick. Lapchick advises Knight that he was going to have a kid who is a pain in the butt, and you're going to be happy to get rid of him. But, you are also going to have a good kid who screws something up. You can't set down rules and then treat guys differently. You decide, based on your knowledge of the situation, what would be best for the kid and the team, and you go from there, advised Lapchick.

Another indication that Bobby Knight is a situational leader is that among his four coaching "cornerstones" one is dedicated to the continually changing nature of leadership in his profession. Knight's third coaching cornerstone is an appreciation of basketball as something never to be mastered but always, every day of every year, to be studied with an unflagging zeal for answers—and a duty to pass them on. That was brought into focus for him by playing at Ohio State for Hall of Fame coach, Fred Taylor, and it also gave him a better understanding of what he had learned from other coaches as he was growing up.

Knight also recognizes the importance of adapting one's leadership behavior to the situation in speaking about his relationship with his players. He tries to understand the strengths and the weaknesses of every player who plays for him, and make sure they also understand them. According to Knight, what a player can't do is every bit as important for him to know as what he can do. Continuing with this line of reasoning, Knight points out that his team is like a ball of putty. It is always changing form. They might look one way for Iowa, then he rolls the putty around and they look a little different for Michigan. After Michigan, he'll work the putty around again and have still another look for Purdue. For Knight, adapting to different situations is the joy of the game.

On the contrary, Knight is not very situational when it comes to utilizing political frame leadership behavior when appropriate. In fact, he has a definite disdain for acting out of the political frame and seems to consider doing so a compromising of his principles.

STRUCTURAL FRAME

Structural leaders develop a new model of the relationship of structure, strategy, and environment for their organizations. The common perception among followers of Bobby Knight's career is that he is certainly no stranger to the need to behave out of the structural frame to be effective as a leader. His reputation for being well organized, preparing thoroughly, and planning strategically is well earned. This public perception is borne out in Knight's extensive use of structural frame leadership behavior.

One of Knight's boyhood heroes was Ted Williams. Knight modeled much of his philosophy of life after that of the "Splendid Splinter." Knight recalls that as a boy he sat in the stands at Lakefront Stadium in Cleveland and marveled at Williams' swing. He was an Indians fan, but when he saw that classic Ted Williams swing send a baseball screaming into the stands and watched that head-down Williams lope around the bases, he felt privileged. The more he learned about him, the more he revered him—not only as a great baseball player but also as a genuine hero of two American wars; as a master fisherman; and "as one of the rare national figures who absolutely God-damned refused to knuckle under to a hostile press" (pp. 1–2).

Knight attributes his "four cornerstones" on the knowledge of the game of basketball and his philosophy on how it is to be taught to four individuals: Joe Lapchick, Clair Bee, Fred Taylor, and Pete Newell. As with Ted Williams, Knight learned the importance of structural leadership behavior as a means to being an effective basketball coach primarily from these four men.

Knight indicates that of the four cornerstones he had about coaching basketball, one of them is the idea of how to run a basketball team—team rules, his approach to training, and the need to clear away inconsequential matters to allow good decision-making, all of those things were influenced by talking with and observing a master of the game—Joe Lapchick. Knight maintains that for his forty plus years as a college basketball coach, his primary goal was focused on getting players to reach their potential. This, he knew, would give him a chance to have a team that was as good as it could possibly be. This, of course, is prototypical structural leadership behavior.

According to Knight, his former coach, Fred Taylor, was very well organized, and he was very articulate in his explanation of how to play and what he wanted. He was the first to tell Knight the familiar story of the six honest men.

> All my life, I've had six honest serving men.
> They taught me all I knew.
> Their names were What, Where, and When;
> How, Why, and Who.

As a basketball coach, Fred Taylor put every one of those "serving men" to work for him. Maybe as important as anything Knight had ever learned from him was that a coach should never be afraid to ask questions of anyone from whom he could learn. That's what he did to improve his defense to the point where he raised the level of the whole Big Ten through his teams' consistent success. Other teams had to try to match him if they ever hoped to beat him or compete with him for championships.

As far as Clair Bee's influence on Knight is concerned, Knight learned that the very first thing you had to be was a teacher. According to the very successful Bee, you had to teach them the *game*. You couldn't ever assume that they knew what they needed to know, or that they were going to do the right thing, unless you had taught them the right thing.

This was a coach who early in his coaching career developed a way to teach the two-handed set shot, which up until World War II was the basic method of outside shooting in basketball.

However, people familiar with the history of basketball will remember hearing about the 1934 game between Clair Bee's Long Island University team and the visiting Stanford team, featuring All-American Frank Liusetti. Liusetti was famous for having perfected the one-handed set shot. After Stanford ended Long Island University's (LIU) 43-game winning streak before 17,623 fans at Madison Square Garden, Knight noted that the loser of the game, Clair Bee, immediately became one of the best teachers of the one-handed set shot.

The fourth cornerstone of Knight's philosophy of coaching and leading was the legendary Pete Newell. Newell was known for his thorough preparation, according to Knight. Of the things that influenced Knight's philosophy, he believes that the most important was the importance of preparation. Everybody has the will to win, but not everone has the will to *prepare* to win. Knight thinks that it is his fault if the ball is in the hands of a poor free-throw shooter at a critical time at the end of the game and he's fouled. He thinks that it is his fault if he doesn't have the right defensive match-up. According to Knight, if any of these things happens, it is because of poor preparation.

According to Knight, the phrase never uttered in teaching kids how to play a sport is, "Don't think, just do it." In his opinion, if you don't think, you can't really play. Think about those things that opponents do that you don't like to play against, he tells his players. Then do those things yourself. To Knight, concentration is basketball in a nutshell. He maintains that concentration leads to anticipation, which leads to recognition, which leads to reaction, which leads to execution. In typical structural leadership fashion, Knight believes that you should never apologize to anybody for really wanting to win or for hating to lose. However, Knight believes that winning is not enough. Over the course of a season a team has to develop a sense of pride in *performance*. Winning is the last of all criteria that he uses to evaulalte how well his team is playing. When the way you've won a game just isn't acceptable, you show your players why: You talk about turnovers, missed blockouts, fast-break points allowed, fouls committed, etc. You need to demonstrate to your team that you are not as interested in winning as you are in their quality of play.

For Knight, the hardest part of his job is waiting to play—the final preparation. Once the game starts, he's fine. No problems, even when things aren't going according to plan. It's the time leading up to the games that gets to him. He can't wait until the games start. He knows what his problem is. The difference between winning and losing is so great—such a tremendous emotional difference—that it really affects him in a negative way.

However, in typical structural frame fashion, Knight concludes that he likes his system and way of doing things. He's always looking for new ways to be better. He cries when his ideas work in a game, and when he sees his players execute what they've been working on, he admits that there is no finer feeling in the world.

Knight continues in this vein when he stresses a point in almost every talk he gave during his winter out of coaching. You can't go into a sales situation or a negotiation and try to run it by the seat of your pants. In any walk of life, the best-prepared person creates advantages that help him or her be the most successful.

HUMAN RESOURCE FRAME

Human resource leaders believe in people and communicate that belief. They are passionate about *productivity through people*. Although Bobby Knight is not known as a human resource leader, there are instances when he behaves out of the human resource frame. For example, he recalls an incident relating to one of his mentors, Clair Bee. Bee's LIU team was one the first Eastern powers to have a black player. LIU was playing Marshall in basketball at Huntington, West Virginia. At the hotel where the LIU team stayed, the black player was told he could not eat with the team in the hotel's dining room. According to Knight, Coach Bee once marched his entire team into the kitchen, sat everybody down, and said, "Serve us." There was never a thought in Clair Bee's mind about color or religion. Coach Knight has tried to follow Bee's example.

Knight could be criticized for not behaving out of the human resource frame often enough, but he knows himself and sees that deficiency in his character. He says that he has never allowed himself to dwell enough on games his teams won. He has always felt winning is what you're supposed to do. Winning is a by-product of preparation and work in practice, all the things leading up to a game. He immediately forgets the games he has won and gets into the next game right away. He does not intend to change and admits that he will do that as long as he coaches. However, he was so conscious of getting on to the next game that over the years he feels certain that he did not publicly give kids as much credit as he should have for a games they won. He believes that he had shortchanged kids in that regard.

Nevertheless, he always tries to let opposing coaches know when he thinks they have done a good job with their team, or that their team was difficult to play against, or that their team has played well against him. He did the same thing many times with individual players from teams he played. The last time they played against kids (usually from Big Ten Schools) who were seniors whom he thought had showed a great competitive spirit and attitude over the years, he enjoyed telling them how he felt about them. He would often do so during pre-game warm-ups or after the game.

Knight was equally interested in a recruit's human side as he was in his basketball ability. For example, some years ago he was in the home of a top-rated recruit. Knight had been there just a few minutes when he heard him talk to his mother in a way that he should not. As of that moment, Indiana was no longer recruiting that kid, though he wound up playing in the Big Ten and doing pretty well. However, on the basketball court, he also ended up showing the undesirable character traits that had come through that night. Lastly, his former player and assistant coach Mike Krzyzewski recalls an incident when Knight clearly acted out of the human resource frame. "Coach Knight drove me to the airport, when my father had a brain hemorrhage and drove out later that evening to spend a couple of days with my family" (Krzyzewski, 2000, p. 56).

THE SYMBOLIC FRAME

In the symbolic frame, the organization is seen as a stage, a theater in which every actor plays certain roles and the symbolic leader attempts to communicate the right impressions to the right audiences. Admittedly, Bobby Knight is a devotee of symbolic behavior. He is always posting things in the locker room. One was the quote from Ralph Waldo Emerson in the epigraph of this chapter.

From his well-known "four cornerstones" to his "basketball credos," Bobby Knight positions himself as a no-nonsense perfectionist whose nickname, The General, befits him. One could even argue that some of the famous incidents, like throwing a chair across the court to protest a referee's call during a Purdue game and assaulting a police officer during the Pan American Games in Puerto Rico, along with his alleged physical abuse of some of his players, were instances of Knight behaving out of the symbolic frame and perpetuating his strict disciplinarian image. His appearance as the central character in the reality show for ESPN *Knight School*, which followed a handful of Texas Tech students as they competed for the right to join the Red Raiders as a nonscholarship player, also reinforced the Knight image.

On the other hand, Knight has a reputation of personal and moral integrity. He is recognized as running a "clean" program and he admittedly has never understood how anybody who cheated to get a player, or players, could take any satisfaction whatsoever out of whatever winning came of it.

He also has a reputation of being a very patriotic person, perhaps because of his years coaching at Army. Knight asserts that he's a pretty appreciative guy, especially where his country is concerned. It's nothing he has to think about. He has always felt that way. For example, in the summer of 1984 when he was coaching the U.S. Olympic team, every stop he made, every group he talked to, he mentioned what he considered the eight greatest words any American ever put together: "America, America, God shed His grace on thee". (p. 1).

Knight is widely recognized as a "basketball genius." Again, his symbolic frame behavior reinforces that image. His well-known "basketball philosophy" stresses motion offense and emphasizes post players setting screens and perimeter players passing the ball until a teammate becomes open for an uncontested jump shot or layup and requires players to be unselfish, disciplined, and effective in the setting and use of screens to get open. His defense, in which players are required both to tenaciously guard opponents man-to-man and to help teammates when needed, is replicated by coaches across the country. In and of itself, this philosophy is not unique. However, Knight's ability to get his team to execute his philosophy so precisely sets him apart from most of his coaching counterparts. In addition, his pregame preparation and strategies and in-game ability to respond to the tactics of the opposition are unparalleled in his profession. Joe Falls of the *Detroit News* wrote the following about Knight: "'Knight is the king of all he surveys. And what he surveys—what he is the absolute ruler of—is the finest basketball program in the land. The Dukes come and go. North Carolina is always a threat. Michigan has its moments. Keep an eye on Kentucky. But year in, year out, this [Indiana U.] is the place they respect, the place they envy, for it is here that success is defined in ways that no one else has been able to match for nearly a quarter of a century'" (as cited in Knight & Kimmel, 2002, p. 35).

THE POLITICAL FRAME

Leaders operating out of the political frame clarify what they want and what they can get. Political leaders are realists above all. They never let what they want cloud their judgment about what is possible. They assess the distribution of power and interests. Bobby Knight simply refuses in any way to compromise his principles and utilize the political frame of leadership behavior to any great degree. He used Ted Williams as a model. Knight points out that the more he learned about him, the more he revered him—not only as a great baseball player but also as a genuine hero of two American wars; as a master fisherman; as one of the rare national figures who absolutely refused to knuckle under to a hostile press.

We can get a keener insight into why Bobby Knight steadfastly shuns the use of political frame behavior by looking at an exchange that he had with the legendary coach Joe Lapchick. In a conversation with Knight, Lapchick said, "How important is it to you that people like you?" Knight responded, "I hadn't thought about that. I did for just a minute or so and said, 'I'd like to be respected as a coach, but I'm not concerned about being liked.'" Lapchick said, "Good. If you worry about whether people like you or not, you can never make tough decisions correctly" (p. 15).

On the contrary, no leader reaches the status of a Bobby Knight without some use of the political frame, even if it is only in one's own salary negotiations and in one's relationships with one's colleagues and superiors. Still, suffice to say, political frame leadership behavior is not one of Bobby's Knight's preferred styles.

CONCLUSION

Although there is evidence that Bobby Knight operates in all four leadership frames, one could argue that his leadership behavior is very strongly structural in nature. There is ample evidence that he also utilizes the symbolic frame, and some evidence that he behaves out of the human resource frame, when appropriate. However, there is little evidence of political frame leadership behavior.

One could question how Knight could be so successful while making such limited use of two of the leadership frames. There are two possibilities here. Either Bolman/Deal's leadership theory is flawed, or Knight manipulates the "situation" so that he is almost exclusively dealing with individuals and groups that are susceptible to structural frame leadership behavior. I believe it is the latter.

There is much evidence that Bobby Knight surrounds himself with athletes and coaches that think as he does, which is to say that they have a high "readiness level" or predisposition for accepting structural frame leadership behavior. Knight's depiction of his recruitment efforts gives us an insight into his thinking. His approach to recruiting is a little different from the norm. He knows what type of kid he wants. He knows what kind of athlete he needs to compete at the Division I level. In many cases, it was the life-long dream of athletes to play for Bobby Knight, knowing full well what they were getting themselves into. This was the case with two of his more famous recruits, Steve Alford and Randy Wittman. Knight said once that recruiting Steve Alford cost him about forty-seven cents. Alford had always wanted to go to Indiana, and all they had to do was mail him an application form. It was similar when Knight recruited Randy Wittman. Wittman had attended Knight's summer camp as a seventh-grader, and during the camp, his assistant coach Bob Donewald told Knight that he had seen a a kid who looked like someday he would be an outstanding player. Knight asked Wittman if he would be coming to Indiana when he got old enough. Wittman answered in the affirmative. Five years later, Randy Wittman was a freshman on Indiana University's basketball team.

One could speculate that if Bobby Knight had applied more political frame behavior in his dealings with the press and with his superiors, he could have avoided some of the controversy that surrounded some of his behavior and have been even more effective as a leader. For example, women's groups nationwide were outraged by Knight's comment during an April 1988 interview with Connie Chung in which he said, "I think that if rape is inevitable, relax and enjoy it" (*USA Today*, 2006, p. 12). Knight's comment was in reference to an Indiana basketball game in which he felt the referees were making poor calls against the Hoosiers. In this case, if Knight had used more politically acceptable language, he could have avoided the backlash that occurred. At any rate, there is much to be learned from analyzing Bobby Knight's leadership behavior, even if in some cases, we learn what not to do.

7

MIKE KRZYZEWSKI

I look at each year in basketball as an integral part of life. Every season is a journey. Every journey is a lifetime.

—Mike Krzyzewski

BACKGROUND

Mike Krzyzewski was born on February 13, 1947, in Chicago. Often referred to as Coach K due to the difficult pronunciation of his surname, he is the head coach of the Duke University men's basketball team. The program has been one of the most successful college basketball programs in the nation for the past 25 years. He has been selected coach of the United States national basketball team through the 2008 Beijing Olympics.

Krzyzewski, the son of Polish immigrants, attended the U.S. Military Academy at West Point, New York, and played basketball while training to become an officer in the army. He was captain of the army basketball team in his senior year, 1968–69, leading his team to the National Invitation Tournament (NIT) at Madison Square Garden. From 1969–74, Krzyzewski served in the army and directed service teams for 3 years, and then followed that up with 2 years as head coach of the U.S. Military Academy Prep School at Fort Belvoir, Virginia.

In 1974, he resigned from the army, having attained the rank of captain. Bobby Knight, his former coach at Army, called and offered Krzyzewski, then 26 years old, a graduate assistant position at Indiana University. That 1975 squad posted an 18-0 Big 10 mark and a 31-1 overall record. Next, Krzyzewski spent 5 years building the program at his alma mater in West Point. He led the Cadets to two NIT berths and left with a 5-year record of 73-59.

In 1980 he took over as the head coach at Duke University. Duke lost in the National Collegiate Athletic Association (NCAA) championship game in 1986 and then made five consecutive Final Fours starting in 1988, the last two of which resulted in NCAA titles. In the 1992 off season, Krzyzewski served as an assistant on the Dream Team, the legendary U.S. Olympic basketball team that was the first to feature National Basketball Association (NBA) players. Krzyzewski also led Duke to Final Fours in 1994, 1999, 2001, and 2004, with another national championship in 2001. With 68 career wins in the NCAA tournament, Krzyzewski is the winningest coach in the history of the event.

During his years at Duke, Krzyzewski has led the Blue Devils to 11 Atlantic Coast Conference (ACC) regular-season titles and ten ACC tournament titles. In addition, Krzyzewski has won 12 national coach of the year awards. On February 18, 2007, Krzyzewski earned his 700th victory at Duke with a 71-62 victory over Georgia Tech.

Krzyzewski has totaled 775 career victories and is only the 17th coach in NCAA history to reach that milestone. Other such coaches included Bobby Knight, Dean Smith, Adolph Rupp, Eddie Sutton, Jerry Tarkanian, and Lute Olson.

During his long tenure at Duke, Krzyzewski has been given the opportunity to coach in the NBA three times. The first time came after the 1990 season when he led the Blue Devils to their third straight Final Four appearance. The Boston Celtics offered a coaching position to Krzyzewski, but he declined the offer. The next season, Krzyzewski proceeded to lead the Blue Devils to the first of two straight national championships. In 1994 the Portland Trail Blazers pursued him, but again he chose to stay with Duke. In 2004 the Los Angeles Lakers, following the departure of high-profile coach Phil Jackson, interviewed Krzyzewski.

He was given a formal offer from Lakers general manager Mitch Kupchak, reportedly for 5 years and $40 million, but again he turned down the NBA.

On October 26, 2005, Krzyzewski was picked to coach the U.S. national team at the 2008 Beijing Olympics. In the 2006 Fédération Internationale de Basketball (International Basketball Federation or FIBA) World Championship, the team won a bronze medal after losing in the semifinals to his old friend Panagiotis Giannakis and his Greece team and then beating Argentina for third place. Krzyzewski was named the 2006 USA Basketball Coach of the Year and the Men's Senior National Team was named USA Basketball Team of the Year. Krzyzewski also was the head coach of the U.S. national team in the 1990 FIBA World Championship, when he led a team of American collegians to a third-place finish.

Krzyzewski's coaching success has given him opportunities outside of sports. In recent years, Krzyzewski has become a very popular speaker to corporate management groups. Krzyzewski's speaking fee is $100,000 per session. Additionally, American Express and General Motors have featured Krzyzewski in major national advertising campaigns. Critics contend that Krzyzewski's media and corporate exposure give him an unfair recruiting advantage, but Krzyzewski argues that any such advantage is due to the high level of success achieved by the Duke basketball program over the past 20 years.

Krzyzewski has also been an active community leader and philanthropist. In the autumn of 2005, he and his family celebrated the opening of the Emily Krzyzewski Family LIFE Center, a community center named in honor of his late mother. Although most of the center's funding was raised through private out-of-town donations, grassroots fund raising also contributed to the center (e.g., Duke for LIFE bracelet). Krzyzewski is often seen wearing a Duke for LIFE bracelet.

SITUATIONAL LEADERSHIP ANALYSIS

Situational leadership models differ from the earlier trait and behavioral models in asserting that no single way of leading works in all situations. Rather, appropriate behavior depends on the circumstances at a given time. Effective managers diagnose the situation, identify the leadership style or behavior that will be most effective, and then determine whether they can implement the required style.

Mike Krzyzewski understands that one's leadership behavior should be adapted to the situation and he is a master at doing so. In commenting on the need for rules in order to be successful, Krzyzewski asserts that too many rules get in the way of leadership. "They just put you in a box, sooner or later, a rule-happy leader will wind up in a situation where he wants to use some discretion but is forced to go along with some decree that he himself has concocted" (Krzyzewski, 2000, p. 10; all cites in this chapter, unless otherwise noted, are from this source).

Early in my own career as a teacher and coach, I found myself in the situation that Coach K describes above. I had this hard-and-fast rule that if a player was suspended from school, he was suspended from the team—a rule that on the surface makes sense. However, one of my players was suspended for not cleaning his homeroom classroom after school. Ordinarily, this offense would not warrant a suspension, but the teacher involved wanted to make an example of this student and got the school to agree to suspend him for two days. It just so happened that my team was playing for the league championship on one of those days. Abiding by the rule, I did not allow him to play. He also happened to be our top scorer, and as a result, we lost the championship game by two points. Ever since this experience I have taken Mike Krzyzewski's suggestion and made my rules flexible enough, in both basketball and nonbasketball situations, so that I would no longer back myself into a corner.

In this same vein, Krzyzewski points out that the truth is that many people set rules to keep from making decisions and avoid confrontation. Not Coach K. He doesn't want to be a dictator. He wants to be a leader—and according to him, leadership is ongoing, adjustable, flexible and dynamic.

In a situation similar to my own, Krzyzewski points out that at times there may be extenuating circumstances for a person violating a rule. Take being late for practice. If a senior like Tommy Amaker, who's done everything right for four years, is suddenly late for a bus or a team meeting, Krzyzewski would make an exception and wait for him.

In another example of Krzyzewski being situational in his leadership approach, he alludes to a conversation with one of his star players, Grant

Hill. Grant Hill once perceptively remarked that every team he played on during his four years at Duke was coached differently. That's because each year brings with it a new team, with new people who have different personalities and different skills and different needs.

Other instances when Krzyzewski is thinking situationally include the way he treats his team. He is tough on them, but he doesn't want fear to be the primary motivator. According to Kryzewski, being a good leader is looking beyond what your team is doing now. Every long-term strategy must be adjustable and the people on the team must be prepared accordingly.

According to Coach K, leaders should be reliable without being predictable. They should be consistent without being anticipated. "Instead of providing a spawning ground for creativity, a leader may be so structured, so ruled, so totally predictable, that he completely erases any enjoyment on the part of the team" (p. 99). Speaking of the need to be a little unpredictable, Krzyzewski recalls an instance during a game when he stepped into the huddle, looked at the players, then pulled back and sat down on the bench without saying a word. At that moment, he decided to coach by not coaching.

When Chris Laetner, one of his star players, came to him after a long and grueling season and said that he did not want to participate in the Pan American games because it would tire him out for the upcoming season, Krzyzewski made an exception so that Laetner would not miss out on a unique opportunity. He told him to play in the Pan American Games. Laetner didn't have to participate in the preseason program so he would have the summer off but he'd still participate in the Pan American Games. Coach K felt that that would help the team and show great leadership.

Coach K claims that a leader cannot motivate people by simply writing something down on paper, handing it out, and then saying, "Here do this!" The leader has to know his people. You've got to do different things in different situations. In general, his style is flexible and versatile. He thinks there's a time to get in someone's face and there's a time when you express yourself without yelling. There's also a time for a pat on the back or a hug.

In conclusion, he says that continuous learning is a key to effective leadership because no one can know everything there is to know. In leadership, things change. Events change, circumstances change, people change. Krzyzewski believes that leaders take people to places they've never been before. It is obvious from these examples that Mike Krzyzewski has a situational leadership approach whereby he applies different leadership behavior to different situations.

THE STRUCTURAL FRAME

Structural leaders develop a new model of the relationship of structure, strategy, and environment for their organizations. Mike Krzyzewski sets the tone early regarding his use of structural frame behavior. At his first meeting with his players, he gives the team only one rule to live by. The rule involves not doing anything detrimental to yourself or the team. But it cover a multitude of issues. He also tells them that he believes that a team that does its best is a winner, even if they are a loser on the scoreboard. The responsibility of the leaders is to assess the quality of the team, set the standard of excellence, and then work with the team to achieve that standard—to be the best they can be every time they play a game.

Much of Krzyzewski's respect for structural frame leadership behavior came from his experience in the army. One of the first things he learned was that he could answer a question in one of only three ways: "Yes, sir," "No, sir," or "No excuse, sir." He recalls an incident when he and his roommate were walking along and his roommate stepped into a puddle and splashed mud on Krzyzewski's shoes. When he was stopped by a superior officer and asked why he had mud on his shoes, he was tempted to tell his story, but ended up saying, "No excuse, sir." This rule was designed to get people to take responsibility. The way the army looked upon it was that he should have gone back to the barracks and polished his shoes. Reflecting on this incident and applying it to basketball, Krzyzewski believes that no matter what happens, it's his team, and he is responsible. There's no excuse.

According to Krzyzewski, we cannot allow others, like the media, the fans, or even our superiors to define success because doing so almost always leads to conflict. According to Krzyzewski, the only way to get around such an unhappy ending is to continually define your own success. His passion as a coach is to do things to the best of his ability and to have his team get better every day. If his team can do that, the winning will take care of itself. Every time they play a game, he wants it to be a masterpiece.

Krzyzewski was influenced by one of his former coaches, Bobby Knight, in developing his structural frame behavior. Bobby Knight always thought that everybody had the will to win, but not many had the will to prepare to win. Coach K learned a great deal about organization and preparation from Coach Knight. He taught him that goals are important in leadership. They should be realistic, they should be attainable, and they should be shared.

Coach K also sees the value of promoting a learning organization where individuals are taught, allowed to take risks, and if they fail, to learn from their mistakes. He claims that to teach is to learn twice. While coaches teach their players, they are also learning from them. He also points out that coaches cannot be afraid to let someone else educate members of his team. True leaders should have confidence enough not to see learning from someone else as a threat to their authority. Finally, he asserts that as teachers, coaches and leaders, we should remember that when mere winning is our only goal rather than continuous improvement, we are doomed to disappointment and failure.

The value of continuous improvement, which is prototypical structural frame behavior, is a Krzyzewski priority. "When I won a second national championship in 1992 at 45 years old, I wondered, 'Where do I go from here?' 'How does a successful leader get better?' I feel that I still have more potential to fill. And I often ask myself if anyone can really fulfill his potential. There always seems to be something that can be done better" (p. 230). We can readily see why Coach K has the well-earned reputation for being well organized, well prepared, and continually seeking perfection, all structural frame attributes.

THE HUMAN RESOURCE FRAME

Human resource leaders believe in people and communicate that belief. They are passionate about *productivity through people*. Human resource leadership behavior is an important part of Mike Krzyzewski's overall leadership style. In his initial meeting with his new recruits, he makes his concern for their well-being clear to them. He points out to them that each of them is special to him, and he never wants them to forget it. He works hard to get to know each and every one of his players personally. And even though he may not know every aspect of their personality, he does know their character and prides himself on getting to know them as both players and people.

He tries to teach the need for the human touch to his players, not only among themselves, but also with the "least of our brethren." He tells them to remember that even the managers are part of the team and to treat them accordingly. In Coach K's mind, everyone in the program is equal and should be treated as such.

In the building of trust and respect, which is a human resource frame goal, Krzyzewski is a master. He sees himself as a coach and a leader and is responsible for providing a safety net—a family support system. The way he looks at it, all he is really doing is passing along something that was given to him many years ago by his family. He shares with his players how he is going to treat them. He uses a "fair, but not equal policy" that allows him flexibility to make exceptions based on personal circumstances when they are warranted. The "handshake agreement" that he has with his players is a clean and honest one, with no hidden agendas. This approach works in all walks of life, according to Krzyzewski. When you treat a person like this, he or she knows that the leader not only cares about their performance but also cares about them on a personal level. He believes that such human resource behavior helps motivate individuals to do their best.

Krzyzewski advises that besides talent, we should look for other character traits in the individuals we recruit as players or as employees. He believes in recruiting great individuals who are willing to be part of the team and who are coachable. Almost everything in leadership comes back to relationships. And, naturally, the level of cooperation on any team increases tremendously as the level of trust increases. Leaders have to give time for relationships, Coach K believes.

As part of his human resource frame behavior, one of the first things that Krzyzewski tries to do is find the "heart" of his team—the player or players that are recognized by their teammates as the core of the family. In referring to one of his star players, Bobby Hurley, he indicates that Hurley's daring is easy to see. But the quiet heart isn't seen or understood very often. And while the coach has to look for it, it's always known by the players on the court—always. According to Krzyzewski, people have to be given the freedom to show the heart they possess. "I'm always searching for that in a team. I'll even watch the kids I am recruiting while their parents speak" (p. 38). Sometimes he finds it at that time.

Identifying the "heart" of the team helps to build trust and respect. There need to be mutual trust between the players and the coach. The players must have the discipline to believe and trust in what the coach says to them at a moment's notice, especially in a crucial part of a game. As coaches and leaders, we need to communicate in ways that are more direct than most people are used to. This only works if we tell the truth, and learn to trust one another and to understand that we're not trying to hurt each other with our words. He believes that most people will respect and appreciate someone who is honest with them. Coach K also believes that in leadership, there are no words more important than trust. In order to succeed, every great team possesses: communication, trust, collective responsibility, caring, and pride.

Krzyzewski practices what he preaches in citing an instance where he was trying to transition freshman Grant Hill into the team of veterans. Instead of trying to do it himself, he empowered two of his players to do so. He involved Bobby Hurley and Chris Laetner in the process and by doing so, showed that he had confidence in both of them. Using this strategy allowed him to bring Grant Hill further along than just working with him one-on-one.

Care of the person is an important part of Krzyzewski's leadership behavior. He practices human resource behavior because he cares about his job and because he cares about the people with whom he works. In no small way, caring can be a powerful motivational factor on any team, he believes. At Duke, he tries to prevent anyone from being just a number. Rather, he tries to plant seeds that help people grow. He tries to give every individual the freedom to develop their full capabilities. He believes that we need to care for each other because by ourselves, we can never reach our potential. Good players usually know when they have talent. But a great player realizes that he can achieve greatness only if he has other good players around him. Michael Jordan realized he needed players like Scottie Pippen and John Paxon for him to reach his potential. Jordan used human resource leadership behavior with them, knowing that in the long run, it would benefit all of them. Krzyzewski learned many of the subtleties of human resource behavior from interacting with some of his coaching mentors. "If I didn't give Coach Iba or Newell the right answer, they'd ask me another question in an effort to lead me to the correct solution. But always, always they would make sure that I came up with the solution myself . . . and I would never forget it" (p. 99). These same men also taught him the need for adding the human touch to his dealings with his players. Coach K learned that while it's important for a leader to focus on the technical details of his industry or business, it is also vital to focus on details related specifically to people in the organization. And that might mean challenging them, chastising them or simply putting an arm around them and giving them a smile.

Another way of behaving out of the human resource frame is to admit when you are wrong. Krzyzewski says, "Over time I was able to build it up [trust], in part by admitting that I was wrong when I screwed up" (p. 152). "He remembers a time when he asked a player to play a certain way in a game. The players did exactly what he was asked to do, but it didn't work. So, at halftime, Krzyzewski apologized to the kid in front of the entire team. Coach K believes that establishing a sense of trust is essential. The players will not believe you unless they trust you. If you get into a crisis and you have no trust among the members of your team, then you might be in a hopeless situation, asserts Krzyzewski.

Krzyzewski's sensitivity to others is embodied in his personal philosophy of life. He says that friendship is a matter of the heart, and all of his friends remain in his heart forever. He believes further that a leader must be committed to helping people grow. His commitment to each of his players to help him realize his full potential. After the last game of the year, win or lose, he makes sure that he thanks his team for their efforts during the season. He often thinks about the guys who fought in Vietnam who came home to no parades, no celebrations, no thank yous.

Recognizing the need for human resource behavior, but also the need to be situational, Krzyzewski says that some people respond positively when criticized. And some go into a shell with even the slightest bit of criticism. The leader of the team is responsible for getting to know the players well enough to understand what methods are the most effective for each individual—as well as the team as a whole. Krzyzewski is grateful to his wife, Michie, who frequently reminds him to have a different player over to the house each week for a session of individual instruction or for just conversation.

Krzyzewski considers himself both a teacher and a coach. He consciously surrounds himself with other good teachers on his staff. Their whole approach to coaching revolves around teaching. . . . And teaching is an art. A coach may have plenty of basketball knowledge, but his teaching ability will be judged by what his players know and what they are able to achieve under game conditions. As mentioned before, he believes that to teach is to learn twice. Suffice to say that human resource behavior is an important part of Coach K's overall leadership strategy.

THE SYMBOLIC FRAME

In the symbolic frame, the organization is seen as a stage, a theater in which every actor plays certain roles and the symbolic leader attempts to communicate the right impressions to the right audiences. Coach K is a master at using the symbolic frame of leadership.

From the very first time he meets his team, Mike Krzyzewski makes much use of symbolic frame leadership behavior. "It's important to begin using plural pronouns right away. 'Our,' instead of 'my.' 'We,' instead of 'I.' 'Us,' rather than 'me.' I don't want the guys thinking this is 'my' team—Coach K's team. I want them to believe it's 'our' team" (p. 7).

Krzyzewski's use of the symbolic frame is also seen in an incident that he describes. During practice, he dropped a cup of water. Justin, one of his players, ran over and said "'Let me get that coach." Coach K said. Just give me the towel," and wiped it up himself. The morale of the story, according to Krzyzewski is that even a CEO of a company, you should clean up your own mess. Another instance of using symbolic frame behavior is his use of the "fist" as a symbol of the value of teamwork. He looks at the members of his team like the five fingers of a hand. Some have small fingers, others have large, but they are never as strong as when they come together as a fist. And, when you point blame at someone else, one finger sticks out—and you no longer have a fist.

Along these lines, Krzyzewski often tells the story of his mother being mugged, but holding onto her purse and using it as a weapon to ward off the mugger. "Now, guys, if a 75-year-old lady is going to fight for her purse, you 19- and 20-year-olds aren't going to fight for a loose ball?" (p. 80).

Krzyzewski often uses spontaneous symbolic leadership behavior to motivate his team. In a locker room speech before an important game, he wrote "45 MINUTES" on the blackboard and circled it. He then said, "All right, listen up, fellas. In 45 minutes you're going to be dead. You're going to heaven or hell. Where do you want to be?" "That's what I do," he says, "I coach by feel. I follow my heart" (p. 125). By the way, Duke won the game 87-79.

He also used the image of a train as a symbol of a team's season long journey. At the beginning of the season, he wants everyone to board the the Duke Train. During critical periods of the season, he might indicate that the train is moving fast right now and everyone needs to stay on board. Everyone needs to be on the Duke train and not on another train. He says that the train stops at each game, when we can get off the train to see how we are doing. Games, however, are not our final destination; they are just checkpoints on our progress. The final destination is the NCAA Championship. Sometimes they reach their destination and sometimes they don't.

Coach K recalls another situation when he acted out of the symbolic frame. Duk had lost a few games in a row. The team was gathered in the locker room for the standard pregame talk. Krzyzewski turned out the lights and walked in with a lighted candle in his hand. He said that he was just an old Polish coach looking for a few players with heart. That was his entire pregame oration. And all of the players who were in that locker room that day still talk about it. It is important, says, Krzyzewski, that you demonstrate to your team that you're worthy to lead them. He suggests that we stand tall, stay stoic or smile as the situation warrants. Keep your face clean. Keep your uniform clean. Don't show any mud on your shoes. Portray an image that gives your team whatever they may need at that moment: a smile, a frown, emotion, anger, a joke.

Still another use of the symbolic frame of leadership is in the way Krzyzewski organizes his end-of-the-year basketball banquets. He instituted a form of awards banquet, with a family-type atmosphere, honoring seniors, videos of the journey, and so on. He patterned it after the graduation parade at West Point. At the end of every year, the corps of cadets comes out onto the reviewing field. The graduating seniors separate, march straight ahead, and then turn around and face the rest of the cadets and then the corps passes in review of the senior class.

Krzyzewski uses the symbol of the "sixth man" to show his appreciation for the Duke fans. He knows that it is easy to see the contribution of the members of your team. It's not so easy to recognize all of the other people who contribute to the success of an organization—people from the community, fans, supporters, students. He refers to the students and the fans as Duke's "sixth man" to recognize their contribution.

Coach K often tells the story of the "three baskets of potential" when exemplifying the symbolic frame. When we are born, he says, we are given three baskets of potential. Do we stay with three baskets our entire lives? Or when we fill up two of those baskets, have we developed even more possibilities so that now we have eight baskets of potential? Maybe one of the potentials in the third basket is to learn how to make more baskets.

His deceased mother was a great Duke fan, according to Krzyzewski. Before every game, he put her rosary in his shirt pocket so that it was close to his heart. And when his team is warming up out on the court, when he was all alone, he'd put his hand over his shirt pocket and say a prayer in honor of his mom. He asked God to look out after her and he would say, "Please, God, help me do my best, help me be myself, and help me lead with my heart" (p. 284).

THE POLITICAL FRAME

Leaders operating out of the political frame clarify what they want and what they can get. Political leaders are realist above all. They never let what they want cloud their judgment about what is possible. They assess the distribution of power and interests. Mike Krzyzewski makes use of the political frame, as needed. He certainly would not be the almost universally admired coach that he is without having been able to employ the political frame of leadership behavior when the occasion called for it. For example, he recalls an instance of reporters asking him how he thinks his Duke team will fare in the Final Four match-ups. He said to his team, "Don't even listen to what I say publicly. Just listen to what I tell you face-to-face. Then I went out and portrayed us in the media as the poor underdogs" (p. 174).

CONCLUSION

Coach Krzyzewski's image as one of the best college coaches in the nation is well earned. He could be the poster child for the effective use of situational leadership theory. He shows signs of operating out of all four leadership frames in appropriate situations. He is knowledgeable, well organized, and well prepared, which are all structural frame behaviors, and he treats his players with human dignity, being sensitive to their individual needs, which is emblematic of human resource frame behavior. His use of symbolic frame behavior is prolific, and his use of political frame behavior, although not frequent, is appropriate. His balanced application of leadership behaviors is a model for all leaders and aspiring leaders. There is much to be learned about effective leadership from Coach K.

8

DEAN SMITH

Don't let one day pass without doing something for a person who cannot repay you.

—Dean Smith

BACKGROUND

Dean Smith, born on February 28, 1931, is the retired head basketball coach at the University of North Carolina. Originally from Emporia, Kansas, the members of the Basketball Hall of Fame have called Smith a "coaching legend." Smith is best known for his successful coaching tenure at the University of North Carolina (UNC) at Chapel Hill for 36 years. Smith coached from 1961–97 and retired as the National Collegiate Athletic Association (NCAA) Division I men's basketball coach with the most wins ever, with 879 wins. Bobby Knight later surpassed the record in 2006. Smith has the ninth highest winning percentage of any men's college basketball coach at 77.6%. During his time as head coach of UNC, the team won two national titles and appeared in 11 Final Fours.

Smith is also known for running a clean program and having a high graduation rate among his players, with 96% of his players going on to graduate. While at UNC, Smith helped foster desegregation by recruiting UNC's first African American scholarship player, Charlie Scott, and promoting equal treatment for African Americans by local businesses. Smith coached and worked with numerous individuals at UNC that went on to achieve notable success in basketball, as either players or coaches or both. Smith retired as head coach in 1997, saying that he was not able to give the team the same level of enthusiasm that he had given it for years. Since retirement, Smith has been involved with various charitable ventures and political activities.

Both of Smith's parents were public school teachers. His father, Alfred, coached basketball and lead the Emporia High Spartans to the 1934 state title in Kansas with the first black basketball player in Kansas tournament history. While at Topeka High School, Smith lettered in basketball all 4 years and was named All-State in basketball as a senior. Smith's interest in sports was not limited only to basketball. Smith also played quarterback for his high school football team and catcher for the high school baseball team.

After graduating from high school, Smith attended the University of Kansas on an academic scholarship where he majored in mathematics and joined the Phi Gamma Delta fraternity. While at Kansas, Smith continued his interest in sports by playing varsity basketball, varsity baseball, and freshman football. During his time on the varsity basketball team, Kansas won the national championship in 1952 and finished second in 1953. Smith's basketball coach during his time at Kansas was the legendary Forrest "Phog" Allen, who in turn was coached in college by James Naismith, the founder of the game of basketball. After graduation, Smith served as assistant coach at Kansas in the 1953–54 season. Ironically, after leaving Kansas, Smith watched with disappointment as the University of Kansas team that he had helped coach lose to UNC in the 1957 national championship game in triple overtime.

Smith next served in the U.S. Air Force in Germany, and then worked at the U.S. Air Force Academy as head coach of its baseball and golf teams. In 1958, North Carolina University coach Frank McGuire asked Smith to join his staff as an assistant coach. Smith served under McGuire for 3 years until 1961, when McGuire was forced to resign in the wake of recruiting scandals. At age 30, Smith became the head coach.

Smith's first years as head coach were difficult. In his first season, there was a national point shaving scandal that involved three North Carolina State players and a UNC player. As a result of the scandal, both North Carolina State and UNC deemphasized basketball by cutting their regular season schedules. In Smith's first season, UNC played only 17 games and went 8-9. It was the only losing season that Dean Smith ever had. After this slow beginning, Smith turned the program into a consistent winner. His first major successes came in the late 1960s when his teams won three consecutive regular season and tournament championships in the Atlantic Coast Conference and went to three straight Final Fours. It took Smith seven trips to the Final Four before winning his first national title, and then it took him nine more years to return, and two more to get another national championship.

His first national championship occurred in 1982, when the team was comprised of future National Basketball Association (NBA) players such as Michael Jordan and James Worthy. The Carolina squad faced a Georgetown team that featured future NBA star Patrick Ewing. The climax of the game occurred when Jordan, with 18 seconds left on the clock, caught a pass and made the shot with time running out. His second and last championship run in 1993 almost began with a tragedy. One of the Carolina players during an invitational tournament in Hawaii nearly drowned while parasailing. North Carolina beat Michigan for the title.

Smith announced his retirement on October 9, 1997. His announcement was a shock to the basketball community and fans, as he had given little warning that he was considering retirement. Smith had been the only coach many UNC fans had ever known. His long-time assistant, Bill Guthridge, succeeded him.

Smith is credited with creating or popularizing several basketball techniques: the "tired signal," in which a player would used a hand signal (originally a raised fist) to indicate that he needed to come out for a rest, huddling at the free throw line before a foul shot, encouraging players who scored a basket to point a finger at the teammate who passed them the ball, instituting a variety of defensive sets in one game, having the point guard call out the defense set for the team, and creating a number of defensive sets, including the point zone, the run-and-jump, and double-teaming the screen-and-roll.

But strategically, Smith is most associated with his implementation of the four corners offense, a strategy for stalling with a lead near the end of the game. Smith's teams executed the four corners set so effectively that, in 1985, the NCAA instituted a shot clock to speed up play and minimize ball control offense. Smith is also the author of *Basketball: Multiple Offense and Defense*, which is the best-selling technical basketball book in history.

Smith also instituted the practice of starting all his team's seniors on the last home game of the season (Senior Day) as a way of honoring the contributions of the subs as well as the stars. In one season when the team included six seniors, he opted to put all six on the floor at the beginning of the game—drawing a technical foul—rather than leave one of them on the bench.

Smith received a number of personal honors during his coaching career. He was named the National Coach of the Year four times and ACC Coach of Year eight times. Smith was also inducted into the Basketball Hall of Fame on May 2, 1983, two years after being enshrined in the North Carolina Hall of Fame. On November 17, 2006, Smith was recognized for his impact on college basketball as a member of the founding class of the National Collegiate Basketball Hall of Fame. He was one of five, along with Oscar Robertson, Bill Russell, John Wooden, and James Naismith, selected to represent the inaugural class.

SITUATIONAL LEADERSHIP ANALYSIS

Situational leadership models differ from the earlier trait and behavioral models in asserting that no single way of leading works in all situations. Rather, appropriate behavior depends on the circumstances at a given time. Effective managers diagnose the situation, identify the leadership style or behavior that will be most effective, and then determine whether they can implement the required style.

Dean Smith is very astute at utilizing all four frames of leadership behavior suggested by Bolman and Deal. One need only look at the way Smith-coached teams varied their style, depending on the players Smith had available. He generally featured a fast-break style and half-court offense that emphasized the passing game and an aggressive trapping defense that produced turnovers and easy baskets. However, he is also known as the creator of the four corners offense, which was very deliberate, and oftentimes the player did not even shoot the ball until time almost ran out. Smith clearly used different tactics in different situations, a characteristic of a situational leader.

In fact, Smith decried the use of the term *system* when referring to his offensive and defensive schemes. "One book called us the Big Blue Machine. But I disliked those terms because I felt they were inaccurate. We had a philosophy of basketball, not a system. A system would imply that we used the same offensive and defensive strategy every season. Actually we were very flexible in our strategy and it changed from year to year, depending on the individuals in our program and their strengths and weaknesses." As the coach of the U.S. Olympic team, for instance, "We had to build a team in a short period of time. Our Carolina philosophy wouldn't help us here" (Smith, 1999, p. 120; all cites in this chapter, unless otherwise noted, are from this source).

THE STRUCTURAL FRAME

Structural leaders develop a new model of the relationship of structure, strategy, and environment for their organizations. Dean Smith was known for being knowledgeable, well prepared, and well organized. His teams played in a very disciplined manner, all indicative of his use of structural frame leadership behavior.

Smith's respect for the need for appropriately used structural frame behavior became obvious early on in his professional career. He recalls that one day during summer basketball tryouts in physical education, a first-year cadet just didn't get it. The thought of passing the ball and sharing it with his teammates never entered his mind. After putting up with it for some time, Smith finally pulled his four teammates off the court. "'Okay, play them by yourself' I said. He gave me a quizzical look. 'Who takes the ball out of bounds, sir?' he asked. 'Good,' I said, 'Now, you've learned that you need two, anyway'" (p. xvi).

Smith modeled an internal locus of control, which is a structural frame leadership trait. He says, as the coach, he remembered all the losses. Why? Because he held himself responsible for them. He told his players from the outset that if they did what he asked, the victories will belong to them and the losses would belong to him. He sincerely believed that when his team lost, it was his fault. "Smith's definition of good coaching means teaching your players how to play individually and unselfishly as a team. If players do that and play hard in the process, then losing should not be so debilitating, although he admits that it is much easier to say than to live it. For example, Smith played an injured Kenny Smith in a championship game and lived to regret it. He noted that bringing Kenny Smith back with a cast in the 1983 championship, lost the championship for North Carolina. He felt absolutely awful for his players and blamed himself.

Establishing goals and planning strategically are structural frame behaviors. These behaviors are exemplified in Smith's program. His philosophy at UNC was: 1) play together unselfishly, 2) play hard and with maximum effort, 3) play smart and properly execute. He pointed out to his team that seldom, if ever, had there been a leading scorer in the country who played for a ranked team, and certainly not a championship team. Smith was very demanding, but he also held that demands must be coupled with true caring for the students, which couples structural behavior and human resource behavior.

Smith's identification of players who would respond to structural frame behavior started with the recruiting process. He checked carefully in his recruiting process to be sure the players he brought in were compatible with Carolina's philosophy. He never made recruiting promises. He simply told them what Carolina had to offer, and he hoped they took it.

In true structural frame fashion, Smith used his practices to instill in his players the attitude that he was seeking. To Smith, practice, preparation and planning was the foundation of everything. In practice it was extremely important to praise and use positive reinforcement to promote unselfish play. Positive reinforcement is crucial to building a team. Blow the whistle and acknowledge a good screen, he suggested. Smith made sure that he punished as a team, not individually. For instance, if one player didn't hustle in practice, the whole team ran sprints.

THE HUMAN RESOURCE FRAME

Human resource leaders believe in people and communicate that belief. They are passionate about productivity through people. Dean Smith is a very human resource–type leader. There are numerous instances of his operating out of this frame. He expresses his feelings regarding human resource behavior when he indicates that the hardest thing about writing his biography was deciding what to put in and what to leave out. That was particularly hard for him because he had thirty-six teams at North Carolina, and each team and each player was important to him.

Smith worked hard to create a family atmosphere among his teams and players. He recalls that King Rice, class of '91, didn't play with Michael Jordan, class of '85, but when King called for play-off tickets to a Bulls' game, Jordan not only got him two good seats, but after the game took him and his wife to his restaurant for dinner. It's that "Carolina Family" atmosphere that Smith constantly promotes. Smith indicates that his players develop a feeling for their teammates that is unique. For example, they are often in each other's wedding parties. When Henrik Rodl was married, George Lynch was his best man. Henrik is white, George is black. Henrik is from Germany, George is from Virginia. They had a bond from their days as Carolina basketball players, and that would be for a lifetime.

Smith's penchant for operating out of the human resource frame carried over to his behavior regarding segregation. According to Smith, some people have given him undue praise for integrating North Carolina's basketball team in the early 1960s. He says that his father was the family's true reformer, however, and taught him to value each human being. He was taught to believe in the dignity of the human family, and other than that there wasn't talk about it. Racial justice wasn't preached around the house, but there was a fundamental understanding that you treated each person with dignity. Smith gives another example of the kind of coach and person his father was. Smith would be credited years later with inventing the practice of having a scorer point to the passer to thank him for the assist. However, his father did it long before he did. Still, Smith was influenced by his father to such a degree that he used many of these same practices, and Smith is duly credited with recruiting the first black player, Charlie Scott, in North Carolina basketball history.

An indication of the racially charged atmosphere that Smith and Charlie Scott were in at the time is reflected in Smith's recollection of an incident that occurred in Scott's senior year. Scott had a quick first step, was a great defensive player, and had a soft jumper with which he averaged 22 points and 7 rebounds a game. He was an Olympian. But, then came the announcement: Scott had lost the ACC Player of the Year Award to John Roche of South Carolina, who was white, a sophomore whose team finished in 2nd place to UNC in the league.

Smith's concern for the person is so strong that he practices it even when it can be detrimental to him personally. For example, he has long been an advocate of early entry into the professional drafts for certain undergrads. If a player is drafted in the top five, he is financially secure for life. Smith's attitude is that he can always come back for an education. On the other hand, as far as freshmen being eligible to play on the varsity, he is against it. In his view, it may be good for the team, but not for the player.

Another instance of Smith's reliance on human resource behavior is in his philosophy regarding how to treat his players. He always felt that it was important not to embarrass players in public. His college coach at Kansas, Phog Allen, at times would substitute for a player because of a mistake—and the player would play tentatively as a result. Thus, Smith learned not substitute for mistakes. Considering these many examples, it is quite obvious that Dean Smith had great respect for human resource frame leadership behavior.

THE SYMBOLIC FRAME

In the symbolic frame, the organization is seen as a stage, a theater in which every actor plays certain roles and the symbolic leader attempts to communicate the right impressions to the right audiences. Dean Smith is a great advocate of and makes much use of symbolic frame leadership behavior.

Once again we find that Smith's family background had a great influence on his leadership behavior, most especially on his symbolic behavior. He was taught as a boy to never, ever brag about myself. His father claimed that the more you brag, the less you have to brag about.

Someone genuinely secure in his or her abilities has no need to brag, the elder Smith held. Smith comments further on his father's influence on him by noting that he had never heard profanity in their home. His father would not allow him to take a summer job as a caddy at the Emporia Country Club, because he knew he'd be around a kind of language he didn't condone. Tobacco and liquor were forbidden in his household as well, Smith noted.

Smith was also influenced by the strong Christian faith of his family. He had always been aware of the Holy Spirit, but he had never truly given himself over to Christ. So often in his life he thought he was self-sufficient. The key to a fruitful life, he suddenly understood, lay in surrendering his life and his daily choices to the gift of the power within. Every work his minister wrote seemed to have particular relevance for him. "'No sinner is hopeless, no situation is irretrievable. No cause is past redeeming,' I read. A setback, Reverend Marshall wrote, 'is actually the crucible out of which victory could rise.' Finally she quoted Jesus in John's gospel, 'I am the vine; you are the branches. Apart from me you can do nothing'" (p. 79).

On the other hand, Smith says, that the thought that God has given a victory has always bothered him. His Methodist minister always said, "God answers prayers in four ways: yes, no, wait, or you gotta be kidding." When we pray for victory, Smith thinks the Lord responds with "you gotta be kidding." Smith's use of symbolic frame behavior is evident in some of the unique rituals that he employed. For example, one of the things that he did was institute the "tired signal." When a player was tired Smith told him he could pull himself from the game. All he had to do was hold up a clenched fist. Smith also had a "Thought of the Day" at the top of each daily practice plan. One of them was: "You can tell more about a person from what he says about others than what others say about him." Another was the epigraph to this chapter. Also, "Never judge your neighbor until you have walked in his moccasins for two full moons" (p. 127).

The "Blue Team" was another of Smith's symbolic leadership devises. He says that one of the best things that he ever did to bring a team together was to go to the Blue Team in 1969. He would have a mass substitution for two minutes in each half. This ritual reflected Smith's belief that every man on the team should be a go-to guy and was important.

He believes that rituals are tools in building family life, church life, teamwork, and even company life.

Smith cared deeply about his team's image. He made certain that their collective demeanor was modest and neat. It was his hope that their appearance would bespeak achievement without showing it. The first time he saw a player "showboat" after making a spectacular play, he admonished the player and told him to try to act as if he had done that before. To Smith's way of thinking, a teammate is the most important person in the world. So when a player comes out of a game, his teammates showed their appreciation by standing and applauding. This did wonders in promoting unselfishness, Smith believes. In practice, he had his coaches run over and pick up the player who drew the charge.

Other symbolic behavior included sprinting to the bench. On substitutions and time outs, he instructed his players to sprint to the bench. Before taking the court prior to tip-off and after time-outs, they would stack hands as a sign of unity. And, signaling the priority of academics, Smith made sure that his players never missed a class and scheduled early flights so they could get back to class. Smith also demands punctuality of himself and his team. To Smith, showing up late is disrespecting the person or persons you are meeting. Thus, to him showing up late is selfish and arrogant. Finally, he had the practice of sharing the money he made advertising for Nike with the entire staff. All of this symbolic behavior was designed to create of culture of trust and caring.

THE POLITICAL FRAME

Leaders operating out of the political frame clarify what they want and what they can get. Political leaders are realists above all. They never let what they want cloud their judgment about what is possible. They assess the distribution of power and interests. Dean Smith makes use of the political frame when needed. During his time as head coach at North Carolina, he was almost universally respected and liked. One does not gain this kind of reputation without the astute application of political frame leadership behavior. In addition to the political relationships that we can only speculate about, there was at least one instance when Smith recalls using political frame behavior. On Smith's first fund-raising assignment, the institutional development officer with whom he was working only gave him broad guidelines regarding the fund-raising process and his part in it. So when the donor prospect said to him, "What do you think I should give?" Smith said, "I don't know, how about $10,000?" The development officer immediately excused himself and took Smith aside. "When we went back in he asked the man to ask the question again, this time I was instructed to say $250,000" (p. 220).

CONCLUSION

Dean Smith makes appropriate use of all four leadership frames suggested in Bolman/Deal situational leadership theory. He believes very strongly in thorough preparation and practice. He obviously has an extensive knowledge of the game of basketball and is demanding of his players. All of these structural frame traits have served him well. In addition, he believes strongly in "productivity through people." He treats his players and everyone else with human dignity.

Smith's use of the symbolic frame, reflected in his "Thoughts of the Day," his "Blue Team" concept, and the clasping of hands as a sign of unity, is well noted. Although his use of the political frame is not frequent, he does use this frame when appropriate. This balanced approach to the use of the four frames of leadership has helped Dean Smith become an icon among basketball coaches. He is an exemplar of how one can become an effective leader, using situational leadership theory.

9

PAT SUMMITT

If you can't take the heat, get out of the kitchen.

—Harry Truman

BACKGROUND

Pat Summitt was born on June 14, 1952, in Clarksville, Tennessee, and has been the coach of the Tennessee Lady Vols basketball team for 33 years. Her entire head coaching career has been at Tennessee, and her career record is currently (2006–7) 947-180. As a player and a member of Chi Omega sorority at the University of Tennessee–Martin, Summitt was an All American and cocaptain of the 1976 Olympic basketball team. She has written two books (with S. Jenkins), *Reach for the Summit* and *Raise the Roof*.

In the 1974–75 season, Pat Summitt took over a 25-2 Lady Vols team. In her first season, the Lady Vols won the Tennessee College Women's Sorts Federation (TCWSF) Eastern District Championship for the third straight year. However, the team finished only fourth overall in the TCWSF and was not invited to the Association for Intercollegiate Athletics for Women (AIAW). After finishing 16-11 her second season,

Summitt directed two 20-win teams, winning back-to-back AIAW Region II championships. In 1976 the Lady Vols defeated three-time AIAW champion Delta State, and received Tennessee's first number one ranking. In 1978 Lady Vols participated in their first AIAW Final Four, where they finished third. Summitt also recorded her 100th win during this season. Tennessee finished the 1970s by winning the first ever Southeastern Conference (SEC) tournament, and returning to the Final Four, where they finished runner-up to Old Dominion.

During the 1980–81 season, the Lady Vols went 25-6 and avenged their championship game loss to Old Dominion by defeating them three times. The team made it to the AIAW Final Four for the third straight year, but finished runner-up for the second consecutive year, losing to Louisiana Tech. The 1981–82 season featured the first ever National Collegiate Athletic Association (NCAA) women's basketball tournament. The Lady Vols were one of 32 teams invited. In the regional championship, the Lady Vols upset first seeded (USC)University of Southern California (USC) in overtime to advance to the Final Four. They would again lose their Final Four match-up with Louisiana Tech, who ended up winning the tournament.

The 1983–84 season saw Tennessee start out poorly. However, Summitt got her team together and finished 22-10, for her eighth straight 20-win season, a streak that was still ongoing in 2007. Tennessee not only made it to the NCAA Final Four for the second time out of the three tournaments, but also made it to the title game. However, Tennessee lost to USC, who had also won the title the previous year. Pat Summitt earned coach of the year honors. This season was followed up by another 20-win year in which Tennessee earned both the regular season SEC title and the tournament title. However, the Lady Vols fell in the NCAA tournament to Mississippi during the Round of 16. The next season was a similar story—the Lady Vols had a decent regular season, played a great tournament, but fell in the Final Four.

In 1988–89, after years of trying, the Lady Vols finally broke through and defeated perennial power Louisiana Tech for their first NCAA title. During this season, Summitt also earned her 300th win. The next year, the Lady Vols were poised to repeat, as the third-ranked and top seeded Tennessee made it to the Final Four yet again. However, Louisiana Tech avenged their championship loss with a 9-point win for the title.

In 1988–89, the Lady Vols made it to the Final Four for the fourth straight year, and as a first seed for the second straight year defeated Auburn for the title, and Tennessee took home its second title in three years. Record wise, this was Tennessee's best season yet, as they won 35 games while dropping only 2.

Despite winning neither the SEC regular season championship nor the tournament championship, Tennessee was given a top seed in the 1991 National Consortium for Academics and Sports (NCAS) tournament. In the national semifinals, the Lady Vols beat Stanford to earn the opportunity to avenge the previous year's tournament loss against Virginia. Just as the previous year's game had gone into overtime, so did this one. Down one at the half, the Lady Vols managed to tie the game at 60 by the end of regulation. Tennessee escaped in overtime with a 70-67 win, and their third national title in 5 years.

In 1995–96, with freshman Chamique Holdsclaw and senior Michelle Marciniak, the Lady Vols won the SEC tournament and made a second straight Final Four. Tennessee won their fourth NCAA title easily, with an 83-65 win over Georgia.

In many respects the 1997–98 team was Summitt's best. With the top-ranked recruiting class as well as Chamique Holdsclaw, the Lady Vols ran the table to a 39-0 season while playing one of the top-ranked schedules in the country. Only three teams came within ten points of beating them, and the Lady Vols won a 93-75 victory over Louisiana Tech for their third straight national championship.

Pat Summitt and her Lady Vols continued their success into the new millennium. During the 2002–3 season, Summitt earned her 800th win, the coach to reach this milestone most quickly. The 2003–4 season was quite similar to the previous year. The Lady Vols defeated most of their opponents, including Duke and Louisiana Tech, but dropped games to University of Connecticut and Texas. The Lady Vols again went 14-0 in the regular season against SEC competition and again fell in the tournament. And once again, the Lady Vols won five games in the NCAA tournament only to lose in the championship game to their new rival, Connecticut.

In the 2004–5 season, Pat Summitt gained her 880th win, breaking North Carolina coach Dean Smith's record of 879 wins, making her the all-time winningest coach in basketball history. The next year was Candace Parker's first year as a college athlete. However, Tennessee lost early in the NCAA tournament, not making the Final Four for the first time in 5 years. But in the 2006–7 season, lead by Candace Parker, Tennessee once again made it to the Final Four. In that championship game against Rutgers, Tennessee finally won its seventh title.

Pat Summitt has seven national championships, which is the most among all women coaches. In all of college basketball records, only John Wooden has more with ten. She has appeared 17 times in the Final Four. She was also named the Naismith Coach of the Century. She is a 7-time NCAA Coach of the Year, and was inducted into the Basketball Hall of Fame in 1990, making her one of the most honored coaches in history.

SITUATIONAL LEADERSHIP ANALYSIS

Situational leadership models differ from the earlier trait and behavioral models in asserting that no single way of leading works in all situations. Rather, appropriate behavior depends on the circumstances at a given time. Effective managers diagnose the situation, identify the leadership style or behavior that will be most effective, and then determine whether they can implement the required style.

In reality, Pat Summitt is the epitome of a situational coach, even though she is oftentimes thought to be someone who almost exclusively operates out of the structural frame—the strict disciplinarian—the George Patton of women's basketball. But Summitt learned early on that she had to vary her leadership behavior to be successful. When she first started coaching, "I was hard on them and myself and everyone around me. I thought I had to be. I thought that's how you commanded respect" (Summitt & Jenkins, 1998, p. 11; all cites in this chapter, unless otherwise noted, are from this source). However, at the end of a particularly grueling practice, a group of four young ladies were running together. When they got to the end of the line, they just kept on running. They ran out the door and up the steps, and Summitt never saw them again. Her ideas about how to command respect have changed since then. She learned that you can't demand it, or hit them on the head with a cinderblock. You have to cultivate it, in yourself and those around you.

Even before she began coaching, she realized that different situations called for different responses. She was raised to respect authority, but sometimes it has to be tempered with human kindness. Summitt remembers how the men in her family were treated with such deference. When her family sat down at the dinner table, Summitt saw blind authority at work. "They [the men] wouldn't say a word. They'd just lift their glasses, and shake them until my mother served them. It was their way of saying, 'Come fill my glass.' I can still see those hands, holding up their glasses, rattling the ice. My mother waited on them. And I thought, *That isn't right*" (p. 22).

Pat Summitt also realized that in order to meet the differing needs of her players, a situational approach was required. Tennessee has had its share of individualists over the years. According to Summitt, Chamique Holdsclaw was one. She's proof that being a creative, expressive individual is not incompatible with being responsible, as so many people, especially kids, seem to think, Summitt asserts. At Tennessee Summitt increases her players' responsibilities to each other slowly, incrementally, over four years. Buy the time they are seniors, she assigns them mentoring roles; they each have the personal charge of an incoming freshman. They are responsible for seeing that their freshman gets to class and eats lunch and all the other things that will lead to success as a student-athlete.

In some cases, the need to be situational in one's leadership behavior was learned the hard way. Summitt says, "From 1974 to 1986, we reached the Final Four a total of seven times, and lost. We couldn't win the big one. And some of that was my fault. I was wrong when I thought I had to intimidate my players into obeying me. I was wrong when I overcoached. I was wrong in some of my game plans in those early national championship games when I insisted the Lady Vols play a highly structured half-court game" (p. 34).

But Summitt learned from those mistakes. Now, she not only behaves situationally herself, she also depends on it from her assistants. Her assistants have a complementary chemistry with her. When she is strict, they're compassionate; when she's punishing, they're soothing. They have patience when she does not, humor when she or the players need it, and good judgment when she lacks it.

Summitt has come to know that each situation requires a different nuance. We all know people who yell at every opportunity. They yell in the office, at home, in a restaurant. After a while, we tune them out. Too much of one thing tends to dull your listener's sensibilities. That's why, sometimes, saying nothing at all can be just as powerful as yelling, Summitt believes.

For example, in the 1977 season, Summitt received word that the team had been out late drinking one night. They had had a big party and stayed up until 4 a.m., even though they had an early practice scheduled for the following morning. They had violated just about every one of the team policies. Summitt was upset, and she was ready and waiting for them when they arrived at the gym the next morning.

She considered verbally abusing them as she usually did in like circumstances. But she decided that one more lecture from her would not make the point effectively enough. Instead she decided not to say a word. Instead, she placed four plastic trash cans at the four corners of the court. A suicide drill is a sprint in which you have to run from the baseline to the free throw line and back, then to half court and back, then to the far free throw line, and so on. Summitt required them to run four suicides in a row.

Considering that the players were out partying until 4 a.m., one can imagine that those four trash cans were well used. She had made her point and never had to utter a word. She employs many different modes of communication as a coach. In a game, she issues blunt commands and motivates players to conquer adverse situations. Circumstances dictate how you need to speak, or whether you need to just keep quiet and listen. Once a player or an individual starts to slide in a downward direction, then it's time to examine your methods, says Summitt. Challenging a player might be a good strategy, or then again, it might be a confidence breaker. The goal of coaching and leading is always to motivate, not to demoralize.

In another instance in dealing with one of her star players, Michelle Marciniak, Summitt further manifested situational leadership behavior. She spoke with Michelle regarding the need to distribute the ball and not constantly look for her shot. Michelle did not respond, "And I benched her. Well, that pushed Michelle further into the tank." Seeing that that approach did not work, Summitt tried another. She said to

Michelle, "If I could choose any player in the county, I'd choose you," she said. "There's no one else I'd rather have run this team. The next year when we were in another tight NCAA tournament game against Connecticut, I knew what *not* to say to Michelle (p. 77). Tennessee went into overtime in that game because Michelle did not guard a Connecticut player close enough to prevent a game-tying three pointer. Summitt's instinct was to go straight at Michelle and overreact again. But she decided not to say a word to her. She talked to the team calmly, and let Michelle regain her composure—and won the game, 88-83 in overtime. A day later Tennessee beat Georgia for the title.

In thinking about the application of situational leadership behavior, Pat Summitt gives the following advice: One does not always have to make the right decision. There's always a judgment involved. You need to ask yourself what the person needs today, right now? And you have to watch his or her body language. The trick to communicating with a group is balance both praise and criticism. Too much praise loses effectiveness—just as too much criticism does. For example, Summitt does not feel that she has to go rah-rah every time the team sprints down the floor, because you're *supposed* to sprint.

Fifteen years earlier, she would have gone off on a team just to feel better. But now it wasn't about her any longer—it was about trying to determine how to get a team to come around and respond. She wanted them to figure it out for themselves. She didn't want to call another exhausting meeting, and give them all the answers, or try to pull the answers out of them. She had done that in the past, but sometimes the players need to talk amongst themselves and come up with their own answers. Why? Because in recent years Summitt has tried to understand that more is not always better. You don't beat a dead horse. Sometimes you step back, create some space and silence and let things solve themselves. Sometimes, a simple gesture can be worth a thousand words.

According to Summitt, a leader needs to use his or her competitive instinct situationally. She recalls two incidents when her competitiveness had to be held in check because of the situation of the moment. Tennessee's most recent archrival for national prominence is the University of Connecticut. Summitt says that her competitive instinct is to actually *hate* UConn. But she realizes that in this situation, that would not be appropriate leadership behavior, because there wasn't a team the

Tennessee respected more than UConn. It got their competitive juices flowing. Tennessee has a great rivalry with UConn. Summitt likes and respects the Connecticut coach, Geno Auriemma. They recruit a lot of the same players, and their games are usually close and hard fought. Competitiveness needs to be tempered with affection in these situations. It is a sign that Summitt values the need for situational leadership behavior.

In a second example, Summitt cites her relationship with her longtime husband, R. B. "There is a time and place to be a competitor," she says. "I've had to learn to leave my competitive instincts at the office at the end of the day, because they are hard on my marriage. R. B. and I used to play racquetball all the time. I taught him how to play, and we would go into the basement of the Alumni Gym and wail away with those rackets until we were both drenched in sweat. You could hear our sneakers squish when we walked. At first I beat him like a drum" (p. 210).

But R.B. got better and started beating her in racquetball. And she didn't like it one bit. She discovered that she couldn't play racquetball with him and then go home and cook his dinner. If she lost, it made her tense. She couldn't separate the two. Finally, she had to stop playing. So, she struggles to keep her competiveness in check, but does not ever want lose it, or be self-conscious about it, because it has served her so well in surviving the tough times. And she knows that the young women who play for her may need it in their lives at some point down the road. However, says Summitt, "Competitiveness is not meant for peacetime" (pp. 212–213).

Pat Summitt speaks eloquently about the need to adapt to the given situation to be a truly effective leader. For years her mentality was the opposite. She and her teams were very predictable. She was extremely structured early in her career. She had a system and did not stray from it. But it was a system with no flexibility—and it was limiting as a result. She had to learn the value of strategic change and the element of surprise. At one time, she actually wanted to control the way her players thought. But basketball is a game of quick and fluid changes. Players often do not have time to think about what Pat would do in this situation. They need to be allowed to be creative.

Today, Summitt considers herself to be a much better teacher. She imparts what she knows about the game and lets them make intelligent decisions on their own. She believe *that's* real teaching. Not until she had the willingness to change was she a real success as a head coach. In her first few seasons, Summitt admits that Tennessee was woefully easy to scout and prepare for. She employed only one defense and one offense. They were a slow, plodding, methodical half-court team. She says they deserved the nickname "corn-fed chicks." Their predictability worked against them in at least two ways. Not only were they incapable of altering their strategy, but when people changed up against them, they'd panic. Summitt's inflexibility and resistance to change cost them games.

Change is a risky business. But after losing so many times in the Final Four, Summitt decided that change didn't seem nearly as risky as being static. After a loss to Connecticut in the 1995 NCAA championship game, she decided that they had to revise their offense and defense. Summitt believes that as a result of this change, Tennessee won back-to-back national championships.

She says that it was defeat that forced her into trying something new. They had suffered a string of losses to UConn, and it bothered her to no end. She had a choice. She could resent UConn's success. Or she could learn something from it. She decided to be situational and learn.

Summitt learned even more about the use of situational leadership theory upon talking with Phil Jackson, the successful professional basketball coach of the Bulls and the Lakers. She learned in the meeting that Jackson has the capacity to allow people space; he had a patience and a tolerance for individuals, without abandoning his team principles. For her, that was an area in which she had to change. The most important thing she learned from that afternoon with Jackson wasn't a strategy or a scheme. It was the simple truism that it's what you learn after you know it all that counts the most.

So, Pat Summitt learned that despite all the reasons we resist change, like fear, laziness, caution, and lack of confidence and control, the reality is that one is in greater control when one is open to needed change. It allows the leader to remain in control even in a different situation.

THE STRUCTURAL FRAME

Structural leaders develop a new model of the relationship of structure, strategy, and environment for their organizations. Pat Summitt shows indications that she makes liberal use of structural frame leadership behavior. In one of her books, *Reach for the Summit*, she makes it very clear where she stands relative to the use of structural frame behavior. "That's who you're dealing with here," she says. "Someone who will sell her house to own your farm. Someone who will push you beyond all reasonable limits. Someone who will ask you to not just fulfill your potential, but to exceed it. Someone who will expect more from you than you may believe you are capable of." Her motto is: "Discipline yourself so no one else has to" (p. 2).

In typical structural fashion, Summitt believes that respect is essential to building group cohesion. People who do not respect others will not make good team members, and they probably lack self-esteem themselves. You don't have to like each other. But you do have to respect your colleagues' opinions and decisions, because whether you as a leader are successful depends on the loyalty and effort of your followers.

In referring to Abby Conklin, one of Summitt's star players, she says that she felt that Abby didn't respect her. Abby felt that Summitt did not respect her either, because Summitt was always getting on her back in front of the team. It turned into an epic battle of wills. In reality, Abby lacked respect for her own abilities. But it manifested itself as a lack of respect for Summitt and her game plan, and in that she made a big mistake.

One day, in front of the entire team, Abby challenged Summitt and indicated that she did not agree with her regarding the game plan. The problem was that Summitt counted heavily on Abby as her "coach on the floor." Abby's most critical responsibility as a leader was to back up the coach up, no matter what. If she wasn't going to respect the game plan, chances were that no one else was.

Summitt believes that when you lose the support of your leaders in front of the whole team, you might lose the team altogether. By taking her on like that, Abby jeopardized everything they were working toward. But Summitt feels that she should have gone ahead and let her have it, instead of bottling it up, in light of what happened next. After practice, Summitt went into the locker room, where Abby started to apologize. She was sipping from a cup of water at the time. But it wasn't cooling her down any. She ended up throwing the cup across the room. She admits that she shouldn't have thrown the water, of course. It was hardly an example of mutual respect. But in true structural fashion, she felt that she had to do something to impress on Abby the seriousness of the situation. Having gotten the team's attention by using structural behavior, Summitt then applied some human resource behavior to the situation, and sat down with Abby and really communicated with one another for the first time.

Summitt attributes her dependence on structural frame leadership behavior to her father. While she loved and respected her father, she also feared him. Over the years her father steadily built up a thousand-acre farm. At one point they had sixty-four milk cows. Then he bought a general store and opened a hardware store, a feed mill, a gas pump, and a laundry. He also got into the construction business. So when Summitt talks about self-respect, it comes from someone who belongs to a family of self-made overachievers.

Her father demanded respect with his belt. The children got regular whippings—hard ones. For example, once when she was about five years old, her brothers thought it would be funny to teach her an off-color song about beans and bodily functions. If you've got kids, you've probably heard it before. That night at dinner she raised up a spoonful of beans and sang her new song for the family. "Beans, beans, good for the heart, the more you eat, the more you . . ." Summitt, of course, paid the consequences of that little indiscretion.

Summitt says that, to a great extent, her father made her who she is. His combination of love and discipline was hard to take, but in the end she was grateful for it. He gave her strength. Today, they are at peace with one another because Summitt learned that the application of structural leadership behavior is essential for success.

Summitt comments further on her father's influence on her by recalling that he once built a basketball court in the top of a hayloft for his kids. He put up an old iron rim, and strung lights so they could play up there at night. They'd climb up the 20-foot barn ladder and have heated contests of 2-on-2. Her oldest brother, Tommy, would team with her, the smallest, against the middle boys, Charles and Kenneth. As one would imagine, Summitt became a force to be reckoned with. Once, she remembered, Charles locked himself in her parents' bedroom so he could use the phone to talk to his girlfriend. She wanted to use the phone too. She got so mad she told him she was going to kick in the door, which she promptly did, putting a three-foot hole in it.

The epigraph to this chapter is a typically structural leadership behavior statement by former president Harry Truman. Pat Summitt is in that mold. She says that if one doesn't want responsibility, don't sit in the big chair. According to Summitt, to be successful, the leader must accept full responsibility; responsibility for everything from headaches to major crises. And to add insult to injury, she believes that the more successful you are, the more responsibility you must assume. According to Summitt, responsibility never ends. It's not a step, or just a chapter. You don't finish it and then move on to something more fun or interesting. "Responsibility is a constant state of being" (p. 29).

As a structural leader, Pat Summitt places much emphasis on structure and discipline. She has her share of team rules, one of which is "no tattoos," which is difficult to enforce these days. But there are no exceptions. According to Summitt, All-American Chamique Holdsclaw has a tattoo down around her ankle. When she goes to Summitt's office, Chamique knows to to pull her sock up or put a bandage over it. Summitt's thinking is that things like tattoos are the height of conformity. She believes that she is in the business of producing leaders, not followers.

Summitt admits that Tennessee has strict rules. Her competition tries to make something out of that. They oftentimes say that Tennessee is too rigid and call them a "cookie factory." They say the players act like they came out of cookie cutters. While it is true that Tennessee's players buy into the system and are expected to be more mature than their peers. The fact is, by comparison, they don't have many rules. Summitt believes that the fewer the rules, the fewer that will be broken. One of the rules that she does have, however, reflects her focus on taking responsibility for one's own actions. Walking with what she calls the "loser's limp" is intolerable. Here definition of the loser's limp is blaming something else or someone else for what's going wrong instead of being accountable for your own actions. Summitt just will not tolerate the "loser's limp."

Structural leadership behavior in the form of strict discipline is important to Summitt. Preemptive discipline is what happens when the mere thought of the consequences—like, facing her—is enough to prevent a problem from occurring in the first place. The ultimate goal of discipline is to teach *self*-discipline, she asserts. She believes that discipline is the basis of leadership. Discipline is the internal mechanism that motivates one to get out of bed in the morning. It gets you to work on time, and it tells you when you need to work late. It drives you. It is essential to success, whether individually or in a group. Discipline is all about trust and respect, according to Summitt. She asks her players to believe and trust that she has their best interests at heart.

To Summitt, enforcing a code of conduct is a necessary evil. The truth is that she dislikes punishing her players. She hates punishing her own son, too. However, while she doesn't want her players or her son to be afraid of her, she does want them to have a healthy respect for the consequences if they cross her. Recognition of the consequences is the surest way to instill discipline. Too many people don't think about consequences, or if they do, they don't care, she claims. In order to teach that concept, she sometimes has to play the role of disciplinarian. "Our Tennessee players have to think that just about anything is better than facing me" (p. 93).

She believes that discipline is important for any job. You can't just freelance and hope your talent will make up for lack of discipline. Not letting an unforeseen bad break, an official's call, or some obnoxious crowd take you out of your game plan is another form of discipline. And it takes discipline to understand that it's a 40-minute game, and that you must do the things that will allow you to win all game long, not just in the closing seconds. It takes discipline not to panic in the stretch. Discipline is what helps you finish a job when you're tired and ready to go home. However, punishment in order to maintain discipline will only work temporarily, according to Summitt. It is only when the disciplined behavior becomes internalized that it is instinctive.

At Tennessee, disciplined behavior is in fact internalized. "We could change uniforms and come out on the floor in purple, and you'd still be able to pick us out—just look for the more disciplined team," Summitt says. "Tennessee discipline has acquired a certain mystique on a national level. That's good and bad. It scares off some prospective recruits, which is unfortunate. But it also makes opponents respect us. Whenever our players are on national teams in the summer, women from other programs barrage them with questions. 'What is it like?' they ask, awed. Actually, it's a compliment." However, "as a leader, you cannot develop discipline if you don't have self-discipline" (p. 98). It is an old adage, a leader must model desired behavior.

A strong work ethic is another structural frame behavior that Pat Summitt endorses. By her own admission, however, she sometimes goes overboard. She once had a full-length practice immediately upon returning to campus after a loss. It was several years ago, back in the days when she thought terrorizing a team was the same thing as coaching it. Tennessee had lost a game to Vanderbilt on the road, thanks to a lackadaisical effort on the part of Tennessee. If there is one thing that Summitt cannot tolerate, it's lack of effort. The team went right back to campus in the team bus. Her husband was with them, and made the mistake of asking where the team was going for dinner. Little did he know!

Summitt prides herself in not being outworked. She believes in constantly trying to be more thorough, more conditioned, and more knowledgeable. Her staff realizes that they are expected to outwork everybody in college basketball, and her players take pride in knowing they can outlast their opponents. Summitt believes that any first-class and effective organization is committed to maintaining its work ethic.

In typical structural leadership form, Summit is always looking for something more to do, because it's those small things that can make the difference. She compares hard work to having a baby. It's like being in labor. There is no fun about it while it's happening. But you forget about the pain when you see that child. You forget about the long practices when you win championships.

Summitt says that we have to watch her team practice if we want to understand them. We have to see the intensity level with our own eyes to believe it. She challenges people to be the best they can be—every day. In practice, she expects the team to perform at a certain level, and she cannot abide them not giving their best effort because they only practice two hours a day. When they step off the floor, she doesn't demand that they spend their leisure time thinking about basketball or doing extra drills. She leaves them alone to live their college lives. But when they're on the court, she expects concentration and effort. So if you are selfish or you are lazy, you won't make it with Pat Summitt. Another structural frame behavior that Pat Summitt practices assiduously is planning. A lot of people say that they want to be the very best and win a national championship. Who wouldn't. But, according to Summitt it's not enough to say it, or even to mean it. If you want to succeed, you need to plan for success. Plan your work, and work your plan. You work every day in a disciplined and systematic way. The effective leader has to focus small, because attention to everyday, ordinary detail is what will separate you from everyone else. Everybody wants to win; but very few people are willing to *prepare* to win. Tennessee expects to win because they prepare to win in practice.

A competitive spirit is another structural trait that Summitt espouses. She has always understood that competitiveness is the first cousin to leadership. Blazing the trail is hard. You have to be competitive to do it. In Summitt we're talking about somebody who would fight a bear with a switch. She's known to be a competitor She is willing to take on all comers, whether it be cooking, or jogging, or arm wrestling. Competitors seek revenge for losses, she says. The secret to Tennessee's success in the post season is that they will have already played most of the teams they will face. Since Tennessee had often lost to some of them, they have a competitive advantage in the rematch, according to Summitt's way of thinking. Summitt had one player in particular, Shelley Sexton, who was especially "well-mannered" and in her mind, noncompetitive. "You know what happens to nice girls?" Summitt said, "they finish last" (p. 199).

Competitiveness is why Summitt stresses defense at Tennessee. They pride themselves on being very aggressive on defense. Summitt has to drum her defensive philosophy into her players' heads, and it's not fun for her. People don't naturally want to play defense. It's tough, and it takes a long time to teach. She has to convince them of its importance year in and year out. "Offense sells tickets, defense wins games, rebounds win championships" (p. 221).

Summitt also sees herself as a change agent, another structural frame behavior. She believes that change is good. However, she believes that it is also underrated. It's got a bad name. But how can you grow, if you never change? Without changing something almost every year, Tennessee would never have won five national championships, Summitt claims. If they had not changed, they would still be losing the big one. But breaking out of old habits, or cycles is hard work, and frightening. We naturally resist it out of laziness, or fear, or insecurity. She believes that the willingness to experiment with change may be the most essential ingredient to success at any endeavor.

Finally, in true structural frame fashion, with a hint of symbolic frame behavior thrown in, Summitt espouses her "Definite Dozen" as a road map to success:

1. Respect Yourself and Others
2. There Are No Shortcuts to Success
3. Develop and Demonstrate Loyalty
4. Learn to Be a Great Communicator
5. Discipline Yourself So No One Else Has To
6. Make Hard Work Your Passion
7. Don't Just Work Hard, Work Smart
8. Put the Team Before Yourself
9. Make Winning an Attitude
10. Be a Competitor
11. Change Is a Must
12. Handle Success Like You Handle Failure

THE HUMAN RESOURCE FRAME

Human resource leaders believe in people and communicate that belief. They are passionate about *productivity through people*. Although Pat Summitt's public image is one of a strict disciplinarian, privately, she makes liberal use of human resource leadership frame behavior. For example, she recalls her first encounter with a new team. Summitt didn't know them very well yet. And they didn't really know her because she was still treating them nicely. Hanging over them were pictures of dozens of past All Americans and the ten Olympians she have produced at Tennessee—more than double any other school. Among them were Nikki McCray, Carla McGhee, Bridgette Gordon, Daedra Charles. These players had all been undergraduates once—drilled relentlessly in the Definite Dozen and yelled at by Summitt at one time or another. But they were also like daughters, each with her own place in her heart.

One of Summitt's star players, Abby Conklin, had the following to say about Summitt's use of human resource frame behavior. "[I liked playing for Coach Summitt] because she makes you better. And she cares about you. I mean it's genuine, I love her to death. As hard as she is on you when you're on the court, she cares. She teaches more than basketball. She teaches you the things that are going to get you through the rest of your life" (p. 9).

Once again, Summitt's knowledge of how to lead was ingrained in her at an early age. She says that there is no such thing as self-respect without respect for others. It may sound like a riddle, but it isn't. She says that she does not know anyone who has succeeded all alone. Individual success is a myth, according to Summitt. We are all dependent on those around us. This is a fundamental truth that she learned growing up on a farm. It applies elsewhere, too. Especially in her locker room. So, her first rule is to respect others, no matter what their place on the team or in society, because respect is the first step toward team building. Treat people the way you like to be treated. It sounds simple enough. But she is always surprised at the ill manners some full-grown people can display, and how it can interfere with group solidarity.

Summitt believes that there are some simple ways to build mutual respect in a group. To her, eye contact is a sign of both self-respect and mutual respect—it demonstrates that you are confident enough to look at the person who is speaking and that you will give that person your full attention. Another simple matter of showing respect is being on time. When you think about it, being on time shows that you respect the other person. According to Summitt, lateness sends a message that you are either too sloppy, too careless, or too special to be on time. If your teammates or colleagues always have to wait on you, rancor builds and egos clash. "We have enough trouble putting twelve big egos together as it is" (p. 12).

Summitt is well aware of the need for human resource behavior, when appropriate. She says, that it may look like she is taking responsibility for some things that are none of her affair. But when you are the leader, you will be held responsible for everything, however trivial. If there's a problem with a player, everyone will hold the leader accountable. They will expect the leader to have done something to prevent the problem. So the players' personal problems are the coach's problems, too. Summitt assures her recruits and their parents of what to expect at Tennessee: tough love and constant monitoring. For these four years, it will be her responsibility to know, within reason, where they are and what they're doing. Summitt is convinced of that. "Because what it says is that

Tennessee doesn't just produce great players, we turn out people who are capable of assuming that kind of responsibility" (p. 31).

Pat Summitt also practices concern for the person in regard to setting the team rules. She consults with the players on most of the rules, so that they take some responsibility for *making* them, as well as *following* them. When players have input into establishing their own rules, suddenly the rules become "ours" rather than "hers." And they'll be responsible to each other, rather than solely to the coach.

Summitt tries to foster a family atmosphere among her team and the basketball community, which is another indication of her reliance on human relations behavior. She believes in the "family" model as being the most conducisive to success. She believes that it is easier to work with someone you have a regard for and a relationship with; someone you have shared good and bad with, and have developed some trust in and loyalty to. She thinks that the single most common reason organizations self-destruct is disloyalty, especially when they are made up of young people who have a tendency to talk behind each other's backs. In the family model, you can count on each other and the above is less likely to occur, she asserts.

In order to build a sound organization she believes that you must surround yourself with people who share the same basic values, people who are constant and who will be true to the organization. Creating a family atmosphere is, as far as she is concerned, the surest way to do that. Over the years at Tennessee, she has prided herself on the relationships with the families of the student athletes. Recently, at the suggestion of the team's sports psychologist, Dr. Nina Elliott, they held a team meeting in which all of the players and coaches brought in pictures of their families. They sat together and showed each other the pictures and talked about their parents and brothers and sisters, and described how they all grew up. Some of them cried. But at the end of that meeting they all knew each other a lot better, according to Summitt. They had created a support group. The next time someone is in a bad mood, or low, or struggling, they know which questions to ask in order to make the individual feel better.

Continuing in this vein, Summitt indicates that, for the purposes of creating a family atmosphere, she insists on being addressed on a first name basis by her players. She likes the way it sounds when she hears it.

It sounds like you came into her office to talk especially to her. You might not feel comfortable talking to Coach, or Head Coach, or Mrs. Summitt. You might not want to confide in someone that you had to call "Coach," but you most likely would in someone you could call "Pat." The application of human resource behavior does not only apply to her players. She feels the same way about her staff. She is often asked how she keeps her staff year-after-year and why they are so loyal? Her reply is how do you keep your family? You take care of your family, and you protect your family. How do you do that, she is often asked. Paying people well is a start, she says. That's why she has the highest-paid nanny in Knoxville. It's also why she fights for every available raise for the staffers she values. She insists that you must find a way to show that you appreciate them. Even with a simple gesture like buying them lunch.

Summit says that if you want to develop loyalty, the first thing you have to do is demonstrate it. Too many people use the term unilaterally. Especially bosses. They demand loyalty, without reciprocating. According to Summitt, you win with people. She doesn't care how good you are or what kind of a genius you may be. If you don't have a good, loyal staff, you will not succeed, she asserts.

Pat Summitt even gets her familial family involved in her human relations framed behavior. As Tyler, her young son, has grown up, he has become part of the fabric of the team. She worries that he sometimes has too many "aunts" and "sisters." But then she sees how much love and attention he gets, and how many wonderful relationships he is developing, and she feels great. For his first birthday, his "Aunt Mickie" gave him a pilot's crumpled flight plan from that fateful trip to the Final Four. There are times when Tennesse is on the road that Tyler insists on sleeping in Mickie's or Holly's room, instead of his mother's. Summit is not suggesting that you "live" with your players, but those shared personal experiences, whether they are shared arguments, laughs, weddings, funerals, births, wins, or losses, are the only way that she knows to build genuine long-term loyalties.

Continuing this thought, Summitt says, "My son is the one who finally taught me how to be freer with my feelings. I talked to Tyler every day when I was pregnant. When I took those daily walks, I chatted out loud to him the whole way. I'd talk about what we were going to do with our day, and how I couldn't wait until he got here. I'd tell him I thought he was probably going to be a red headed little boy with a temper, because there's a lot of redheads in our family with tempers. Things like that" (p. 74).

Another practice Summitt has that occasions the use of human relations behavior is the meetings that she has with each of her players. She meets four times a year with each player on her team, individually. She looks "eyeball to eyeball" and talks about everything from their fears to their ambitions. She clearly spells out what the player's role is and exactly what is expected of her, but more important, Summitt asks what *she* wants. After those talks, Summitt feels more in tune with the player. She knows what the player needs to hear to help her performance. "And I have heard *her*," she says (p. 69).

Another incident that Summitt recalls in which she displayed her propensity for human relations frame behavior was when she had one of her players, Bridgette Gordon, in her car and she decided to show Bridgette the other side of her personality. In general, her players were afraid to ride with her because she was so intense. In an empty parking lot she did some 360s with her car. She did it again, and then again, and then again. She did several 360s in that empty lot before she got tired of watching Bridgette Gordon's eyes widen. Nobody believes she is capable of that sort of behavior, but she is. But it took her a few years to get to the point where she would do something as spontaneous as that. She felt so consumed with work that it was difficult for her to develop relationships with her players—much less have fun with them. "You could practically see my gears grinding and the smoke pouring out from under my hood," she says. (p. 136).Making that breakthrough was a bonding experience for Summitt and Gordon. They became especially close. She practically became part of Summitt's family. And, her players will ride with her now. But it's not nearly as easy as it sounds, according to Summitt. Human beings are not socket wrenches. "They are extremely complicated, enormously inconsistent, and they change emotional shape on you all the time" (p. 138).

Summitt learned that hard work wasn't much use without intelligence and understanding. In the early years, she ran her teams ragged. She was not fully conscious of just how hard she was working her players until they walked off the court. But it hit her as soon as she left the arena.

Her point guard, Dawn March, said, as she limped on to the team bus. "Boy, that was a hard practice." All of the sudden Summitt felt poorly about it. She knew she had asked too much of them. Summitt had not appropriately supplemented her structural frame behavior with her human resource frame behavior.

Another time when Summitt learned the need to temper her leadership behavior with human relations behavior was when she called a time out in a crucial game and set up a play for one of her star players, Pat Hatmaker. But, instead of shooting, Hatmaker passed the ball to a teammate. As a result, the play backfired and Tennessee lost the game to Louisiana Tech. Reflecting on that incident, Summitt says, "And the person who learned the most that day was not Pat Hatmaker. It was the other Pat. Me" (p. 142).

She benefited more than anyone else that day, because she realized that she had not done a good job of understanding the personnel with whom she was working. And she really had not understood an individual's specific reaction to pressure situations. Everyone handles pressure in a different way. That's when people will hide from responsibility or bend under the fear of failure. Prior to even getting on the court, you must have a working knowledge of how people will respond to pressure. What Summitt learned was she was the person at fault. She admits that no coach, leader, or manager should be that ignorant of their personnel. Tennessee was playing in the semifinal game of the Final Four, and Summitt's whole offensive strategy was designed to get the ball to Pat Hatmaker, and Pat didn't want the ball. Not once had Summitt sat down with her and asked, "Pat, how would you feel if we were in this situation?" Seven years into her coaching career, Pat Summitt admitted that she should have known better.

Summitt believes that it is the responsibility of a leader, or manager, or CEO to know who you can delegate to and when. The obvious question is, how can you know these things? By talking with people, first and foremost, she suggests. But there are also some tools that can help. One of them is the Predictive Index, which Summitt has used for the last ten years in an attempt to understand her players better. A personality profile gives a coach a tool to determine how and when she needs to reach a player. If all her life she's thrived on approval, then you would use that to motivate her. Summitt searches for ways to draw the best out of her players. She also makes it a point to hire people who have qualities in which she is deficient. By evaluating her own strengths and weaknesses, she is able to put people in a position to complement her personality traits.

According to Summitt, teamwork does not come naturally. It needs to be fostered by human resource frame behavior. Summitt points out, that when two or more children get together in one room, what do they fight about? Sharing, that's what. They hate to share. Tears roll down their faces over the cheapest plastic toy, simply because another child wants to play with it. She has witnessed entire teams acting in this way. And, in most cases, those teams lost. Her point is, teamwork is taught. Teamwork is really a form of trust. She says that teamwork is what makes common people capable of uncommon results.

In the same vein, Summitt recalls another instance when the application of human resource behavior fostered teamwork. It occurred when she was coaching the U.S. Olympic team and needed to make the final cut. She allowed the players to make a crucial decision in shaping the team during the Olympic Trials. The team was down to eighteen players, and a decision had to be made to cut the roster down to twelve. She told *them* to do it. It meant that the squad went to the Olympics believing that it was *their* team. Not Summitt's. They felt that all-important sense of ownership and were willing to play their assigned roles without complaint. She took the twelve players they wanted. It preempted potential problems. She believes that if you want to have a real team, you have to involve the team members in the decision-making process.

In true human resource fashion, Pat Summitt tells her players, "My real victories and championships are not made of polished wood and metal. My victories are you." She continues, "If there is one thing I would like to be more successful at, it's this: I would sincerely like to develop a greater understanding between me and our players" (p. 254).

So, where does Pat Summitt derive her human resource behavior tendencies? One of her players, Carla McGhee, believes that she has the answer. "Let me tell you something," she says. "There is one person who really has her number. Tyler. He's the only person who keeps her in check. She's a total sucker for him. She thinks she's in charge of that relationship, but she's not. That boy is running things" (p. 250).

THE SYMBOLIC FRAME

In the symbolic frame, the organization is seen as a stage, a theater in which every actor plays certain roles and the symbolic leader attempts to communicate the right impressions to the right audiences. Pat Summitt clearly knows how and when to use the symbolic frame of leadership. When asked to explain her success, she uses the symbol of her "Definite Dozen," described earlier. Whenever she is asked to explain the remarkable accomplishments of her teams, she points to a placard posted in the most central place in our locker room. It says, THE DEFINITE DOZEN. The Definite Dozen is a set of commandments. It is Tennessee's most basic set of rules. Summitt believes that it is her blueprint for winning.

Summitt is careful in the way she presents herself because of the symbolic effect that it might have. She says that she realized that presentation counts very early in her career. She says that for better or worse, strangers made sweeping judgments based on her appearance and demeanor. She responded by beginning a process of self-transformation. In her mind, dressing appropriately for a role can help you play it better. It has certainly helped her, whether as a coach, a mother, a teacher, or a speaker. She cares about clothes and other external things because they help form a perception, but she also cares about them because she seeks perfection whether it about her shoes or her grammar. Her quest for self-improvement has never really ended, and is symbolic of her reputation as a perfectionist.

Summitt knows full well the need to model desired behavior. She says that two things must happen before she can demand responsible behavior from the team at large. (1) She has to demonstrate to her team that she will fulfill her own responsibilities. For instance, she admits to not being the most punctual human being. But she makes it a point never, ever to be late for a team meeting or a practice. (2) She must make sure that the responsibilities of her players and staff are clearly delineated and that everyone understands them. Another form of symbolic behavior that Summitt applies is that shown in her locker room. There is a pole on which the players are permitted to place their signatures only if they graduate. A visitor to the locker room can see the graffiti autographs of all the former Tennessee greats in magic marker. It has become a ceremonial honor to leave a signature on that pole. But if you don't graduate with a degree, you can't sign. Summitt says that people were shocked by that. It made *USA Today* and ran on the wire services and generally contributed to her reputation as the General George Patton on women's basketball. But she had made her point: If you don't fulfill your responsibilities, you will be held accountable. Tennessee's locker room is a privilege, a mark of excellence. And Summitt did not feel that they were being excellent in any way if they did not graduate.

The effect of Summitt's symbolic behavior is reflected in the reaction of her players. At times, Summitt says that all she has to do is *look* at somebody to make her hear her. Niya Butts says about her: "She has that stare. I don't know how she can stare at you for so long without blinking. She must have had surgery (p. 66)." Another symbolic gesture on the part of Summitt is her insistence on sitting in the middle of the bench rather than at the end. She sits herself right smack in the middle of the bench, with her assistants on either side of her. The reason that she does so is that she wants to be able to "get at" her players. She wants to look them in the eye and communicate with them. Secondly, she doesn't want players sitting at the end of the bench, complaining and inattentive. She hates the effect that it has on the team, and she hates the way it looks to the fans.

At the beginning of each season, Summitt gives her players a sheet of paper and asks them to list their values. The sheet is blank, with the numbers one through ten. She asks them to list their values in order. She tells them they don't have to list all ten. She just wants to know a few of the things that are important to them. This practice is another instance of symbolic leadership behavior.

In making her point about the power of teamwork, Summitt again uses symbolic frame leadership behavior. Summitt gives all 12 players on her team a pencil. Then she asks them to break the pencils. They do so with no problem. But what if we take twelve pencils, and bind them together with a rubber band? Now try to break them. You can't. That is the basic principle of teamwork.

Summitt's religious faith has a great effect on her use of symbolic behavior. She considers herself a believer. She believes in God. There are a lot of skeptics in this world, she says, but she is not one of them. She considers herself to be reverent to the bone. She attended Mount Carmel United Methodist Church every Sunday morning, and on a lot of weekday evenings too. She believes that belief is a fairly practical matter. Most people think of it as something mystical, or, at least, highly conceptual, she points out. She doesn't, however. To her, the strongest kind of belief is one grounded in reality.

Applying her religious beliefs to her practice, Summitt says that with a combination of practice and belief, the most ordinary team is capable of extraordinary things. Every day she handed out a thought for the day. One of them said, "Fate saves a warrior when his courage endures." What it means is, if you keep fighting, blindly, in a positive and courageous way, sometimes chance will rescue you" (p. 178).

In still another example of symbolic leadership behavior, Summitt posted the following poem in her locker room:

> You can love me
> But only I can make me happy.
> You can teach me
> But only I can do the learning.
> You can lead me
> But only I can walk the path.
> You can promote me
> But I have to succeed.
> You can coach me
> But I have to win the game.
> You can even pity me
> But I have to bear the sorrow.
> For the Gift of Love
> Is not a food that feeds me.
> It is the sunshine
> That nourishes that which I must finally harvest for myself.
> So if you love me
> Don't just sing me your song.
> Teach me to sing,
> For when I am alone,
> I will need the melody.
>
> —Dan Baker

According to Pat Summitt, "The meaning of the poem is this: I can challenge you, and teach you and discipline you. But ultimately it's up to each of you to make the right choices" (p. 256).

THE POLITICAL FRAME

Leaders operating out of the political frame clarify what they want and what they can get. Political leaders are realists above all. They never let what they want cloud their judgment about what is possible. They assess the distribution of power and interests.

Needless to say, for a woman like Pat Summitt to have succeeded the way that she has in a historically male-dominated sport like basketball, she must have made good and frequent use of political leadership frame behavior. Her attitude toward the advancement of women's causes is typical of a leader operating out of the political frame. "There are two ways to break through a glass ceiling," she says. "You can scream and kick at it and try to shatter it with your high heels. Or you can learn to cut glass. I chose to be a glass cutter" (p. 151).

She continues in this vein indicating that if the men's basketball team got twenty new pairs of game shoes, she didn't go to the administration and make a scene, demanding twenty pairs of game shoes for the women. She only asked for three pairs, because that was all that they needed. If you ask for what you need, and no more, people will be inclined to give you what you want. And they'll be more inclined to listen to you on those occasions when you do take a stand, Summitt maintains.

CONCLUSION

Despite Pat Summitt's self-described image as the General George Patton of women's basketball, there is abundant evidence that she appropriately utilizes all four frames of leadership behavior described by Bolman and Deal. Although it can be said that she is primarily a structural leader, which leads to her reputation as a strict disciplinarian, her use of the human relations, symbolic, and political frames is also apparent.

This apparent contradiction speaks to Summitt's contrasting public and private images. Her public image is undoubtedly one of a strictly structural leader. However, when one examines her more private behavior, it is quite obvious that she effectively balances her leadership behavior, depending on the circumstances, and is therefore a truly situational leader. This balanced approach toward the application of leadership behavior is something to be admired, and it makes Pat Summitt someone for leaders and aspiring leaders to emulate.

JOHN THOMPSON

> John Thompson is a great coach and a better human being.
>
> —Dean Smith

BACKGROUND

John Thompson was born on September 2, 1941, in Washington, D.C., and he is a former basketball coach of Georgetown University. He is now a professional radio and television sports commentator. In 1984 he became the first African American head coach to win the National Collegiate Athletic Association (NCAA) Men's Division I Basketball Championship when Georgetown defeated Houston University.

After attending Archbishop John Carroll High School in Washington, D.C., Thompson went to Providence College. At Providence, Thompson was part of the 1963 National Invitation Tournament (NIT) Championship team, and was part of the first Providence NCAA tournament team in 1964. He was an All-American in his senior year. He graduated as the school leader in points, scoring average, and field goal percentage, and second in rebounds. He played 2 years in the National Basketball Association (NBA) for the Boston Celtics in 1964–66. At 6 feet 10 inches, 270 pounds, he backed up Bill Russell, the Celtics' star center, en route to two championships. Nicknamed "The Caddy" for his secondary role to Russell, he retired in 1966 to coach at Saint Anthony High School near Washington, D.C. After accumulating an impressive 122-28 record as a high school coach, Thompson was hired to become the head coach of the men's basketball team at Georgetown University.

Thompson, an imposing figure on the sidelines who towered over many opposing coaches, was often noted for the trademark white towel that he carried on his shoulder during the games. Inheriting a Georgetown team that had been just 3-23 the year before, Thompson quickly and dramatically improved the team, making the NCAA tournament within three seasons. Over the following 27 years, Thompson's Hoyas went an impressive 597-239, running off a streak of 24 postseason appearances—20 in the NCAA tournament, 4 in the NIT—including a 14-year streak of NCAA appearances from 1979–92 that saw three Final Four appearances in 1982, 1984, and 1985, winning a national championship in 1984 and narrowly missing a repeat the next year by losing to underdog Villanova in one of the greatest upsets in college basketball history.

Thompson still holds conference records for most overall Big East wins (231), most regular-season Big East wins (198), and conference championships (seven regular season, six tournaments). He won seven coach of the year awards: Big East (1980, 1987, 1992), U.S. Basketball Writers Association and the *Sporting News* (1984), National Association of Basketball Coaches (1985), and United Press International (1987). Thompson coached many notable players, including Patrick Ewing, Sleepy Floyd, Alonzo Mourning, Dikembe Mutombo, and Allen Iverson.

Thompson, who had served as an assistant coach for the gold medal winning team in the 1976 summer Olympics, coached the U.S. team at the 1988 summer Olympics. Although favored to win the international tournament, the United States was narrowly defeated by the Soviet Union in the semifinals, marking the first time the United States did not reach the gold medal game. The team proceeded to win its final game against Australia to secure the bronze medal.

On January 8, 1999, Thompson shocked the sports world by announcing his resignation as Georgetown's head coach, citing marriage problems. For those who knew him well the announcement seemed odd and ill-timed, since the family problems he cited had been in the public eye since November 17, 1997, the date on which Gwendolyn Thompson first filed for divorce. Both these issues fueled speculation that Thompson was being forced to step down. The legendary coach was inducted into the Basketball Hall of Fame on October 1, 1999. Thompson was replaced by longtime assistant Craig Esherick, a popular player's coach. Esherick, however, would not be able to sustain Thompson's success and was fired in 2004 and replaced by John Thompson III, the former coach's eldest son. At the time the elder Thompson was serving Georgetown in what Leo J. O'Donavan, university president, referred to as a "coach emeritus" position, assisting on academic, athletic, and community projects.

After retiring from coaching, Thompson continued to be active in basketball as a commentator for both professional and collegiate games. He also hosts *The John Thompson Show*, a sports talk show on Sports-Talk 980 (WTEM-AM) in Washington, D.C. Thompson signed a lifetime contract with Clear Channel Radio and SportsTalk 980 in February 2006. He continues to spend a lot of time around the Georgetown basketball program, including traveling to road games and participating in press conferences.

SITUATIONAL LEADERSHIP ANALYSIS

Situational leadership models differ from other trait and behavioral models in asserting that no single way of leading works in all situations. Rather, appropriate behavior depends on the circumstances at a given time. Effective managers diagnose the situation, identify the leadership style or behavior that will be most effective, and then determine whether they can implement the required style.

John Thompson's image is that of the prototypical structural leader. He is perceived as a strict disciplinarian and very demanding person. However, when one looks more closely, we find that Thompson is very situational in his approach to leadership. For example, when Thompson talks about the people who played critical roles in his life, Red Auerbach's name is usually mentioned. "As much as anybody that I look back on, he made the adjustments over different periods of time. He passed from era to era extremely well. He manages and handles men, and the other responsibilities that go with coaching as well as anybody" (Shapiro, 1991, p. 52; all cites in this chapter, unless otherwise noted, are from this source).

Thompson's own philosophy reflected the situational nature of Red Auerbach's approach. Describing that coaching philosophy, Thompson said, "I like to run and do a lot of things defensively, but what style of play we would use ultimately would depend on the type players we could bring to Georgetown" (p. 89).

Thompson is often criticized for not being situational especially in coaching the Olympic team the way he did at Georgetown, emphasizing an intricate full court–pressing defense that would be difficult to teach a team of all-stars in such a short time. There was even talk that some of Thompson's Olympic players were not particularly happy being berated Georgetown style in ruggedly physical practice sessions that summer. On the other hand, Mitch Richmond, one of his Olympic team members, said, "After we lost to the Russians, I guess we all thought that he would go off on us. It was our first loss, and some of us knew how he would react. I didn't know whether he'd start screaming and yelling or throwing stuff. Some guys were probably afraid. But he calmed us down a lot. He just said we worked hard and it wasn't meant to be. That's all" (p. 255).

Questioning Thompson's situational abilities, *Philadelphia Daily News* columnist, Dick Weiss, wrote, "The international game is a game for the offensive-minded. That was something Thompson never grasped. The Americans' ball movement on offense was a disaster" (p. 256). This criticism was reinforced by University of Pittsburgh basketball coach, Paul Evans who said, "It's very tough to teach his style of defense. I don't know if you can coach his style of play in such a short time, get kids like that gung ho to play that style" (p. 257).

However, many of Thompson's coaching colleagues have since stood up in his defense. Dean Smith and many others insisted that the improvement in international basketball had been phenomenal over the past decade and that American teams no longer were guaranteed victory anytime they walked on the court, and Thompson's failure to adjust had nothing to do with the loss. As a matter of fact, this loss lead to the decision to allow American professionals to play in the Olympics and spawned the participation of the "Dream Team" in the next Olympics.

Despite this criticism of Thompson's ability to adjust his leadership style to the situation, we will see that Thompson is relatively adroit at appropriately operating out of all four frames of leadership.

THE STRUCTURAL FRAME

Structural leaders develop a new model of the relationship of structure, strategy, and environment for their organizations. As we shall clearly see, John Thompson makes abundant use of structural frame leadership behavior.

John Thompson often talked about the concept known as "bogarding," a distinctively Washington, D.C., term that goes a long way in defining his philosophy of life. Patterned after the on-screen persona of Humphrey Bogart, "bogarding" meant taking control of the situation, walking and talking with authority, and being prepared to back it up, on and off the basketball court. It was playground power, pure and simple. According to Leonard Shapiro, in his book, *Big Man on Campus*, "John Thompson learned all about that at the very early age, and, in a sense, he has been bogarding his way through life ever since" (p. 5).

It is well known that Thompson focused on structural leadership behavior. Thompson preferred to jam the ball inside to a big man, crash the boards nonstop, and run a controlled, disciplined fast break when the opportunity presented itself. On defense, his teams were always superbly conditioned and kamikaze oriented—diving on the floor for every loose ball, trapping and pressing full court, and capable of smoothly switching back and forth from a variety of zones and man-to-man formations designed to confuse their opponents. This system became known as the "Georgetown Way."

According to Shapiro, a longtime observer of John Thompson, Thompson's players come mostly from Black America, some with subpar high school grades and educational skills that would seem certain to spell failure at such an elite, prestigious Jesuit University as Georgetown, a school with an impeccable academic reputation for producing diplomats, doctors, lawyers and leaders of industry, commerce and high finance. Yet when his players leave Thompson and his program after four years, 98% have earned their diplomas, an enviable record in almost two decades of big time college sport rocked by scandals as diverse as point shaving, blatant cheating to recruit athletes, academic fraud to keep them in school, the use of illegal drugs and more felonies and misdemeanors, right up to rape, armed robbery, and murder than occurred in all of amateur American sports before 1973. His mentor, Red Auerbach, influenced Thompson in his strong use of structural behavior, with a sprinkling of human relations behavior. Red Auerbach's genius as a coach was mostly based on his skills as a motivator. He was a master psychologist who knew that there are as many different ways to psyche people. He knew that he had to yell at Heinsohn, whereas he bullied Satch Sanders, and Don Nelson in a cruel, offhanded, matter-of-fact way. With K.C. Jones you had to be honest and leave him alone; he'd do the rest. Thompson watched Red spend time with the Celtics who played the least, the guys at the end of the bench. He expected them not to smolder all season over their lack of playing time, but he always talked to them enough to remind them how important substitutes are to a team. He tended to be more supportive of them than he was of the regulars.

Thompson grew to respect Auerbach's ability to distill the game of basketball to its essence and patterned his leadership behavior after that of his mentor. Auerbach said that he had never been much for Xs and Os and all kinds of fancy diagrams. Throughout his career, he believed that mastery of the *fundamentals* of the sophisticated game basketball is still what separates the men from the boys. Keep it simple; that was his rule. Auerbach was talking about the Celtics philosophy of course, but clearly all of those concepts were incorporated into Thompson's system.

Other structural-type behavior came from Thompson's friendship with Bill Russell. Bill Russell once said about Thompson that they were philosophical allies. Thompson noted that Russell was black before it was fashionable to be black. Both men have developed their own standards as opposed to accepting the standards of others. Thompson believed that Russell came as close to anybody in his life who did what he wanted to do the way he wanted to do it.

Another person who influenced Thompson in his use of structural frame leadership behavior is Dean Smith, the former North Carolina coach. When Thompson assisted Smith with the U.S. Olympic team, he learned the nuances of the game of basketball. Smith was a superb teacher, and Thompson was taking notes on his principles of pressure defense, his use of run-and-jump traps, his disguising defenses, his four-corners offence. As much as the players were learning Thompson was also getting the benefit of a two-month, 24-hour-a-day coaching clinic from a master of the game. When Thompson returned to Georgetown, in fact, many of Smith's drills were incorporated into his practice session, and he would take the Smith Philosophy and blend it with his own to the point where some would say Georgetown became the Carolina of the North.

Thompson's structural frame philosophy was made clear in his recruitment of Patrick Ewing. Thompson's "pitch" stressed academics, but touched on all aspects of his philosophy. He told Ewing that education is about change—if you have the potential, it would be Thompson's job to make Ewing reach that potential. Thompson demanded that players travel in coats and ties in public because they have a responsibility to represent Georgetown. Mary Fenlon, his academic coordinator, became his conscience. Freshman were required to meet with Mary every day. They had to answer questions in Thompson's book concerning academics: cutting classes, grades, class work. Thompson warned them against signing the book if there were any lies in it. Further, Thompson feels that no one should take the place of your parents. He is not a player's father and Mary is not his mother. But they are there to help guide them and to aid their development. Shapiro says of Thompson, "'God help anybody who is black.' John says, 'I will not give you anything because you are black, or take away anything because you are white.' He has no athletic dormitory. He wants you to meet people and make contact with people other than athletes who will help you find human resources for the future. Georgetown's responsibility is to protect your individuality and not let the public out there know everything that goes on concerning you as a person" (p. 176).

As a result of this structural behavior approach, Thompson's teams are disciplined, incredibly conditioned and thoroughly relentless, particularly on defense, where Thompson truly excelled.

THE HUMAN RESOURCE FRAME

Human resource leaders believe in people and communicate that belief. They are passionate about *productivity through people*. Although John

Thompson is a coach with a stern image usually associated with leaders who operated almost exclusively out of the structural behavior frame, there is much evidence that Thompson realized that to be a truly effective leader, he must appropriately utilize human resource behavior. He can be the compassionate coach who once seemed to hug a player to death after the poor soul threw a pass to an opponent that cost his team the national championship and the man North Carolina's Dean Smith describes as a great coach and a better human being. Even in college, he would always stay and sign autographs for the kids. He only had a problem when he thought that people wanted to be with him or around him just because he was an athlete.

There is much evidence that Thompson did enjoy working with children. In his senior year he was a student teacher at Central Junior High School in East Providence, and he made a significant impression. He was assigned to a class of children with low IQs, some ranging between 60–80. Thompson said that he enjoyed seeing the smiles come across the children's faces when they finally understand the point being made. They appreciated the help so much that it gave him a feeling of great satisfaction. He did not know at the time if he had the right temperament or the necessary patience to teach these children, but he wanted to try. Thompson's supervising teacher at the time, Julia Sanderson, noted that Thompson was so tall, such a celebrity, yet he walked down the aisle and got down on his knees to help a little boy or girl with arithmetic. She observed that they all loved him so.

Red Auerbach once observed of Thompson's human side, that some people say he is a hostile man. But he is a very caring man. He acts the way he does because he does not want people getting too close. He learned that from Red Auerback and Bill Russell; be in control and put the others on the defensive. However, one of Auerbach's other priorities was creating a family atmosphere among the players, which Thompson emulated. He believed in making a basketball team a family, keeping private matters inside the family, keeping insiders in and outsiders, particularly the media, outside.

Another instance of Thompson using human relations leadership behavior was in his insistence that his athletes do well academically. Even as a high school coach, Thompson's players knew that unless they performed in the classroom, they would not be allowed to practice or play in the games. He checked their work, stayed in touch with their teachers and monitored their grades. Donald Washington, one of Thompson's players at Georgetown, missed a few classes during his freshman season. Thompson's friend, Dean Smith, found out about it and reported it to Thompson. Thompson was at Washington's residence by ten o'clock that night. He said to him that unlike some of his buddies whose fathers are presidents of companies and when they goof off, they still have a job, he didn't have that luxury.

Father R. J. Henle, the president of Georgetown who hired Thompson, said that he offered him the job and Thompson said he wanted to add a new staff member, an academic advisor, to the team to ride herd on the players. Fr. Henle said, "you've got it!" Thompson said that he wanted to be known as an educator. He wanted them all to get a Georgetown degree.

Further evidence of Thompson's concern for human resource behavior even this early in his career came from one of his Saint Anthony High School players Greg Brookes. Brookes recalled that when John took the Georgetown job, it was a foregone conclusion. His players respected him enough that if he wanted them to go to Georgetown, they would have pretty much followed him anywhere he wanted them to go. Thompson, himself, tried to assuage their fears, telling them they had a chance to get in on the ground floor of the program, that it would be a struggle but that he would be there with them every step of the way. Another of his players, Mark Edwards, said of Thompson that he took some players who really needed his guidance, people like John Smith and Merlin Wilson, and literally changed their lives.

A more dramatic incident that demonstrated Thompson's deep concern for his players and others' welfare and operating out of the human relations frame was when, after a couple of key loses early in his career at Georgetown, some students rolled out a sign that read: THOMPSON, THE NIGGER FLOP, MUST GO!

Reverend Ed Glynn, then a Georgetown administrator and later president of Saint Peters College in Jersey City said that it would be difficult to articulate how stunning that episode was to the Georgetown community, and particularly to John Thompson. But Thompson's first reaction told Fr. Glynn and the Georgetown community a lot. He said, "Those little kids that saw that—it'll be in their memory banks forever (p. 113).

Felix Yeoman, another of Thompson's Georgetown players, recalls the time when Thompson once again acted out of the human resources frame. Larry Long, a starter, missed three crucial games with a foot injury. However, only at a team meeting did they find out from Larry that he had been unable to play because of serious academic problems. Thompson never told them because he didn't want Larry to be publically humiliated. Making this known would have taken the pressure off of Thompson. But once again, John Thompson was just the opposite of a "nigger flop." Yeoman noted that all of the team members knew of many such personal instances when Thompson protected them from public criticism and shouldered the blame himself.

Steve Martin, one of Thompson's players who ultimately graduated from Georgetown, said that it seemed like Thompson could tell when an individual player was down. He always stayed in touch. According to Martin, he wanted to make sure his players were not discouraged. There were times when Martin was second-guessing his decision to attend Geogetown. At one point, he almost left. But one day he had a long conversation with Thompson. Thompson called him into his office and talked him into staying. Martin considers it the best decision that he has ever made.

Thompson also extended this human side to those outside the immediate Georgetown community. For example, when Mitch Kupchak, the North Carolina star that Thompson met when he was coaching the U.S. Olympic team, was recovering from a serious knee surgery a few years later, Thompson allowed him to rehab at Georgetown. At the time, Kupchak was a pro and Thompson had no responsibility to him, but he treated him as one of his own and allowed him to rehabilitate his injury at Georgetown. In a similar instance, when Lefty Driesell was under siege in the wake of the cocaine-induced death of his star player Len Bias, Thompson publicly defended him and criticized the school for firing him. Thompson said that he "bled" for Driesell at that time.

Numerous other instances when Thompson operated out of the human resource frame include his relationship with his star player Patrick Ewing. Mike Jarvis, Ewing's high school coach, remembered that Ewing instantly trusted Thompson, and felt he had a coach he could talk to and confide in, a man who would understand from firsthand experience what it was like to be 7 feet tall in a much smaller world. Another similar instance involved Fred Brown throwing the ball away and losing the NCAA Championship game against North Carolina. Instead of throwing a tantram, Thompson told Brown that he had won more games for him than he had lost and he was not to worry. It was just one of those human errors.

Immediately after that same game, Thompson once again demonstrated human resource behavior, not to his own player, but to the opposing coach. After the final buzzer, Thompson smiled and lifted Dean Smith off the ground in an embrace that clearly was from the heart. His old friend had finally won a national championship, and with Patrick Ewing around for another three years, there would still be time for John Thompson and the Georgetown Hoyas to win one of their own in the near future.

Lastly, there are a number of Thompson observers who have witnessed the the soft and soppy side to the man: John Thompson who cried the day his first recruiting class graduated; the man who lovingly cared for his mother over the last years of her life, lifting Anna Thompson in his arms to her daily morning bath; the man who once called a nervous young colleague who had just been named head basketball coach at a local university to offer encouragement and some advice. That young coach, Ed Tapscott, the first black coach at American University, received a call one night just a couple of days after he had been hired at American. Much to his surprise, on the other end of the line was John Thompson. Like any 28-year-old in that kind of position, he was a little nervous, wondering what he had gotten himself into. But on the other end of the line he heard a deep voice that he vaguely recognized, with a slightly bemused tone. Thompson asked Tapscott if he was still awake. Because if he was not, there was no way in which he would beat Georgetown next year when they played their traditional game. That gesture was so reassuring to Tapscott that he remembers it to this day.

THE SYMBOLIC FRAME

In the symbolic frame, the organization is seen as a stage, a theater in which every actor plays certain roles and the symbolic leader attempts to communicate the right impressions to the right audiences. John Thompson makes significant use of the symbolic frame of leadership behavior, beginning with his trademark white towel draped over his shoulder to indicate that he is your typical "blue collar" coach and that he is working just as hard as his players.

Thompson learned to utilize the symbolic leadership frame early on in his career. At Georgetown he took over a foundering program, but he made sure that when the team opened its first season against Saint Francis of Loretta College, there were plenty of changes. The locker room, once a dingy little space with cold concrete floors, had been enlarged and new carpet had been put on the floor. The basketball court had been reconditioned with a picture of the school mascot, a bulldog, painted at midcourt.

Even in his days at Saint Anthony High School, Thompson liked to use symbolic leadership behavior, when appropriate. Thompson was fond of displaying a deflated basketball on his office shelf. When high school recruits inquired about the ball with no air, John Thompson asks them if they have thought about life after basketball. Perhaps it is a little obscure, but still thought-provoking. He continued to display that deflated basketball even when he was at Georgetown.

Another use of the symbolic frame was how Thompson created and maintained his team's image as an indomitable force to be reckoned with. In years past, particularly during the Patrick Ewing era of the early 1980s, they played a confrontational style of basketball that enhanced their image as a swaggering bunch of bullies, an image that even now makes Georgetown jackets and tee shirts the fashion of choice among young people from coast to coast, not to mention countless kids from Harlem to Watts who dreamed of playing for the big man with the perpetual scowl on his face and the trademark towel draped over his shoulder.

Sometimes, however, the use of symbolic behavior was less than effective. Pat Ewing's menacing demeanor and the hard-nosed style of play his teams exhibited also created a downside for Thompson and his program. In many quarters he was no longer "St. John," the altruistic educator. By the mid-1980s he was "Big Bad John" the head paranoid of a team that thrived on secrecy, intimidation, and aggressive physical play.

Thompson openly acknowledges his use of symbolic behavior when he indicates that there are great individuals and teams with an abundance of talent that don't win. He tells his kids that it is as though they're putting on a play. He's the director. He's going to pick the script and he's going to give them their roles. They're the actors. Their job is to learn their roles—that's what practice is all about. When they go out on the basketball court, that's their stage. Out there, he wants them to perform as they practiced—no improvising.

There are those who believe that Thompson's 1983–84 national championship team symbolized "The Georgetown Way," and its performance in the Big East tournament that same season was a classic example of the intimidating style of play that sent shivers of fear throughout college basketball

Another instance of Thompson's use of symbolic frame behavior was after Georgetown had been upset by Villanova in Thompson's pursuit of a second consecutive national championship. After the game in the Georgetown locker room, John Thompson told his players they learned how to win a national championship the year before, and now it is time to show the world they know how to lose, with style and grace as well. When the game was over, the Georgetown players huddled at the foul line briefly, then stood at their bench and applauded respectfully as the Villanova supporters mobbed their team on the court. Thompson instructed them: "We know how to win, now we have to know how to lose" (p. 235).

Thompson used a combination of symbolic and political frame leadership behavior in protesting the passage by the NCAA of Propositions 42/48, which increased the academic requirements for student-athletes. Thompson thought it was particularly unfair to minority athletes.

In reaction to the news, he left the building and got into his car, driving around the city and listening to the games on the radio. He decided to boycott the team's next game four days later at Providence. This time, he never left Washington, though his trademark towel was draped on an empty chair in the middle of the Georgetown bench area where Thompson normally would be sitting. Thompson's protest resulted in almost immediate reaction from the NCAA. A day after the Providence game, Albert White, the president of the NCAA, announced that he would recommend legislation that would postpone any changes in Proposition 48, including Proposition 42, until the NCAA had finished studying the relationship of academic success in college to high school grade point average and standardized test scores.

THE POLITICAL FRAME

Leaders operating out of the political frame clarify what they want and what they can get. Political leaders are realists above all. They never let what they want cloud their judgment about what is possible. They assess the distribution of power and interests. John Thompson makes very astute use of political behavior. The above case regarding his protestation of the passage of Propositions 42/48 is typical.

According to many observers, Thompson trusts few people, but he seems intensely loyal to many of his friends. His program is criticized for having been almost entirely black, yet Mary Fenlon, his longtime academic coordinator and assistant coach and perhaps his best friend and alter ego, is white, as are his chief recruiter, his longtime trainer, and his top assistant coach on the Olympic team, a college teammate who worked as an assistant at Georgetown for ten years. One could easily speculate that Thompson was operating out of the political frame in forging these relationships. This assertion would be reinforced by what Vinnie Ernst, a teammate of Thompson's at Providence, had to say about him. "I always had the sense that he was afraid people wanted to use him" (p. 48).

Much of Thompson's political frame behavior can be attributed to the mistrust that he allegedly had for much of the establishment. For instance, Thompson has also said he would never have taken the assistant's job at the Olympics for any other coach but Dean Smith. Thompson claims that too many black coaches in the past became symbols as the U.S. Olympic basketball team assistant. He was not interested in being the "token" black.

Thompson used political frame behavior in making a name for himself. He was learning the fine art of making friends and influencing people to enhance his chances of landing better players. For example, Georgetown was a very good customer of Howard Garfinkel, the New Yorker who ran all-star summer camps where Thompson could recruit great players. With four subscriptions to Garfinkel's newsletter, when one would have been more than sufficient, he endeared himself to this very influential man.

Thompson used political behavior in his dealings with Lefty Driesell, the coach of Maryland and his archrival in the recruiting wars in the

Washington, D.C., area. By the time Thompson became coach at Georgetown, Driesell had long been recognized as the powerbroker of college basketball in the Washington area. So, here was Thompson, the upstart threatening Driesell's stranglehold on Washington area basketball interests. As a result, their relationship was always strained. Still, Thompson was careful not to offend the big state university down the road, and acted out of the political frame by paying a visit to College Park to learn more about the marketing tools former Maryland promotions director Russ Patts had used to help sell out Cole Field House, where Maryland played its home games.

During the 1980 season, Thompson and Driesell got into a shouting match during a regular season game between the two rivals. Thompson refused to shake Driesell's hand after the game. However, Thompson once again used political frame behavior to help resolve the situation. Maryland and Georgetown did meet once more that same season in the NCAA tournament, with Georgetown prevailing again. Before that game, however, Thompson publicly apologized to Driesell for the incident months earlier. He took complete responsibility for the incident and admitted he was wrong. Case closed!

Thompson consciously utilized political frame leadership behavior in order to get his points across. He maintains that he abhors the advice of those who suggest that he stick to sports and not speak out about issues in which he is not expert. He responds that if he has to do something controversial to get attention for his players, he will continue to do so. He also used political frame behavior in his negotiations with Georgetown and other universities regarding his services as a coach. Thompson had many job offers over the years, but one in particular, an offer from the University of Oklahoma, demonstrated Thompson's use of the political frame. He was very impressed by his trip to the Southwest and the basketball facilities and the salary increase available there. For several days back in Washington he agonized over his decision. Could he uproot his wife and the two boys? What about his staff at Georgetown and the players he had recruited? And what about his loyalty to Georgetown, a school that had taken a huge chance on him light years before, supported him in the terrible times, and allowed him to build a program his way, with virtually no interference? So, he decided to stay and in the process built up even more political capital for himself.

CONCLUSION

John Thompson makes use of all four leadership frames as discussed by Bolman and Deal. There are clear indications that he utilizes structural leadership behavior, when appropriate, in that his teams are well drilled and well disciplined. However, there is ample evidence that he balances his structural behavior with human resource behavior. As a result, he gets maximum effort from his players, and they remain loyal to him long after they graduate.

The use of symbolic frame behavior is also evident in his leadership style. It starts with the wearing of a white towel over his shoulder to signify his work ethic and continues with his insistence on his players doing things "The Georgetown Way" and his rather brash assertion that "Auerbach is the Celtics and I am Georgetown" (p. 55).

Thompson's predisposition was to perceive the world as a basically hostile place, which is typical of a leader operating out of the political frame. This worldview is most likely due to his being an African American in an era when the presence of white coaches clearly dominated college basketball. In this environment, he took advantage of his 6 feet 10 inches frame and did not seem adverse to presenting an intimidating presence to his players and opposing coaches. Although he used different tactics to make his points, Thompson found himself in a situation similar to that of Pat Summitt as a "pathfinder" in their sport. John Thompson's record of success speaks for itself. Albeit somewhat controversial at times, there is much to be learned from observing his effective application of leadership behavior.

JOHN WOODEN

> There is nothing stronger than gentleness.
>
> —Abraham Lincoln

BACKGROUND

John Wooden was born on October 14, 1910, and is a retired UCLA basketball coach. He is a member of the Basketball Hall of Fame as both a player and a coach. He was the first person ever enshrined in both categories. He is widely regarded as the greatest college coach in history and his ten National Collegiate Athletic Association (NCAA) national championships while at UCLA are unmatched.

Born in Hall, Indiana, Wooden led Martinsville High School to the state championship final for three consecutive years, winning the tournament in 1927. He was a three-time All-State selection. After graduating in 1928, he entered Purdue University where he was a three-time All-American guard and a member of Purdue's 1932 national championship team. Wooden was nicknamed "The Indiana Rubber Man" for his suicidal dives on the hardwood. He graduated from Purdue in 1932 with a degree in English, and later earned his master's degree at Indiana

State Teacher's College (now Indiana State University) where he spent 2 years as athletic director and basketball coach.

After college, Wooden spent several years playing professionally with the Indianapolis Kautskys, while teaching and coaching in the high school ranks. In 1942 he enlisted in the navy where he gained the rank of lieutenant during World War II.

Wooden coached 2 years at Dayton High School in Kentucky. His first year at Dayton would be the only time he would have a losing record (6-11). After Dayton he returned to Indiana, teaching English and coaching basketball at South Bend Central High School until entering the armed forces. His high school coaching record was 218-42.

After the war, Wooden coached at Indiana State University in Terre Haute, Indiana, for 2 years. Wooden also coached baseball and served as athlete director. In 1947 Wooden's basketball team won the conference title and received an invitation to the National Association of Intercollegiate Athletics (NAIB) National Tournament in Kansas City. Wooden refused the invitation, citing the NAIB's policy banning African American players. A member of the Indiana State Sycamores' team was Clarence Walker, an African American athlete from East Chicago, Indiana. In 1948 the NAIB changed this policy, and Wooden guided his team to the NAIBN final, losing to Louisville. That year, Walker became the first African American to play in any postseason intercollegiate basketball tournament. John Wooden was inducted into the Indiana State University Athletic Hall of Fame in 1984.

During his tenure with UCLA, Wooden became known as the "Wizard of Westwood" and gained lasting fame with the Bruins by winning 10 NCAA titles during his last twelve seasons, including seven in a row from 1967–73. His UCLA teams also had a record winning streak of 88 games, four perfect seasons, and won 38 straight games in NCAA tournament play. In 1967 he was named the Henry Iba Award College Basketball Coach of the Year. In 1972 he received *Sports Illustrated* magazine's Sportsman of the Year Award. Wooden coached his final game in Pauley Pavilion on March 1, 1975. Four weeks later he would surprisingly announce his retirement following a NCAA semifinal victory over Louisville, and before his tenth national championship game victory over Kentucky.

To this day Wooden retains the title Head Men's Basketball Coach Emeritus at UCLA, and attends most home games. On November 17, 2006, Wooden was recognized for his impact on college basketball as a member of the founding class of the National Collegiate Basketball Hall of Fame, along with such college basketball luminaries as James Naismith, Oscar Robertson, Bill Russell, and Dean Smith.

SITUATIONAL LEADERSHIP ANALYSIS

Situational leadership models differ from the earlier trait and behavioral models in asserting that no single way of leading works in all situations. Rather, appropriate behavior depends on the circumstances at a given time. Effective managers diagnose the situation, identify the leadership style or behavior that will be most effective, and then determine whether they can implement the required style.

John Wooden realized the situational nature of leadership behavior early on in his career as a teacher and coach. He speaks of dismissing a student/athlete from his high school team because of a breach of team rules. No longer having basketball as an outlet, the student eventually dropped out of school. Recalling this experience, Wooden said, "A reprimand or a suspension would have accomplished what I wanted, but in those days I lacked the maturity and experience—wisdom—to do that. Everything was black and white. I should have remembered my high school coach's words, 'Be more interested in finding the best way, not just having it your way'" (Wooden & Jamison, 2004, p. 64; all cites in this chapter, unless otherwise noted, are from this source).

Another example of Wooden's awareness of the importance to alter one's leadership behavior depending on the situation is how he handled his players. He admittedly does not hand out praise gratuitously; however, he routinely praised the non-starters more than the starters so that they would feel as if they were an integral part of the team. The starters don't need this type of reinforcement. As leaders, Wooden believes that we need to couple firm discipline with fairness and reason. He says that it took him too long to get a handle on what the appropriate balance was. He taught, not coached, basketball at UCLA for 15 years before the

Bruins won a national championship in 1964. They were a valuable 15 years, Wooden points out, because he *learned*.

One thing that Wooden learned was to be situational in his application of leadership behavior. He was comfortable being a disciplinarian, but did not want to be an ogre. Therefore, when discipline was required, he tried to dole it out in a manner that was firm but fair, with no emotionalism or anger attached. He believes that anger prevents proper thinking and makes one vulnerable. However, when the situation called for structural frame behavior, Wooden did not back off even if he was dealing with his star player. Bill Walton liked to wear long hair. Wooden's dispassionate view was that Walton certainly had the right to wear it long, and he, Wooden, "had the right to choose who would be on the team" (p. 103).

A good parent, teacher, coach or leader—and really they're all the same according to Wooden—must understand human nature. He fully recognizes that no two individuals under his supervision are alike and shouldn't be treated as if they are. He didn't recognize this when he first started out. For example, he believed that the difference between a good team and a great team is usually the leader's ability to understand others—human nature—and teach accordingly.

Gail Goodrich, one of his star players, was very high spirited but had to be worked with in an almost gentle manner, according to Wooden. If he were given a sharp rebuke, he'd go into a shell and almost sulk. On the other hand, his teammate Keith Erickson, could be dealt with in a very direct, almost rude way, and it would bounce off like water off a duck's back. Walt Hazzard was totally different from Gail or Erick. A compliment would go in one ear and out the other. However, if you made him angry at you, he would get better just to prove you wrong.

Continuing on the situational nature of leadership theme, Wooden says, that Walt Hazzard was very flamboyant and he could not see any real advantage to his style. Wooden decided to have him conform to the UCLA style without losing him and called his father to tell the Reverend Hazzard what he was about to do. Reverend Hazzard agreed. When Hazzard called home after he was benched and said he was quitting, his father told him not to come back home because the door will be locked. Wooden says that Hazzard toned it down but did not stop all the fancy stuff; but now it was Wooden's time to compromise—also something he only learned along the way.

Wooden recalls another player on that first championship team, Jack Hirsch, who tested him. Hirsch was the only fellow he's ever coached who called him John. In his early years, he would not have tolerated such informality, but by this time in his career, he somehow felt that if it made Jack feel good, what was the harm?

Referring once again to his superstar player Bill Walton, Wooden describes how he had to be "situational" in dealing with him. Bill Walton required special care because he seemed to lead two separate lives; All-American athlete, coachable player, anti-establishment protester lying down in the middle of Wilshire Boulevard, disrupting classes and closing administration buildings. How a nonconformist rebel conformed to his requirements for selfless team play is still a mystery to Wooden. It was not a mystery to Bill Walton, however. To this day, he is complimentary of Wooden's ability to adapt his leadership behavior to what is needed in a specific situation.

THE STRUCTURAL FRAME

Structural leaders develop a new model of the relationship of structure, strategy, and environment for their organizations. John Wooden was known as a taskmaster whose teams were well drilled in the fundamentals of basketball. These behaviors are characteristic of leaders operating out of the structural frame. For example, one of Wooden's favorite expressions is, "Failing to prepare is preparing to fail" (p. 5).

Wooden recalls an insight that he had early in his career that prompted him to see the value of structural leadership behavior such as planning and preparation. In his own estimation, he was a better teacher than he was a coach at that point in his development. In fact, he believes that his coaching skills improved greatly because of what he did in the classroom. Teaching a substantial subject such as English forced him to create a detailed schedule and lesson plan. For example, he had fourteen days to cover Hamlet. In college he had spent the entire semester on one play. For his Dayton High School students to have any chance of learning something about Shakespeare, he had to carefully hone the material. He learned to accommodate the abilities of a wide range of students. He believes that in the first year at Dayton, he learned more about how to work with people and about himself—his temper, stubbornness, impatience, and desire for immediate results—than in any of the thirty-nine years of coaching that followed.

Wooden revered the teaching profession to the point where he insisted on being called the basketball teacher in addition to the basketball coach. When he was coaching at Indiana State, there was a petition on the part of the faculty to take "teacher" out of his title. He explained to the president very nicely that teachers were what the school was producing, not basketball players, and that he wouldn't be working in a place where turning out basketball players was the goal. Needless to say, the university capitulated.

Wooden learned from his teaching days the appropriateness of operating out of the structural frame, even to the point of how his players wore their sweat socks and sneakers. "This may sound trivial," he says, "but sweat socks prevent blisters. Blisters cause pain and pain causes distraction and distraction affects performance" (p. 107). So, Wooden began every season with a lesson on how to put on your sweat socks and how to properly lace up your sneakers.

Wooden doesn't like sloppiness on or off the court. Well groomed, towels into the wall basket, are his credo. He believes that sloppiness in one area breeds sloppiness in another. Equally important, he does not want players to think managers are there to pick up after them. Wooden wanted his players to assume responsibility, and the training process started with what some would consider "minor details." They were not minor to Wooden. He started planning practices down to the exact minute and tolerated no "horseplay" during practice "because you practice the way you want to play." Wooden used "the power of the bench on fellows who were slow learners" (p. 107).

Another indication of Wooden's use of structural behavior is his development of what he calls the "Pyramid of Success." In building your own personal Pyramid of Success, Wooden says one has to include the following attributes: ambition, adaptability, resourcefulness, fight, faith, patience, integrity, reliability, honesty, sincerity, power, confidence, conditioning, skill, teamwork, self-control, alertness, initiative, intentness, industriousness, friendship, loyalty, cooperation, and enthusiasm. The characteristics, according to Wooden, lead to competitive greatness. Schools, companies, service agencies, and others have utilized Wooden's Pyramid of Success concept as a professional development tool.

In addition to his Pyramid of Success, Wooden developed his "Three Principles for Coaching and Winning":

1. Conditioning: Performance diminishes when conditioning is insufficient.
2. Fundamentals: Automatically, instinctively.
3. Team Spirit: Must be eager to sacrifice for the common good.

All of this is reflective of a structural leader. In fact, Wooden describes himself as such. He doesn't consider himself to be a great "game" coach, but thinks of himself as being among the best when it came to conducting practice. And practice is where a championship is won. If he had a "technique," it was his ability to get players to share his belief that a player is a success only when he does his best in service to the team. To him, the star of the team is the team.

Wooden recalls times when he did not use structural leadership behavior when he probably should have. Wooden was concerned about complacency after Bill Walton had led the UCLA Bruins to an NCAA Championship in only his sophomore year. As he had feared, the "Walton Gang" won the following year, but not his senior year. His gut feeling was they were just too sure of themselves, going through the motions. A coach needs to address this and he didn't.

Typical of one operating out of the structural frame, Wooden was demanding of both himself and his players. He demands that each player expend every available ounce of energy to achieve his personal best, to attain competitive greatness. Victory may be a by-product, but not always, he maintains.

Finally, Wooden believes that he and his players have an internal locus of control and take responsibility for their actions. He asserts that there should never be a need for him to give a pep talk to instill motivation. Motivation must come from the player's belief—deeply entrenched—that ultimate success lies in giving his personal best. More than anything, he wanted players to love the process of attaining their personal best. Unlike a pep talk that creates temporary enthusiasm, loving the *process* is enduring.

THE HUMAN RESOURCE FRAME

Human resource leaders believe in people and communicate that belief. They are passionate about *productivity through people*. Although John Wooden considers himself to be fundamentally a structural frame leader, there is much evidence of his concern for the individual and the use of human resource frame leadership behavior.

Again, referring back to his early years in coaching and teaching, Wooden said, "I had yet to learn that the greatest motivator is a well-deserved pat on the back from someone you respect. Instead, I was quick to criticize, slow to commend." Wooden learned that "patience is the most valuable asset for a leader" (p. 56).

Referring to the need to operate out of the human resource frame on occasion, Wooden said he gradually—too gradually—recognized that he was the source of the problem of not advancing in post-season play. He believed his intense preparation was hurting the team—too long practices, too many new plays, playing too many players, etc.

He came to believe that character is at the center of what he considers necessary for an individual to be a team player. A person of good character tends to be more considerate of other people and more giving and sharing. So, his complaining to officials, whining and making excuses subsequently ended. Those good players who were also good people helped him come to that realization.

Wooden believed that an effective coach and an effective leader need to be concerned with every individual on the team, not just the stars. In referring to another of his great players, Lew Alcindor (Kareem Abdul-Jabbar), he pointed out that during interviews after a game in which Alcindor had scored 30 points, he would make a point to first compliment a player who had made a valuable defensive play or set up a big basket. With UCLA's campus being in Hollywood, Wooden was fond of pointing out to his players that there was a star on the screen, but the star is helpless without a good script and co-stars, lighting and make-up artists, etc.

Finally, in human resource frame terms, Wooden ends one of his books, *My Personal Best*, with the following conclusion: "Love is the most important word in the English language, and my journey has been filled with so much love. I pray that yours is too—that your own journey is full of love. And that along the way you never cease trying to be the best you can be—that you always strive for your personal best. That is success. And don't let anybody tell you otherwise" (p. 205).

THE SYMBOLIC FRAME

In the symbolic frame, the organization is seen as a stage, a theater in which every actor plays certain roles and the symbolic leader attempts to communicate the right impressions to the right audiences. John Wooden's use of symbolic frame leadership behavior is nothing short of prolific. Starting with his Pyramid of Success to his Three Principles of Coaching and Winning, he made liberal use of symbolic leadership behavior.

Some of the quotes attributed to Wooden include the following:

- Success is peace of mind which is a direct result of self-satisfaction in knowing you did your best to become the best you are capable of becoming.
- Be quick, but don't hurry.
- Talent is God-given. Be humble. Fame is man-given. Be grateful. Conceit is self-given. Be careful.
- A player who makes a team great is more valuable than a great player. Losing yourself in a group, for the good of the group, that's teamwork.
- Sports don't build character, they reveal it.
- Failing to prepare is preparing to fail.
- Don't mistake activity for achievement.
- The worst things that you can do for the ones you love are things they could and should do for themselves.
- Little things make big things happen.
- It's what you learn after you know it all that counts.
- When everyone is thinking the same, no one is thinking.

John Wooden learned the use of the symbolic frame early on in his coaching career. When he was coaching at Dayton High School, he would urge his team to, "Do your best. The score cannot make you a loser when you do that; it cannot make you a winner if you do less" (p. 6).

Wooden's father had a great influence on him and used symbolic behavior in the process. In those early days, his father's message about basketball—and life—was that you should not try to be better than somebody else, but never cease trying to be the best you can be. You have control over that; the other you don't. Wooden says his father was fond of quoting the following poem to him:

> I'm not what I ought to be.
> Not what I want to be,
> Not what I'm going to be,
> But I am thankful that I'm better than I used to be. (p. 18)

Another part of his father's legacy to him was "Dad's Seven Point Creed" (p. 18):

1. Be true to yourself.
2. Help others.
3. Make each day your masterpiece and give thanks for your blessings every day.
4. Drink deeply from good books, especially the Bible.
5. Make friendship a fine art.
6. Build a shelter against a rainy day.
7. Pray for guidance and count your blessings.

Another of his father's favorite quotes was from Abraham Lincoln, "There is nothing stronger than gentleness." As a high school football coach, Wooden had struck a kid who challenged him. As a newly hired coach, Wooden was no more than two weeks into the job, and he had quickly lost his temper and stooped to violence. After all his father taught him, it troubled him deeply.

Wooden says his high school coach, Coach Curtis, was the first person he knew who used poetry to win basketball games. His poetry got the players to put out more than they knew they had in them, says Wooden. For example:

> For when the one Great Scorer
> Comes to write against your name,
> He writes not that you won or lost,
> But how you played the game.

Wooden adopted Coach Curtis's use of poems, and tacked them on the bulletin board. Examples include, "Discipline yourself and others won't have to." "Respect every opponent, but fear none." "It's amazing how much we can achieve when no one cares who gets the credit." "Time spent getting even would be better spent getting ahead" (p. 110).

One of Wooden's favorite poems relates to his credo of leadership (p. 67):

The Little Chap Who Follows Me

A careful man I want to be.
A little fellow follows me;
I do not dare to go astray,
For fear he'll go the self-same way.
I cannot once escape his eyes.
Whatev'er he sees me do, he tries.
Like me he says he's going to be,
The little chap who follows me.

As part of his symbolic leadership frame behavior, John Wooden always tried to project the image of a God-fearing, strong, and loyal family man. He was especially close to his wife of many years, Nell. After her passing, he believed that when the Good Lord took Nell, He then sent the love of his grandchild, Cori, and great grandchild after great grandchild until their love and the love of all the grandchildren was all around him like a field full of flowers.

THE POLITICAL FRAME

Leaders operating out of the political frame clarify what they want and what they can get. Political leaders are realists above all. They never let what they want cloud their judgment about what is possible. They assess the distribution of power and interests.

There is little direct evidence that John Wooden utilized the political frame of leadership to any great degree. However, one does not attain the reputation as being perhaps "the greatest college coach in history" without being politically savvy when the occasion requires it. For example, in his relationship with his two superstar centers, Lew Alcinder (Kareem Abdul-Jabbar) and Bill Walton, there were times when he compromised some of his minor principles in order to maintain harmony. He readily acknowledged that Bill Walton required special care because he seemed to live two lives—the All-American, coachable player and the anti-establishment protester. Suffice to say that John Wooden most likely employed political leadership behavior when it was appropriate to do so.

CONCLUSION

Mortimer Adler, American philosopher and educator, expresses his thoughts on situational leadership in the following way: "In Aristotelian terms, the good leaders must have ethos, pathos and logos. Ethos is his moral character, the source of his ability to persuade. The pathos is his ability to touch feelings, to move people emotionally. The logos is his ability to give solid reasons for an action, to move people intellectually" (as cited in Seldes, 1985, p. 8).

Using Alder's definition of the good leader, we can readily agree that John Wooden qualifies. His balance of the structural (logos), the human resources (pathos), and the symbolic (ethos) frames is exemplary. It is not difficult to see why he is widely recognized as a great coach and leader, perhaps the best college coach in history.

His teams were known to be well prepared, well drilled, and in excellent physical condition. He was an acknowledged master teacher of the game. These traits are characteristic of a strong structural leader. Likewise, Wooden was known as a compassionate and considerate man who believed that "love is the most important word in the English language." This behavior is endemic to a human resource leader.

Wooden's use of poetry and inspirational quotes, which he posted in the UCLA locker room, are examples of his use of symbolic frame leadership behavior. As a result, he was known as the "The Professor" and the "Wizard of Westwood." Although there is not much direct use of political frame behavior, as was pointed out above, a leader does not reach the standing of a John Wooden without the astute use of political behavior, when appropriate. Suffice to say that John Wooden is the epitome of a situational and transformational leader. He is an ideal model for leaders and aspiring leaders to emulate.

12

BOB HURLEY

> You are Entering a Special and Safe Place. The Streets Stop Here!
> —Sign at entrance to Saint Anthony's High School

BACKGROUND

For 36 years, Bob Hurley has coached Saint Anthony's High School in Jersey City, New Jersey. He has given 24 hours a day, 7 days a week, 365 days of the year to aspiring students from the downtrodden, drug-infested neighborhoods of this city. He has given as a coach, teacher, father figure, advisor mentor, and friend.

    He has nurtured his players with love and nourished them with meals. He has carted them to and from practice and found them jobs. His wife, Chris, has tutored them and prepared them for their Scholastic Aptitude Tests. The Hurleys have transported them to tournaments in California, Hawaii, and Florida and taken them on family vacations to their house on the Jersey shore. And when his players have been hassled, stabbed, or shot at, Hurley has vehemently protected them, standing up to the gang members in the inner-city housing projects.

Bob Hurley is Jersey City through and through. He was born in the Greenville section, in the southern part of the city, raised attending Saint Paul's parish. His father was a Jersey City policeman and his wife, a Jersey City girl, from neighboring Sacred Heart parish. He attended Saint Peter's College, a Jesuit institution of higher education in Jersey City.

During his sophomore year at Saint Peter's, Hurley realized he was not in the Peacocks' plans, so he walked off the varsity basketball team and right into a volunteer job coaching a Catholic Youth Organization grammar school team in his parish. Although he had wanted to be a teacher, a substitute stint after graduation dissuaded him. His father suggested he apply for a position as a probation officer, and he held that post for 30 years until retiring in 2002.

His youngest son, Danny, a former Seton Hall star who is now the head coach at Saint Benedict's Prep in Newark, says his father's greatest gift is his ability to "penetrate the hardest hearts and the stiffest souls," a talent put to the test in the probation department and in coaching. "He has an innate feel for kids and what they can do," Danny says. "He knows how to make the most out of what others see as seemingly very little." Over the years, Hurley has built Saint Anthony's into a national powerhouse team and himself into a mythical figure in high school basketball, amassing over 900 victories over the best high school competition in the nation. His teams have won 24 state championships, which is a national record. In 2007 Hurley became New Jersey's winningest high school coach and gained a nomination to the Basketball Hall of Fame.

He makes a very modest salary (reportedly under $10,000 per year) and ends up spending more than that on basketballs, refreshments, and anything else that fuels teenage boys. He routinely donates much of the money that he makes from his many speaking engagements and basketball camps to Saint Anthony's High School and the basketball program.

Because the school has no gymnasium, the Saint Anthony Friars have practiced at over 25 different facilities over the years. The main practice site is the White Eagle Bingo Hall on Newark Avenue. Hurley renovated the place, refinishing the basketball court and building and adding a weight room in the basement. He raised all the renovation money himself. The Friars have played home games in nine gyms, including the

Jersey City Armory, where Hurley also constructed a court and mounted a scoreboard. The team currently plays home games at the Golden Door Charter School, across the street from Saint Anthony's.

All but one of Hurley's players has gone on to college. Five have played in the National Basketball Association (NBA), including his son, Bobby, an All-America guard at Duke. Two others are playing Major League Baseball: John Valentin of the New York Mets and Willie Banks of the Boston Red Sox.

It has often been said that young people do not play for Hurley, they enlist. A strict disciplinarian, Hurley demands total commitment. His players attend study halls before practice, train all year, and live by a narrow set of rules. But in return, the Hurleys are even more committed, embracing their players as family, showering them with unconditional love and support.

There have been numerous opportunities for Hurley to leave for a lucrative college job, but he has always declined. The closest he came to leaving was in 1985, when Pete Gillen became the head coach at Xavier and asked Hurley to be his assistant. After a weekend touring the leafy suburbs of Cincinnati, he was ready to take the plunge. But when he returned home he was met at the door by an angry Bobby, who was about to enter ninth grade at Saint Anthony's. He reportedly found Bobby in tears over who was now going to be his high school coach and whether his father would ever see him play. And that was the end of that. Bob Hurley remains at Saint Anthony's. His 2007–8 team is currently ranked first in the nation.

SITUATIONAL LEADERSHIP ANALYSIS

Situational leadership models differ from the earlier trait and behavioral models in asserting that no single way of leading works in all situations. Rather, appropriate behavior depends on the circumstances at a given time. Effective managers diagnose the situation, identify the leadership style or behavior that will be most effective, and then determine whether they can implement the required style.

Like many teachers and coaches, Bob Hurley relied almost exclusively on structural frame leadership behavior early in his career. It seemed important to establish a set of firm rules and to focus intently on the planning and preparation required for success. It is usually not until later in one's career that a leader realizes that "one size does not fit all" and one needs to adapt his or her leadership behavior to the situation. Bob Hurley was not different from the norm in this regard.

Adrian Wojnarowski, Hurley's friend and author of *The Miracle of St. Anthony*, chronicles Hurley's evolving leadership style. He says, "Going into the 2005 season, Hurley had already given this team so many second chances, letting kids back whom he would never have before" (Wojnarowski, 2005, p. xiv). Bob Hurley justifies this exception by indicating that there is a little social worker in him. Nonetheless, he seems to have learned that to be truly effective, he needed to adjust his leadership behavior to the changing times. Hurley learned that if he tore into them with anger yesterday, he needed to find an inspirational way to pick them up today.

On another similar occasion, Hurley albeit reluctantly, adapted his leadership behavior to a changing situation. Commenting on reinstating a player whom he had suspended, he indicated that the kid was lucky to have a uniform and that he had never before allowed a player to return to the team like this. Although he saw the need to make an exception in this time and place, he was not at all certain that he was doing the right thing. These are but a few examples of how Bob Hurley adjusts his leadership behavior to the situation.

THE STRUCTURAL FRAME

Structural leaders develop a new model of the relationship of structure, strategy, and environment for their organizations. Perhaps because he is dealing with teenagers from mostly urban neighborhoods who need more structure in their lives, Bob Hurley operates out of the structural frame of leadership more often than most of the coaches profiled in this book. He had been described as driving his team with a tenacity developed during his thirty years on the job as a Hudson County probation officer.

Hurley's reliance on structural leadership behavior is well known to his contemporaries. He is known as the greatest high school basketball coach in the country, but there may be is no stopping there because no one teaches like Bob Hurley. No one inspires kids like him, and no one anywhere in basketball comes closer to perfection under the most imperfect of circumstances. Almost everyone who's watched his teams play through the years comes away convinced that they play harder than any team, on any level, that they've ever seen. In fact, Saint Joseph's University coach, Phil Martelli calls Hurley, "the best pure teacher of basketball I've ever seen" (p. 32).

Hurley felt that he needed to continue using structural leadership behavior because once anyone sees a crack in the foundation, once the discipline is dulled, once the fear of God that his players feel when Bob Hurley walks into the gym is gone, the dynasty may be dead.

One of Hurley's former players, Mark Harris, said that his use of structural behavior was manifested in the way they were prepared; they began to see everything at a different speed. In encountering situations as a firefighter after he graduated he said, that all that flashed into his mind was: "Think before you react! Awareness! Alertness! And it was just like Coach had trained us. Everything turned to slow motion. It was like I was playing ball again." As Mark Harris stood against the Jersey City sky, as flames spit into the air, the chills went up and down his spine. It had hit him, like it would for so many former Saint Anthony basketball players. He looked into the inferno and thought: "Coach Hurley just saved my life" (p. xvi).

We can assess Hurley's teams in this way: Mostly, they won with the principles of Saint Anthony basketball: unselfish passing, unforgiving defense and unparalleled toughness. Almost every player is so well coached, so well schooled in the fundamentals that most coaches agree they arrive at college far more advanced than their counterparts at other high schools.

In true structural frame fashion, no detail is overlooked by Hurley. Hurley instructs his players to tuck in their shirts. He did not want the officials to have to point that out to his kids. He didn't want someone from outside the program to enforce the codes. And he did not waste time in getting his points across. Hurley's practices were planned minute-to-minute, one drill leading into another and to the next lesson, teaching, teaching, and more teaching. During the first two days of practice, Hurley planned very little cerebral instruction. He wanted hard, fast, and emotional practices, where the ferocity would start to shape his team's persona and push leaders to the forefront. The complexity would come later.

Hurley was forever building toward something; dribbling fundamentals, a confluence of the practice ideas that he had picked up through clinics and conversations, or through his own trial and error. He wanted his players to be thinking of what else they could be doing to please him.

Hurley's basic attitude is that of a strong structural leader. In that light, he is fond of saying that there are only five important things in basketball: Rebound, defend, dribble, pass, and shoot. And if one of those does not work, he wants his kids to try the other four.

At times Hurley was inflexible in his use of structural behavior. Once when one of his star players, Elijah Ingram, was charged with rape while he was a player at Saint John's in New York, Hurley simply disowned him. Hurley had dated only one girl in his life, and had married her, and the thought of bringing a woman back to a hotel room to pay for sex was beyond his capacity to comprehend. Bob Hurley was done with Elijah Ingram.

THE HUMAN RESOURCE FRAME

Human resource leaders believe in people and communicate that belief. They are passionate about *productivity through people*. Although Bob Hurley could be described as basically a structural leader, there are many instances where he found the use of human resource frame behavior appropriate. For instance, one of his players, Ahmad Mosby, nicknamed "Beanie," had been thrown out of practice for breaking a team rule. Looking back, Hurley had wished the assistants had stopped Beanie, told him to come to practice the next day, and talk to Hurley after he had cooled down. He would have reinstated him for the state tournament, but it was now too late in the coach's mind. The deed was done. Beanie was gone for the season. But the story does not end here. After the season, preparing for next season, the coaches talked a lot about Ahmad Mosby and kept coming back to one thing. He had nowhere else to go. So Hurley, in a display of human resource leadership behavior, reinstated Beanie.

In another instance, when Dwayne Lee was a freshman at Saint Joseph's University he lost his father and mother. After each death Bob Hurley would go to the Lees' house, sit down with Dwayne, and talk to him about staying the course with his education, and that the best way to be there for his two younger siblings was to get his degree and get a good job. On a personal note, as graduate dean at Saint Joseph's, I was in Dwayne Lee's presence at several university events and the first words out his mouth when speaking with an alumnus were: "Do you have any jobs available?"

According to Wojnarowski, Hurley treated the first and the last man on the Saint Anthony's High School team with equal credit or condemnation, whatever he had earned. In a further display of human resource behavior, Hurley said to one of his players, "Robert, you're never going to get into a game, but I actually believe that it's my job to coach everyone" (p. 65). After graduation everything would once again change between Hurley and his players and there would be a closeness for life.

Hurley's main objective was to prepare young people to be able to handle life's challenges. His greatest satisfaction was not seeing his former players become college stars or professional athletes, but changing their lives for the better. Upon hearing that one of his former players, Otis Campbell, had gotten a substantial promotion to a very responsible position, Otis couldn't see the tear welling in his coach's eye knowing about who Otis Campbell had been and who he had become.

Other instances of how Hurley's use of human resource behavior had an influential and lasting effect include the obervation of Josh Moore, one of Hurley's players who made it to the NBA. Moore believes that Hurley is one of the top five coaches at any level, and he feels he can make that assessment since he is now in the NBA. Moore admits that he should have realized it even back when he was in high school. In still another instance, upon hearing that Hurley had disciplined the entire team over a rule infraction, a Saint Anthony parent responded that they probably deserved it. Saint Anthony parents trusted Hurley so implicitly, they gave him complete freedom to coach his way.

Opposing coaches and players have commented on Hurley's use of human resource behavior. One of them observed that what he really admired is that there are no airs about him. He comes in, beats you and he's never condescending. Most guys would just shake the opposing coach's hand and walk on. Hurley is not like that. He's always looking to teach and help. Dyjuan Wagner (Camden High School/Louisville University) depicted Hurley as the master motivator. He remembered there were one or two of Hurley's players around him everywhere he turned. They played hard. What he remembers is that "those boys didn't want to let that coach down" (p. 335).

Hurley modeled his human resource frame behavior after another great high school coach. Hurley says that he wanted to run Saint Anthony just like Coach Morgan Wooten did at De Matha High School, in Washington, D.C. Wooten always talked about his seniors going to college, not the championships or games they won. In the locker room after winning the state championship game for the 24th time, Hurley urged his assistants to start getting the players visiting colleges now, get their futures in order. "The underclassmen had a taste of it, but I don't know if they'll be good enough next year" (p. 346). Hurley was already starting to coach next year.

THE SYMBOLIC FRAME

In the symbolic frame, the organization is seen as a stage, a theater in which every actor plays certain roles, and the symbolic leader attempts to communicate the right impressions to the right audiences. Bob Hurley used symbolic behavior to create and project a certain image among his players and the outside world. Wojnarowski says that to Hurley, there is something so pure about high school basketball. In Hurley's practice gym, it is always 1965. There are no tattoos on his players, no cornrows, no facial hair. The most improbable dynasty in basketball has survived against the longest odds because Hurley has kept watch on these streets when he could have left to be a famous college coaching star, with a million dollar a year package, a sneaker deal, and a country club membership.

In typical symbolic frame fashion, Hurley liked to make his points by telling stories. As a probation officer he heard his share of horror stories, which he often shared with his players. He says that he would always bring these stories back to practice. He would point to a kid and tell him a story about a man going back to jail out of the housing project where the player was growing up. And every once in a while, he would tell them a story of someone from the projects who had turned his life around through Saint Anthony's basketball.

Hurley always had a purpose or moral behind his stories. Hurley always called Beanie, of whom we spoke earlier, by his given name, Ahmad. Hurley explains, "Beanie was always the guy getting in trouble. I want him to grow up and become 'Ahmad'" (p. 1). To Hurley the ultimate judge of his teaching came not always when he was there to direct his players, but when they were on their own.

One of the assistant coaches at DePaul University had this to say about Hurley after a recruiting visit: "He sits there with such respect for you, such interest on behalf of his kids. How many high school coaches do that anymore?" (p. 3) He is the most consistent guy that this coach ever met. Hurley's attitude is borne out by the saying on the sign that one sees upon entering Saint Anthony's High School, which is the epigraph to this chapter, and reads: You are Entering a Special and Safe Place. The Streets Stop Here.

Hurley made many of his key points through the use of symbolic behavior. The whole mindset of Saint Anthony's basketball hinged on mental toughness. There was no Gatorade, water bottles and a trainer to fuss over players' minor bumps and bruises. "We were a poor school, we had a dumpy little gym, and that was that," says Hurley (p. 39).

Another trait that Hurley tried to instill through symbolic behavior was poise. It is a constant theme in his teaching—and poise for a Saint Anthony's player was never reacting to a referee, an opponent, and most of all, a pressure situation. Saint Anthony's players didn't argue with officials. They didn't trash talk opponents and they never, ever made even the slightest sign of disrespect toward Hurley. This lesson began on the practice floor, where he promised to turn something as seemingly innocuous as a slight sign of exasperation into a what amounted to a capital crime. Still another trait that Hurley tried to instill was teamwork. He and his team worked very hard, and the result was a cohesiveness and team spirit to be envied. Hurley depicted their efforts by holding his right hand in the air, and indicating that five individual finger had become one hand. Other slogans that Hurley used to get his points across symbolically are: "Defense is like your conservative savings. Offense is like the stock market." And, "Even when you're warming up, you're representing Saint Anthony's basketball." Reebok sent three shipments of shoes a season to Saint Anthony's and to Hurley. Showing up without them constituted an act of irresponsibility and ingratitude. Showing up late without them, well, you were testing Hurley's self control. Employing another one of his favorite slogans, he said, "This is like basketball baby sitting right now" (p. 56).

In another instance of symbolic leadership behavior, Hurley routinely swept the basketball court before every practice as a sign that nothing was beneath him. One time, when Mrs. Hurley was diagnosed with cancer, the coach had to miss practice. Upon hearing the news, one of Hurley's players, Ahmad Nivens, walked down to the supply closet, pulled out the broom, and began sweeping the court.

Hurley's own son became a symbol of Saint Anthony's basketball. Eventually, Bobby became the living, breathing embodiment of his father's genius, his tenacity, his love for basketball. Until Bobby, Hurley was considered just another successful high school basketball coach. Bobby changed everything. For a coach and the school with no gymnasium and no money, Bobby was the ultimate personification of his father and his high school's mission of doing more with less. His big shots, peerless passing, and unending nerve earned him a part of three Final Fours, two NCAA national titles, a Final Four most outstanding player award, and the all-time collegiate assist record.

Hurley's devotion to the mission of Saint Anthony's High School was expressed in a symbolic way, also. He passed along thousands of dollars he earned every year conducting clinics to support the school. And when Saint Anthony's was on the verge of bankruptcy several years ago, he campaigned among his friends and contacts to contribute large sums to ensure its continuance. Fordham University's athletic director Frank McLaughlin says, "I just think he has a mission there. I'm not sure there's anybody else in the coaching profession who I admire as much as I do him" (p. 218).

THE POLITICAL FRAME

Leaders operating out of the political frame clarify what they want and what they can get. Political leaders are realists above all. They never let what they want cloud their judgment about what is possible. They assess the distribution of power and interests. When appropriate, Bob Hurley has used the political frame of leadership behavior. In dealing with the reality of little Saint Anthony's having to raise funds for its very existence, he was willing to utilize political behavior in order to address that need. For example, Saint Anthony's participation in state tournaments was one way of garnering some of this much-needed revenue. Hurley was not above using a little hyperbole to bolster attendance. On one occasion, he said, "I'm going to the radio station: Either I'm going to tell them the truth, or lie my [butt] off and help them sell some tickets for the tournament" (p. 95).

In a more traditional way of raising funds, Hurley was also willing to use political behavior if needed. Since Saint Anthony's was in such poor financial shape, it was now time for Hurley to switch roles, and he was in quite a quandary over doing so. Due to a decrease in charitable donations since the 9/11 attacks, Saint Anthony's had fallen into such dire financial straits that it was in danger of closing by the end of the school year. But Hurley did change roles, from coach to fund raiser, using all of his influence to raise money for his beloved Saint Anthony's, by collecting $20,000 from the New Jersey Nets' Kerry Kittles, and $50,000 from his son, Bobby Hurley.

CONCLUSION

It is interesting to analyze Bob Hurley's leadership behavior in that he is in a significantly different "situation" than any of the other coaches profiled in this book. Whereas all of the other coaches are dealing with adults, Bob Hurley is mostly interacting with teenagers. According to the principles of situational leadership theory, Hurley should be operating out of the structural frame more often than the other coaches. Situational leadership theory posits that when dealing with followers with a low "readiness" level, like teenagers, the leader should utilize structural leadership frame behavior in most instances. Nevertheless, situational leadership theory also postulates that structural frame behavior should not be used exclusively. Human resource, symbolic, and even political frame behaviors should also be utilized, when appropriate.

Bob Hurley's leadership behavior accurately reflects these tenets of situational leadership theory. Although his leadership behavior is dominated by the structural frame, he does employ, albeit less frequently, human resource, symbolic, and political frame behavior, when appropriate. We saw that every minute of his practices is planned, with great emphasis on the fundamentals of basketball. No tattoos, facial hair, or body piercings were permitted. This is all structural leadership behavior that may not have been accepted or effective in a different "situation" (i.e., with adults).

However, Hurley made sure that his student-athletes completed their high school education, and he used his considerable influence to secure a college scholarship for as many of them as possible (human resource behavior). He also passed along thousands of dollars to Saint Anthony's from his clinics and speaking engagements (symbolic behavior) and negotiated with corporate contacts and others to rescue Saint Anthony's from bankruptcy (political behavior).

We can conclude, then, that Bob Hurley effectively utilized situational leadership theory. He balanced his use of the structural, human resource, symbolic, and political frames according to the situation. As with all of the coaches profiled in this book, there is much to learn about effective leadership by observing the actions and methods of Bob Hurley.

13

LEADERSHIP LESSONS LEARNED

> The greatest discovery of my generation is that man can alter his life simply by altering his attitude of mind.
>
> —William James

INTRODUCTION

What do we learn about leadership from these ten remarkably similar coaches? First, we learn that situational leadership theory makes eminent sense. Virtually all of these coaches are effective as leaders because they are able to adapt their leadership behavior to changing situations. None of them is "stuck" in one paradigm. Some might be criticized for using one or another leadership frame too exclusively, but the reality is that by and large they are successful because, to a person, they are able to balance their use of the four leadership frames enunciated by Bolman and Deal very effectively.

More specifically, we have learned that there are three requisites for effective leadership:

1. Knowledge and (passion) for one's field (competency),
2. Ability to engender mutual *trust and respect* with one's followers,
3. Ability to apply (situational leadership theory) to one's practice.

LEADING WITH MIND

Knowledge of one's field is a sine qua non for effective leadership. In basketball terms, the leader must have a good command of the Xs and Os. In business terms, the effective leader must have at least an adequate knowledge of the technical aspects of how a business operates and a sense of how to develop a business plan. In education, the leader needs to know how schools and school systems operate and what the best practices in the field are in curriculum and instruction. In a family situation, the leader (parent or guardian) needs to have at least a modicum of knowledge regarding the principles of child psychology to be effective. In short, leaders in any field need to know that field and be able to apply that knowledge through the theory and practice of organizational development, which would include the following:

a. Organizational Structure: How an institution is organized.
b. Organizational Culture: The values and beliefs of an institution.
c. Motivation: The system of rewards and incentives provided.
d. Communication: The clarity and accuracy of the communication process.
e. Decision Making: How and by whom decisions are made.
f. Conflict Management: How dysfunctional conflict should be handled.
g. Power Distribution: How the power in an institution is distributed.
h. Strategic Planning: How the mission, vision, and strategic plan are developed.
i. Change: How change is effectively implemented in an institution.

I will not go into detail about these processes here. If the reader is interested in a comprehensive look at these processes, I would recommend an earlier publication of mine, *Educational Administration: Leading with Mind and Heart* (second edition, 2005). However, included in the Appendix to this book is a survey titled "The Heart Smart Survey" that I developed to help leaders assess the organizational health of their institutions and to identify which of the factors listed above are in need of improvement.

LEADING WITH HEART

In summary, then, the effective leader needs to be *technically* competent. However, being technically competent is not enough. To be truly effective, the leaders need to master the *art* of leadership and learn to lead with *heart*. In effect, leaders need to operate out of both the structural and political frames (science) and the human resources and symbolic frames (art) to maximize their effectiveness. This means that they must be concerned about the person (*cura personalis*). They must abide by the Golden Rule and treat others as they wish to be treated. As we noted in Chapter 2, truly effective leaders treat their employees like volunteers and empower them to actualize their true potential, thus engendering mutual trust and respect among virtually all of one's colleagues.

LEADING WITH MIND AND HEART

So, the truly effective leaders lead with *both* mind (science) and heart (art). One or the other will not suffice. Only by mastering both will the leader succeed. For example, former President William Clinton was rendered ineffective as a leader because of the Monica Lewinsky affair and was almost impeached. Why? Because he suddenly lost the *knowledge* of how government works (science)? No! He lost his ability to lead because he lost the *trust* and *respect* of much of the American public (art). He could still lead with his mind, but he had lost the ability to lead with his heart.

On the contrary, one could argue that former President Jimmy Carter lost his ability to lead because of a perceived lack of competency. The majority of the voting public did not believe that he had the knowledge necessary to manage government operations and effectively lead with his mind. However, virtually no one questioned his concern for people and his ability to lead with heart. Absent the perceived ability to do *both*, however, he lost the election to Ronald Reagan.

Our conclusion, then, is that effective leaders are situational. That is, they are capable of adapting their leadership behavior to the situation.

They utilize structural, human resources, symbolic, and political leadership behavior when appropriate. They led with both mind (structural and political behavior) and with heart (human resources and symbolic behavior). They master both the science (mind) and art (heart) of leadership, and in doing so, they are transformational, leading their organizations to new heights. As Chris Lowney says in his book, *Heroic Leadership*, in a word, these type of leaders are truly "heroic."

Appendix

THE HEART SMART ORGANIZATIONAL DIAGNOSIS MODEL

Just as there are vital signs in measuring individual health, I believe that there are vital signs in measuring the health of organizations. This survey will help identify those vital signs in your school system. The purpose of the Heart Smart Organizational Diagnosis Questionnaire, therefore, is to provide feedback data for intensive diagnostic efforts. Use of the questionnaire, either by itself or in conjunction with other information-collecting techniques such as systematic observation or interviewing, will provide the data needed for identifying strengths and weaknesses in the functioning of an educational institution and help determine whether the leaders are leading with both mind and heart.

A meaningful diagnostic effort must be based on a theory or model of organizational development. This makes action research possible as it facilitates problem identification, which is essential to determining the proper functioning of an organization. The model suggested here establishes a systematic approach for analyzing relationships among the variables that influence how an organization is managed. It provides information for assessment of ten areas of formal and informal activity: structure, identity and culture, leadership, motivation, communication, decision making, conflict resolution, goal setting and planning, power distribution, and attitude toward change. The outer circle in the Figure

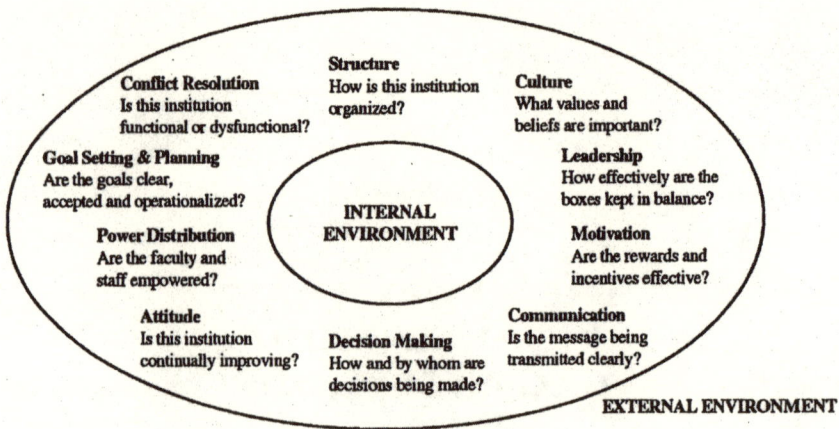

Figure A.1. Organizational boundaries for analysis.

A.1, an organizational boundary for diagnosis. This boundary demarcates the functioning of the internal and external environments. Since the underlying organizational theory upon which this survey is based is an open systems model, it is essential that influences from both the internal and external environment be considered for the analysis to be complete.

Please think of your *present personal or professional environment* and indicate the degree to which you agree or disagree with each of the following statements. A "1" is *Disagree* Strongly and a "7" is *Agree* Strongly.

Disagree Strongly	Disagree	Disagree Slightly	Neither Agree Nor Disagree	Agree Slightly	Agree	Agree Strongly
1	2	3	4	5	6	7

1. The manner in which the tasks in this institution are divided is logical.
2. The relationships among co-workers are harmonious.
3. This institution's leadership efforts result in the fulfillment of its purposes.

4. My work at this institution offers me an opportunity to grow as a person.
5. I can always talk to someone at work, if I have a work-related problem.
6. The faculty actively participates in decisions.
7. There is little evidence of unresolved conflict in this institution.
8. There is a strong fit between this institution's mission and my own values.
9. The faculty and staff are represented on most committees and task forces.
10. Staff development routinely accompanies any significant changes that occur in this institution.
11. The manner in which the tasks in this institution are distributed is fair.
12. Older faculty's opinions are valued.
13. The administrators display the behaviors required for effective leadership.
14. The rewards and incentives here are both internal and external.
15. There is open and direct communication among all levels of this institution.
16. Participative decision making is fostered at this institution.
17. What little conflict exists at this institution is not dysfunctional.
18. Representatives of all segments of the school community participate in the strategic planning process.
19. The faculty and staff have an appropriate voice in the operation of this institution.
20. This institution is not resistant to constructive change.
21. The division of labor in this organization helps its efforts to reach its goals.
22. I feel valued by this institution.
23. The administration encourages an appropriate amount of participation in decision making.
24. Faculty and staff members are often recognized for special achievements.
25. There are no significant barriers to effective communication at this institution.

26. When the *acceptance* of a decision is important, a group decision-making model is used.
27. Mechanisms at this institution effectively manage conflict and stress.
28. Most of the employees understand the mission and goals of this institution.
29. The faculty and staff feel empowered to make their own decisions regarding their daily work.
30. Tolerance toward change is modeled by the administration of this institution.
31. The various grade-level teachers and departments work well together.
32. Differences among people are accepted.
33. The leadership is able to generate continuous improvement in the institution.
34. My ideas are encouraged, recognized, and used.
35. Communication is carried out in a non-aggressive style.
36. In general, the decision-making process is effective.
37. Conflicts are usually resolved before they become dysfunctional.
38. For the most part, the employees of this institution feel an "ownership" of its goals.
39. The faculty and staff are encouraged to be creative in their work.
40. When changes are made, they do so within a rational process.
41. This institution's organizational design responds well to changes in the internal and external environment.
42. The teaching and the non-teaching staffs get along with one another.
43. The leadership of this institution espouses a clear educational vision.
44. The goals and objectives for the year are mutually developed by the faculty and the administration.
45. I believe that my opinions and ideas are listened to.
46. Usually, a collaborative style of decision making is utilized at this institution.
47. A collaborative approach to conflict resolution is ordinarily used.

48. This institution has a clear educational vision.
49. The faculty and staff can express their opinions without fear of retribution.
50. I feel confident that I will have an opportunity for input if a significant change were to take place in this institution.
51. This institution is "people-oriented."
52. Administrators and faculty have mutual respect for one another.
53. Administrators give people the freedom to do their job.
54. The rewards and incentives in this institution are designed to satisfy a variety of individual needs.
55. The opportunity for feedback is always available in the communications process.
56. Group decision-making techniques, like brainstorming and group surveys, are sometimes used in the decision-making process.
57. Conflicts are often prevented by early intervention.
58. This institution has a strategic plan for the future.
59. Most administrators here use the power of persuasion rather than the power of coercion.
60. This institution is committed to continually improving through the process of change.
61. This institution does not adhere to a strict chain of command.
62. This institution exhibits grace, style, and civility.
63. The administrators model desired behavior.
64. At this institution, employees are not normally coerced into doing things.
65. I have the information that I need to do a good job.
66. I can constructively challenge the decisions in this institution.
67. A process to resolve work-related grievances is available.
68. This institution has an ongoing planning process.
69. The faculty and staff have input into the operation of this institution through a collective bargaining unit or through a faculty governance body.
70. The policies, procedures, and programs of this institution are periodically reviewed.

HEART SMART SCORING SHEET

Instructions: Transfer the numbers you circled on the questionnaire to the blanks below. Add each column and divide each sum by seven. This will give you comparable scores for each of the ten areas.

Structure	*Identity and Culture*	*Leadership*	*Motivation*
1 _____	2 _____	3 _____	4 _____
11 _____	12 _____	13 _____	14 _____
21 _____	22 _____	23 _____	24 _____
31 _____	32 _____	33 _____	34 _____
41 _____	42 _____	43 _____	44 _____
51 _____	52 _____	53 _____	54 _____
61 _____	62 _____	63 _____	64 _____

Total

_____   _____   _____   _____

Average

_____   _____   _____   _____

Communication	**Decision Making**	**Conflict Resolution**	**Goal Setting/ Planning**
5 _____	6 _____	7 _____	8 _____
15 _____	16 _____	17 _____	18 _____
25 _____	26 _____	27 _____	28 _____
35 _____	36 _____	37 _____	38 _____
45 _____	46 _____	47 _____	48 _____
55 _____	56 _____	57 _____	58 _____
65 _____	66 _____	67 _____	68 _____

Total

_____   _____   _____   _____

Average

_____   _____   _____   _____

Power Distribution	Attitude Toward Change
9 _____	10 _____
19 _____	20 _____
29 _____	30 _____
39 _____	40 _____
49 _____	50 _____
59 _____	60 _____
69 _____	70 _____

Total

_____ _____

Average

_____ _____

INTERPRETATION SHEET

Instructions: Study the background information and interpretation suggestions that follow.

Background

The Heart Smart Organizational Diagnosis Questionnaire is a survey-feedback instrument designed to collect data on organizational functioning. It measures the perceptions of persons in an organization to determine areas of activity that would benefit from an organizational development effort. It can be used as the sole data-collection technique or in conjunction with other techniques (interview, observation, etc.). The instrument and the model reflect a systematic approach for analyzing relationships among variables that influence how an organization is managed. Using the Heart Smart Organizational Diagnosis Questionnaire is the first step in determining appropriate interventions for organizational change efforts.

Interpretation and Diagnosis

A crucial consideration is the diagnosis based on data interpretation. The simplest diagnosis would be to assess the amount of variance for each of the ten variables in relation to a score of 4, which is the neutral point. Scores below 4 would indicate a problem with organizational functioning. The closer the score is to 1, the more severe the problem would be. Scores above 4 indicate the lack of a problem, with a score of 7 indicating optimum functioning.

Another diagnostic approach follows the same guidelines of assessment in relation to the neutral point (score) of 4. The score of each of the 70 items on the questionnaire can be reviewed to produce more exacting information on problematic areas. Thus, diagnosis would be more precise. For example, let us suppose that the average score on item number 8 is 1.4. This would indicate not only a problem in organizational purpose or goal setting, but also a more specific problem in that there is a gap between organizational and individual goals. This more precise diagnostic effort is likely to lead to a more appropriate intervention in the organization than the generalized diagnostic approach described in the preceding paragraph.

Appropriate diagnosis must address the relationships between the boxes to determine the interconnectedness of problems. For example, if there is a problem with *communication*, it could be that the organizational *structure* does not foster effective communication. This might be the case if the average score on item 25 was well below 4 (2.5 or lower) and all the items on organizational *structure* (1, 11, 21, 31, 41, 51, 61) averaged below 4.

NOTES

CHAPTER I

1. S. A. Kirkpatrick & E. A. Locke. (1991). Leadership: Do traits matter? *Academy of Management Executive, 5*(2), 49.
2. R. M. Stogdill & A. E. Coons, eds. (1957). *Leader Behavior: Its description and measurement.* Columbus: Ohio State University Bureau of Business Research.
3. E. Fleishman, E. F. Harris, & R. D. Buret. (1955). *Leadership and supervision in industry.* Columbus: Ohio State University Press; E. Fleishman & E. F. Harris. (1959). Patterns of leadership behavior related to employee grievances and turnover. *Personnel Psychology, 1,* 45–53.
4. H. Mintzberg. (1979). *The nature of managerial work,* 2nd ed. Englewood Cliffs, NJ: Prentice-Hall.
5. D. McGregor. (1961). *The human side of enterprise.* New York: McGraw-Hill; E. H. Schein. (1974). The Hawthorne studies revisited: A defense of Theory Y, Sloan School of Management Working Paper #756-74. Cambridge: Massachusetts Institute of Technology, p. 3.
6. F. E. Fiedler & M. M. Chemers. (1984). *Improving leadership effectiveness: The leader match concept,* 2nd ed. New York: Wiley.
7. F. E. Fiedler & J. E. Garcia. (1987). *New approaches to effective leadership.* New York: Wiley.

8. N. W. Biggart & G. G. Hamilton. (1987). An institutional theory of leadership. *Journal of Applied Behavioral Sciences, 234,* 429–441.

9. R. J. House. (1971). A path-goal theory of leader effectiveness. *Administrative Science Quarterly, 16,* 321–338; R. J. House & T. R. Mitchell. (1974, Autumn). Path-goal theory of leadership. *Journal of Contemporary Business,* 81–97.

10. V. H. Vroom & P. W. Yetton. (1973). *Leadership and decision making.* Pittsburgh: University of Pittsburgh Press [original version]; V. H. Vroom & A. G. Jago. (1988). *The new leadership: Managing participation in organizations.* Englewood Cliffs, NJ: Prentice-Hall [most recent version].

11. R. H. G. Field. (1982). A test of the Vroom-Yetton normative model of leadership. *Journal of Applied Psychology, 67,* 523–532.

12. P. Hersey & K. H. Blanchard. (1988). *Management of organizational behavior,* 5th ed. Englewood Cliffs, NJ: Prentice-Hall.

13. L. B. Bolman & T. E. Deal. (1991). *Reframing organizations.* San Francisco: Jossey-Bass.

14. R. J. House. (1977). A 1976 theory of charismatic leadership. In J. G. Hunt & Larson, eds., *Leadership: The cutting edge.* Carbondale, IL: Southern Illinois University Press.

15. A. R. Willner. (1984). *The spellbinders: Charismatic political leadership.* New Haven, CT: Yale University Press; A. Conger & R. N. Kanungo. (1987). Toward a behavioral theory of charismatic leadership in organizational settings. *Academy of Management Review, 12,* 637–647.

CHAPTER 2

1. M. DePree. (1989). *Leadership is an art.* New York: Dell Publishing.

2. P. M. Senge. (1990). *The fifth dimension: The art of practice of the learning organization.* New York: Doubleday.

3. A. Solzhenitsyn. (1978). *A world split apart.* New York: Harper and Row, pp. 17–19.

4. W. Glasser. (1984). *Control theory: A new explanation of how we control our lives.* New York: Harper and Row.

5. L. Bolman & T. Deal. (1991). *Reframing organizations: Artistry, choice, and leadership.* San Francisco: Jossey-Bass.

6. DePree. *Leadership is an art,* p. 12.

7. W. Foster. (1986). *Paradigms and promises.* New York: Prometheus Books.

8. D. Griffiths & Peter Ribbins. (1995). "Leadership matters in education: Regarding secondary headship. Inaugural lecture, University of Birmingham, Edgbaston.

9. F. Erickson. School literacy, reasoning and civility: An anthropologist's perspective. *Review of Educational Research, 54,* 525–546.

10. A. Ravier, SJ. (1987). *Ignatius of Loyola and the founding of the Society of Jesus.* San Francisco: Ignatius Press.

11. M. R. Tripole, SJ. (1994). *Faith beyond justice.* St. Louis: Institute of Jesuit Sources.

12. J. J. Toner, SJ. (1991). *Discerning God's will: Ignatius of Loyola's teaching on Christian decision making.* St. Louis: Institute of Jesuit Sources.

13. Tripole. *Faith beyond justice.*

14. Tripole. *Faith beyond justice.*

15. C. Chapple. (1993). *The Jesuit tradition in education and missions.* Scranton: University of Scranton Press.

16. *Documents of the 34th General Congregation of the Society of Jesus.* (1995). St. Louis: Institute of Jesuit Sources.

REFERENCES

Jackson, P., & Delehanty, H. (1995). *Sacred hoops: Spiritual lessons of a hardwood warrior*. New York: Hyperion.

Knight, B., & Hammel, B. (2002). *Knight: My story*. New York: St. Martin's Press.

Krzyzewski, M. (2000). *Leading with the heart*. New York: Warner Books.

McKinney, J. (2005). *Tales from Saint Joseph's hardwood*. Champaign, IL: Sports Publishing.

Ramsay, J. (2004). *Dr. Jack's leadership lessons learned from a lifetime in basketball*. Hoboken, NJ: John Wiley and Sons.

Riley, P. (1993). *The winner within: A life plan for team players*. New York: G. P. Putnam's Sons.

Shapiro, L. (1991). *Big man on campus*. New York: Henry Holt and Co.

Smith, D. E. (1999). *A coach's life*. New York: Random House.

Summitt, P., & Jenkins, S. (1998). *Reach for the summit: The definite dozen system for succeeding at whatever you do*. New York: Broadway Books.

Wikipedia.org

Wojnarowski, A. (2005). *Miracle of St. Anthony*. New York: Gotham Books.

Wooden, J., & Jamison, S. (2004). *My personal best*. New York: McGraw-Hill.

ABOUT THE AUTHOR

Robert Palestini has been dean of Graduate and Continuing Studies and professor of educational leadership at Saint Joseph's University in Philadelphia for the past fifteen years. He has spent more than forty years in basic and higher education. He has been a high school biology and general science teacher, a varsity basketball coach, a principal, assistant superintendent, and superintendent of schools. He is the author of more than ten books on various topics in educational leadership and administration.